AMERICAN
INDIAN
WOMEN

# AMERICAN INDIAN WOMEN

## Telling Their Lives

by
Gretchen M. Bataille
and
Kathleen Mullen Sands

University of Nebraska Press
Lincoln and London

Manufactured in
the United States of America
First Bison Book printing: 1987
Most recent printing indicated
by the first digit below:
5 6 7 8 9 10

*Library of Congress Cataloging in Publication Data*
Bataille, Gretchen M, 1944–
American Indian women, telling their lives.
Includes index.
1. Indians of North America Women—Biography.
2. Indians of North America Women—Biography—History and criticism. 3. Indians of North America—Women—Biography—Bibliography.
I. Sands, Kathleen M.
II. Title.
E98.W8B37 1984
305.4'8897'073 [B]
83-10234
ISBN 0-8032-1159-7
ISBN 0-8032-6082-2 (pbk.)

Publication of this book was aided by a grant from The Andrew W. Mellon Foundation

SIXTH CLOTH PRINTING: 1989

∞

# Contents


Preface vii

1 American Indian Women's Narratives: The Literary Tradition 1

2 The Ethnographic Perspective: Early Recorders 27

3 Maria Chona: An Independent Woman in Traditional Culture 47

4 Culture Change and Continuity: A Winnebago Life 69

5 Two Women in Transition: Separate Perspectives 83

6 The Long Road Back: Maria Campbell 113

7 Traditional Values in Modern Context: The Narratives to Come 127

Notes 143

Selected Bibliography 155

I. American Indian Women's Autobiographies 156

II. Biographies of American Indian Women 173

III. Ethnographic and Historical Studies 181

IV. Contemporary Literature and Criticism 191

V. Additional Articles and Books about American Indian Women 201

Index 207

A Nation is not conquered
Until the hearts of its women
Are on the ground.
Then it is done, no matter
How brave its warriors
Nor how strong its weapons.
Traditional Cheyenne saying

# Preface

The Cheyennes speak for American Indian women of all times and in all tribal communities. But American Indian women have not been spared the attitude that until recently assumed the inferiority of all women. The view that the responsibilities of Indian women were less significant than male roles permeates early writings about native societies and appears in contemporary accounts about the position of American Indian women as well.

The popular view of American Indian women disseminated by historians, anthropologists, sociologists, and educators, as well as novelists, accords women a low status because of the nature of the duties they performed. One anthropologist has written, for example:

> The Indian Country of the Upper Missouri was a man's world before the white man's civilization penetrated that remote portion of the interior of our continent. Indian men were the hunters and warriors. As partisans they led war parties. As chiefs they deliberated in tribal councils and negotiated intertribal peaces. They were the seekers of visions, the makers and manipulators of powerful medicine bundles, and the conductors of prolonged and involved religious rituals. Women, on the other hand, were the diggers of roots and collectors of berries, the carriers of firewood and drawers of water, the dressers of hides and makers of tipis and clothing. As homemakers and housekeepers they performed scores of tasks necessary to the welfare of their families. But their role was a humble one. The Indian woman's inferior status . . . .[1]

Katherine M. Weist, in a study of Plains Indian women, cites examples of the views that have pictured American Indian women as "unfortunate and debased . . . beasts of burden." Although the women may be described as "humane and hospitable," they are also seen as "rude and unpolished." It is clear from Weist's summary of the research that publications about American Indian women, particularly studies of Plains tribes, have either ignored the power of women within tribal structures or undervalued or inadequately evaluated it.[2]

The source of such biased evaluation of the status of women in Indian culture is not difficult to discover. As Clara Sue Kidwell argues convincingly, "The positions of women in European societies, largely derived from Judaic and Christian ideals of womanhood, led European men to overlook the power that Indian women could wield in their own societies." Kidwell further asserts that "the idea of the roles of Indian women in their own societies that emerges from the literature in which women tell their own stories contradicts the usual stereotypes of the subservient and oppressed female."[3] Support for this view comes from other American Indian women today. Bea Medicine, Sioux anthropologist, has said repeatedly in lectures and in print that Indian women do not need liberation, that they have always been liberated within their tribal structures.

If the roles of American Indian women in their own societies and society at large are to be analyzed with fairness and accuracy, we must take a closer look, not from an outsider's viewpoint, but through modes of expression within tribal society. Indian women's autobiographies offer, in both methodology and content, an intimate look into the lives of these women. In the following chapters several autobiographies are discussed in terms of what they tell us about the reality of American Indian women's lives. Some of the life stories are told through editors and reflect the biases of the interpreters; others have been written by an American Indian woman and edited by someone else. Some of the most recent autobiographies have been written by American Indian women who have found autobiography an effective method for self-definition as well as tribal definition. Although definition of these narratives as a genre is complicated by their differences in style and purpose, they all clarify the centrality of women in American Indian cultures.

The preparation of this book would not have been possible without the generous help of a number of people. For her suggestion that a book about Indian women's lives and writing would be a welcome addition to the field of Indian literature, we extend our thanks to Ruth M. Underhill, whose expertise in the field of American Indian studies has been an inspiration to those who have followed her.

We are equally grateful to the women and men who have provided field information and interpretation of some of the works considered in this book: Helen Sekaquaptewa; Allison Sekaquaptewa Lewis; Adeline Shaw Russell; Ross Shaw; Ella Lopez Antone; Nancy Oestreich Lurie; Vine Deloria, Sr.; Adeline Wanatee; Priscilla Wanatee; Leslie Silko; Paula Gunn Allen; Ruth M. Underhill; Michael Taylor; Joyce Herold; and Irma Bizzett.

Research and writing of this text were supported by grants and awards from: Arizona State University Faculty Grant-in-Aid program; Arizona State University Liberal Arts College research award program; Iowa State University Graduate College; and the Department of English, Iowa State University. A. Jean Walker, research assistant in the Department of English at Iowa State University, was diligent in tracing references for the bibliography.

Preparation of the manuscript was also aided by critical evaluation by A. LaVonne Ruoff, University of Illinois at Chicago; Charles H. Mueller, Chicago; and Charles C. Irby, California State Polytechnic University, Pomona. Typing was done by Sheryl Kamps, Marlys Phipps, and Carol Palmquist.

Finally, our thanks to the American Indian women who have contributed to greater understanding of the reality of being female and Indian through the thoughtful expressions of their lives. They and their autobiographies are to be admired.

# American
# Indian
# Women

# 1
# American Indian Women's Narratives: The Literary Tradition

American Indian women have been a part of the storytelling tradition—both oral and written—from its inception, passing on stories to their children and their children's children and using the word to advance those concepts crucial to cultural survival.

Dexter Fisher (ed.), *The Third Woman*

Like most expressions of culture in America, autobiography by American Indian women is a dynamic combination of conservative traditions from transoceanic sources and innovative adaptations to new landscapes and cultural configurations. It is not an indigenous genre of literary expression, nor is it a direct outgrowth of the belle-lettres tradition of European-American personal memoir; it is neither folk art nor "high" art, although it shares elements of both. American Indian women's autobiography defies definition while simultaneously demanding it; the complexity and variety challenge the boundaries of literary categories yet call attention to it as a separate entity in the history of literary expression. It is a problematical form that may best be addressed and analyzed in terms of the process of its creation rather than as an established genre.

Indian women's autobiography has two models: the oral tradition of American Indian literature and the written tradition of Euro-American autobiography. The oral tradition of the indigenous peoples of the Americas is an ancient one—diverse, complex, and enduring. It is based on storytelling—on origin and migration myths, songs and chants, curing rites, prayers, oratory, tales, lullabies, jokes, personal narratives, and stories of bravery or visions. American Indian women's autobiography has not evolved directly from the recognized genres of oral native literatures, for it is not an indigenous oral form. However, it shares with oral forms some basic characteristics: emphasis on event, attention to the sacredness of language, concern with landscape, affirmation of cultural values and tribal solidarity.

These properties of the oral tradition derive from a concern for communal welfare, the subordination of the individual to the collective needs of the tribe.

Such concepts are not the material of autobiography in the Euro-American tradition, with its celebration of individuality and originality. Paradoxically, it is the element of individualism in American Indian women's autobiography that is innovative: the conservative roots of the Euro-American literary tradition provide the tribal narrator with a new element essential to the process of personal narration—egocentric individualism. When the Euro-American tradition is merged with indigenous elements, a unique form of expression results that has been given the implicitly contradictory name American Indian autobiography. How Euro-American individualism is modified and utilized by American Indian female narrators is crucial to understanding the nature of their autobiographical expression.

Autobiography as a literary genre is relatively recent. The term was coined in the first quarter of the nineteenth century in England to denote "a particular kind of self-written life," characterized by "egocentric individualism, historicism, and written text."[1] A development of the emerging romantic tradition in British literature, autobiography is confessional in form, exploring the inner labyrinth of the psyche, recording the emotional vibrations of the writer as well as the cultural milieu, documenting historic events and the autobiographer's relationships with members of society, encompassing both the inner and public lives of the subject over a lengthy period of time. Adapted to the American landscape, autobiography took on a distinctly American character. Thoreau, Franklin, and Henry Adams, all identified with specific American locales, addressed typically American issues—use of the land, acquisition of knowledge and wisdom, development of strategies for dealing with progress, meditation and fostering of virtue—but did little to change the form of autobiography. But another New World form of personal narrative was also an important antecedent to American Indian autobiography.

From colonial times through the nineteenth century, the captivity narrative, usually not termed autobiography because of its incidental nature and its focus on a topical or thematic concern, gained great popularity in published form and was even appropriated by clergymen to inspire rigorous faith in the face of extreme trial.[2] Thus, autobiographers who had public stature and claimed literary fame were balanced by lesser-known returned captives whose exotic experiences fascinated all segments of society. It is, of course, ironic that the written aspect of Indian women's autobiography is in some measure related to the captivity narrative, an intensely confessional form that centers on a theme also addressed by many Indian autobiographies—culture conflict and spiritual trial—but from an opposite perspective. Interestingly, many captivity narratives, including the most famous, Mary Rowlandson's *The Sovereignty and Goodness of God . . . a Narrative of Captivity and Restoration* (first published in 1682 with subsequent editions in 1720, 1770, 1771, 1773), are by women. The captivity narrative was not primarily a self-consciously literary genre but rather a record of spiritual salvation; thus, its relationship to American Indian autobiography is perhaps most directly discernible in the theme of conversion to Christianity that is addressed in a significant number of Indian autobiographies in the later part of the nineteenth and first half of the twentieth centuries.

Spiritual autobiography, the category into which the captivity narrative falls, has been, however obscurely, an important influence on American Indian autobiography. The urge toward spiritual introspection fostered by Puritan doctrine produced such famous works as Jonathan Edwards's *Personal Narrative* and Samuel Sewell's *Diary* and an ongoing tradition of meditative autobiographical explorations. Although this form of writing does not have any significant effect on oral autobiography by American Indians, it has consistently influenced written autobiographies by Indians converted to Christianity and eager to affirm their choice by public declaration. Even such a contemporary work as *Crying Wind* (Crying Wind, Kickapoo, 1977) is more spiritual testament than genuine personal narrative since it focuses almost exclusively on the self-esteem that comes to a Kickapoo woman as she immerses herself in Christianity.

Captivity narratives are the most dramatic of the models of autobiography focused on spiritual development and endurance. They are, if anything, more exotic in their depiction of Indian life than most Indian narratives, but despite their excesses, they are records of personal development and spiritual fortitude that have contributed, along with the more literary and conventional spiritual autobiographies of eighteenth- and nineteenth-century American literature, to the substantial number of conversion narratives in American Indian written autobiography.

In a broader sense, captivity narratives influenced public taste toward both personal narrative and interest in the "mysteries" of Indian tribal life. Although not a source of American Indian women's autobiography, they laid the groundwork in developing literary tastes that accommodated native works that followed, particularly in establishing women's narrative as a New World expression.

The tradition of literary autobiographers like Thoreau and Franklin is perhaps more traceable in Indian male autobiography than in its female counterpart because the subjects of Indian male autobiography are usually figures of some prominence in their tribes: warriors, chiefs, medicine men, army scouts, or renegades. Often they are participants in events critical to the survival of their people and way of life; thus, most Indian male autobiographies reflect the tradition of the memoir with its emphasis on historic context and public event. American Indian male autobiography is similar to published personal memoirs by various heroes of the American West—men of action like Davey Crockett, Daniel Boone, James Beckwourth, and William F. Cody, all of whom published their life stories with the aid of recorder-editors because they were too busy living to take time to write.[3] The process of their literary collaborations exemplifies the process of the greater proportion of Indian autobiographies—both male and female—told by the subject and prepared for publication by a recorder-editor. In this respect, the western hero autobiographies have influenced American Indian female autobiography as much as the male tradition. Like captivity narratives, popular western hero autobiographies and the literary autobiographies that were contemporary with them contributed significantly to the tradition of female Indian autobiographies by forming a taste for personal narrative literature in the American populace.

Another literary parallel to American Indian autobiography is the slave narrative, a major form of black expression. Black writers and American Indian narrators have faced similar problems in attempting to communicate to an audience that has not shared many of their cultural or moral concerns. Furthermore, black slave culture was communal, and thus slave narrators faced "the problem of distinguishing between the individual self and the community self and the desire to present the symbolic nature of one's personal experience while maintaining one's own inimitability,"[4] in much the same way that Indian autobiographers have faced and still face the problem of calling attention to themselves in printed texts while residing in societies which discourage putting oneself forward.

Indian autobiographies, particularly those written in the nineteenth century, share many similarities with slave narratives. Early black writers and, until recently, American Indian narrators, were essentially unaware of the rhetorical conventions and literary models of white society. In many cases they were not consciously attempting to produce literature. Neither group was considered socially or intellectually equal to the whites who constituted their major audience, and generally the subject was looked upon by the audience as an example of the virtues of primitive life, or at least as a typical example of a less-than-civilized society.[5] Thus, the materials published from both groups often focus on experiences that have developed the subject's identity in the group. Indian autobiographies, like slave narratives, chronicle experiences in cultures foreign to a white audience and provide "insight into an individual mind as well as into the structure and working of that individual's society."[6] Both provide an intimate glimpse into an exotic culture at a safe distance. Even today, in both black and Indian autobiographies, the narrators "investigate the process of their spiritual and emotional development and try to assess the effects of social and familial relationship upon the ways in which they see themselves."[7] Like black narrators, Indian narrators have sometimes failed to achieve literary quality in their works. Some of the autobiographies have been "crude in style" and "vague in purpose," interesting only because of the exotic subject matter.[8] However, many black and Indian autobiographers worked consciously or unconsciously in a literary tradition. Nevertheless, even those Indian narratives that achieve literary quality are frequently consigned to the ethnographic areas in libraries on the assumption that they recount tribal life and therefore are social documents, not literature. While the literary tradition of the slave narrative differs significantly from Indian autobiography, primarily in that it is a written form confined to a historical phenomenon which ended in the nineteenth century, it offers insights into Indian autobiography and contributes to an understanding of the forces that have shaped the genre.

Examining the tradition of Euro-American literary autobiography and the distinctly American traditions of captivity narratives, western hero autobiography, and slave narrative, it becomes clear that although Indian autobiography shares some elements with each of these forms, it is quite distinct from the literary traditions that precede and coexist with it. In part, the differences are based on profound cultural differences among whites, blacks, and Indians, but perhaps more important are the differences grouped in the unique process which language and cultural differences forced upon Indian, and particularly Indian women's, autobiography.

American Indian autobiography is a transitional genre, combining elements of tribal oral tradition and Euro-American written tradition, both complex literary traditions when considered separately, but doubly complex when combined and adapted to narration of personal experience by tribal women. Defining just what constitutes an autobiography by an American Indian woman is not a simple task, since there are several kinds of autobiographies by Indian women.

Female autobiographers in general tend toward the tradition of reminiscence with a focus on private relationships and examination of personal growth—personal experience reflected upon.[9] Women's autobiographies generally concentrate on "domestic details, family difficulties, close friends and especially people who influenced them." Women do not "cast themselves in heroic molds," but rather "sift through their lives for explanation and understanding" in order to "clarify, to affirm and to authenticate" themselves.[10] Even where the subject is a woman of stature within the tribe, like Pretty-shield, a Crow medicine woman,[11] the autobiography does not focus on the public role of the narrator, but rather on reminiscences of girlhood, family life, prereservation lifeways, and personal growth. Thus, female Indian autobiographies tend to integrate some elements of historic, ceremonial, and social importance into the narratives but concentrate on everyday events and activities and family crisis events—birth, naming, puberty, marriage, and motherhood. They are private lives, allowing the reader glimpses into the intimate working of individual women's experiences. There is a sense in most Indian women's autobiographies of the connectedness of all things, of personal life flow, and episodes often are not sequential but linked thematically to establish a pattern of character developing through the response to private experience.

To explore the femaleness of Indian woman's autobiography is in no way to judge the quality or significance of either male or female autobiography, but simply to make a distinction that aids in defining a separate tradition within the larger body of Indian autobiography, a

form of literature that shares most of its traditons without regard to gender. It also links American Indian women's autobiographical tradition with the female autobiography tradition that has just recently begun to receive literary attention.

The processes and forms of both male and female narratives are the same, but the focus and the kind of symbolic representation that determine the aesthetic quality of women's narratives are quite separate from their male counterparts'. Although there are exceptions (for example: Albert Yava, *Big Falling Snow,* ed. Harold Courlander, 1978; *Son of Old Man Hat,* recorded by Walter Dyk [1938], 1967; and others), the autobiographies of male narrators usually center on historic events and crisis moments in individual lives and tribal hostory. Many of the day-to-day activities are given only cursory attention, and family and personal relationships are sometimes even omitted. The autobiographies of American Indian women are generally concerned with the more private and intimate aspects of their lives and cultures and with the partnership women share in the structuring and preserving of traditions within their societies. The dynamics of autobiography are similar, but the qualities of Indian womanhood lead to a separate literary tradition, molded from the uniqueness of insight and the pervasive character of womanhood.

The principle that distinguishes Indian autobiography from that of the Euro-American tradition most clearly has no relationship to gender differences; rather, it is a matter of methodology—bicultural composite authorship.[12] While some autobiographies by Indian people have been written solely by the author, even those have in some measure gone through bicultural processing in preparation of the manuscript for publication for a primarily non-Indian audience.

The complicated processes of obtaining Indian autobiographies is discussed at length by Clyde Kluckhohn in his 1945 study of personal documents in anthropology. He distinguishes between true autobiography and semi-autobiography on the basis of the level of involvement of the recorder. He provides a model for the publication of these life stories, admitting, however, to the difficulty of following the model by his own discussion of the variety of forms these materials take. Lewis L. Langness, twenty years later, resurrects the problem of labeling, arguing that the label "life history" is best used to describe any "extensive record of a person's life as it is reported either by the person himself or by others or both, and whether it is written or in interviews or both." And, in his article "The Indian Autobiography: Origins, Type and Function," Arnold Krupat describes written autobiographies as "autobiographies-by-Indians" in which composite composition is not an element.[13] These distinctions, while useful when considering the various types of Indian autobiographies, complicate an already complex consideration of genre.

Essentially, there are two processes that lead to publication of Indian autobiography—oral and written. Both types share in the bicultural composition process, although those few works written with a conscious eye toward production of a literary manuscript generally do not show evidence of editorial intrusion beyond that necessary for publication. The distinction between the oral and written traditions is one of type, not of quality. Furthermore, the terms *oral* and *written* do not presume sequential development of types of autobiography from nonliterate to literate stages among tribal peoples in America, but are two separate processes contemporaneous with each another, and both are viable forms of autobiography today. Some of the earliest autobiographies by American Indian women were written—Sarah Winnemucca Hopkins's recollection of the first white contact with her tribe was published in 1883. Conversely, some of the recent autobiographies by Indian women were narrated—Helen Sekaquaptewa's *Me and Mine* (1969), for example.[14] All forms of Indian autobiography have existed simultaneously, and the oral/written difference alone is not a valid criterion for judgment of literary merit.

The oral/written distinction by itself is an oversimplification, for there are two separate forms of oral autobiography, the "ethnographic" and "as-told-to." These are not mutually exclusive types, since both share in orality and presume a non-Indian partner to effect a completed work. In the ethnographic autobiography, however, the intention of the work is clearly not literary. Usually collected by an anthropologist whose goal has not been to record and publish a literary work but to collect information on the customs, mores, practices, and ceremonies of a specific tribe, the ethnographic autobiography is documentary in nature, valuable not because of its mode of expression, but because of the ethnographic data it contains, a personal document to support anthropological interpretations of social data about tribal peoples. Occasionally, in spite of the scientific purposes for the collection of narrative information, the personality of the narrator breaks through, suggesting the potential for a genuine autobiography, but often this possibility is precluded by the brevity of the account or the concentration of the narrator on one aspect of tribal life in an attempt to elucidate information being gathered by the anthropologist. Ethnographic autobiography does not employ literary techniques, it does not attempt to record a comprehensive story, nor does it develop a literary persona. It is a personal document, edited by the collector to support ethnographic studies of individual tribes; yet, in process it is very similar to the as-told-to autobiography, employing a collaborative effort by interviewer and subject, with the oral narration molded into publishable form for a non-Indian audience.

The as-told-to autobiography is an outgrowth of the ethnographic form. Many of the as-told-to texts in print today were collected and edited by anthropologists: Nancy O. Lurie and Ruth Underhill, for example.[15] The as-told-to autobiographies, however, differ in several ways from ethnographic documents. They are longer, more comprehensive life stories of the subjects; they often employ literary techniques such as dialogue, exploration of inner emotions and responses to events, a first-person omniscient viewpoint, latitude in handling time and sequence of events, and an awareness of audience. These autobiographies use informal, conversational language for stylistic effect.[16] The relationship in the as-told-to autobiography is between a recorder-editor and a narrator chosen because of narrative skill as well as valuable information.

Many of the as-told-to autobiographies of women were collected during the period of the intense acculturation (the late nineteenth and early twentieth centuries), and, while similar in process to the ethnographic narrative, they differ significantly in purpose. The editor-recorder does not simply collect information from a female informant, but works in partnership with the narrator to create a full-length autobiography of a woman, who while she may be representative of the roles of women in her society, is also highly individual and a competent storyteller. This shift in emphasis presumes an altering of the recorder-editor's function in the compiling and editing of the life story, a more intense and intimate relationship with the narrator, and a greater concern for stylistic preservation in the structuring and expression of the narrative.

The relationship between the narrator and recorder-editor is critical for the creation of the as-told-to autobiography, and the quality of the working relationship determines in large measure the impact and validity of the work as both life story and literary text. Within this framework, there is considerable room for variety, and the individuality of the works produced from this method attests to the possible diversity. In Maria Chona's *Papago Woman,* it is obvious that preservation of the oral nature of the narrative is important. Metaphor, Papago respect for language, dramatic dialogue, direct address to the audience, and descriptive detail all attest to the literary sensitivity of the editor. The autobiography of Pretty-shield brings the process of the collection of the content right into the finished text to allow the reader to observe the dynamics of the relationship between Pretty-shield and the recorder Frank B. Linderman. Linderman is present in the text as interviewer and observer of the context of the Indian woman's storytelling, and although this is distracting at times, it reveals how such a work is created. Nancy Oestreich Lurie, editor of *Mountain Wolf Woman,* does not inject her presence into the narrative but provides considerable background information about the narrator, as does Louise Udall, editor of Helen Sekaquaptewa's *Me and Mine,* when she integrates historical material on the Traditional/Progressive conflict at Hopi in 1906 into the narrator's recollections of the event. In each of these narratives, and in such other works as Lowry's *Karnee: A Paiute Narrative* (1966) Polingaysi Qoyawayma's *No Turning Back* (1964), and *The Autobiography of Delfina Cuero: A Diegueno Indian* (1968), the relationship between narrator and recorder-editor is different and leads to a unique expression of the life of the subject, but in every case the methodology is similar. The recorder-editor selects the subject or solicits the narrative, in some cases translating from the original language, usually structuring the materials and presenting them in a stylistically pleasing manner. The narrator offers her life story, and the editor hones it for literary effect.[17]

A natural outgrowth of the as-told-to form is the written narrative, and although there are fewer examples of these works, it is likely that this will become the dominant form of the genre in the future as more and more Indian women find themselves comfortable writing in English and feel less need of a collaborative editor. Not all such works are contemporary, however. From 1900 to 1902, a Sioux woman, Gertrude Bonnin, wrote her youthful recollections in a series for *Atlantic Monthly,*[18] and Sarah Winnemucca Hopkins's written autobiography was published in 1883. This early work is representative of women who spoke for their tribes and were active in efforts to gain redress from the government for hardships imposed upon their people. Their narratives were only secondarily personal life stories.

Written autobiographies may be the result of different processes in much the same way the oral autobiographies can be distinguished from one another according to the mode of composition. One kind of written autobiography is composed in essentially the same way as the as-told-to autobiography: it is drafted in written form by an Indian and edited by a non-Indian for publication. This process assumes the active involvment of the editor, who often is responsible for extensive restructuring of the material and filling in gaps where they occur.

The final category of autobiography by American Indian women is the written autobiography controlled by the writer and literary in intent. Aside from the tribal identification of the writer, this type of autobiography is identical in process to the mainstream of American autobiography. A minimum of editing is done by an assigned editor, and the writer assumes final control over the published material. Although as yet there are few autobiographies in this category, the recent output of fiction by American Indian women suggests that this will be the predominant form of the future.

American Indian women's autobiography is, then, a personal reminiscence that purports to be verifiable, but that subordinates fact to the essential truth of the subject's life. Its literary merit hinges on the narrative skill of the subject and the editorial skill of her collaborator and on the effectiveness of literary techniques employed in both narration and editorial phases. As partners in a bicultural composite work, narrator and recorder-editor attempt the reconstruction of a life and its circumstances with the narrator as the focus. Inevitably, an autobiography is a rationalization of a life. Facts are not the issue. Both narrator and editor search for the truth of a life, a task made doubly hard because of the collaborative process. What makes an autobiography literary rather than simply ethnographic is a search for and development of an inner stance, a sense of discovery of the wholeness of the subject's identity. As a life story the autobiography must have realism; the outer and inner elements must be sufficiently integrated to allow the reader to imagine the life and to comprehend it as a unique experience, not simply a typical representation of a tribal role. Together, the narrator and editor must be both "tender and severe" in articulating the subject's life "from a particular moment in time."[19] The retrospective stance allows the subject to bring new knowledge to bear on her life experiences; the outside view of the recorder-editor allows an objective assessment of the content of the narrative. The separate stances ideally lead to the detection of new significances in the personal experiences reflected upon, imbuing the autobiography with meaning.

The process of articulation and editing encompasses diverse intentions and experiences; but consistently, the act of repeating the past denies time since the narrator and recorder-editor remain in a continual present as the content of the narrative recreates the past; the process leads to a double narrative stance that allows simultaneous exposition of event and evaluation from temporal distance. Like all literature, the as-told-to autobiography creates an enduring present within the illusion of temporal sequence.

Within Indian autobiography the illusion of sequence is often abandoned altogether since oral presentation is often associative. Thus, the post-collection job of the recorder-editor is first one of structuring the narrative material into a pattern of what the nontribal audience perceives as logical sequence. The nonsequential oral process in itself suggests that structural interpretation is an essential element of Indian autobiography. Not until the relationship of all the elements of the oral narrative are discovered can the meaning emerge. It is the job of the editor to order fragmented experience in time and in relation to narrative viewpoint and intention. As one critic points out, "Our sense that there is meaning in something . . . comes only when the elements that go to make up that thing take on a relation to one another; in other words, the meaning emerges with our perception of pattern."[20] Since the patterns of Indian oral literature are not familiar to the nontribal audience, the editor acts as a mediator. Just as the narrator mediates between the world of the past and the accumulated knowledge of the present to form a new entity, a stable symbol of a life in a world of flux, the editor structures the oral narrative from the essential themes, aspects of character, point of view, and experiences of the narrator. Together the collaborators give permanence and reality to the past.

Indian autobiography, particularly Indian women's autobiography, has not received the attention it deserves. Perhaps the greatest barrier has been that autobiography is not a major literary form in

America, and, even more disconcerting, American Indian autobiography does not fit the conception of autobiography held by scholars and non-Indian readers in general. Creative imagination, invention in adaptation, and flexibility in form have been accepted as essential characteristics of poetry and fiction, but the respectability and existence of these qualities are controversial in autobiography. They lead to descriptions like "personal memoir," "reminiscence," or "social narrative." Unfortunately such glib and simplistic terminology obscures more complex and valid definitions.

On the rare occasions American Indian autobiographies have been analyzed and discussed, the results have often been incomplete or muddled, and the analysis is often very selective with important aspects of the genre slighted or entirely overlooked. Autobiographies by American Indian women are almost never considered, or at best are lumped with male narratives and regarded as less important. The result of such casual attention is inherently contradictory, more evidence of the impossibility of systematic appraisal than a confirmation of the literary value of such works. Conversely, sometimes critics are so careful to apply rigorous criteria, perhaps because they are compelled to demonstrate objectivity by suppressing enthusiasm or advocacy of the genre by ignoring its uniqueness, they often squelch recognition of any value.

Not all autobiographies are intentionally literary, certainly not all the texts addressed in this book. Some will not stand up to close literary scrutiny, but this should hardly be surprising or disappointing. Range in direction and quality is inherent in any form of expression. The emphasis in American Indian women's autobiographies is often upon life itself, not on literature, but to some degree, in intention and technique, even the ethnographic autobiography shares in a literary tradition. The balance of emphasis toward document or literary work can be fairly easily discerned as the following chapters in this study will demonstrate. Though every autobiography can be addressed directly, understanding the complex network of processes can help the reader understand, evaluate, and enjoy a given work.

The process of creativity in most American Indian women's autobiographies is dual, but in the production of the work both partners share similar steps: selection and recollection, structuring, and expression. The narrator recalls her life. The incidents are not told exactly as they occurred but are imagined and reshaped in terms of all that has led to the telling. An act of imagination and creative evaluation, critical in nature, has been imposed on each incident, and on the convergence of events that becomes the content of the narrative. The narrator selects the order of event and incident, including or omitting detail, restructuring greatly or subtly the course of her life. The result is a dramatic persona.

The collector-editor follows a nearly parallel process in participating in shaping the work. The editor records the narrative, facilitating the narrator's selection or amplification of incidents through probing or questioning but not pressing so hard to force deliberate distortion or invention. Then the editor provides order to the material. Throughout the process, the recorder is continually involved in fostering and guarding the validity of expression through careful preservation of language, in some cases by meticulous translation as well as transcription of the narrative voice, individual syntax, diction, and emphasis.

The possibilities of error are great, and distortion and misrepresentation are confronted at every moment because two creators are at work simultaneously. But where this creative collaboration is careful, and at least occasionally inspired, the form and content merge, and the work admits the nontribal audience into the life and ways of an individual Indian woman within her culture in a mode that is dramatic and stylistically satisfying.

While seeming to be wholly factual and straightforward, the autobiography is an imaginative work of literature and provides an opportunity for evaluating the value of this genre as both informational and aesthetic. Autobiography "imposes a pattern on life, constructs out of it a coherent story," because consciously or unconsciously, it "establishes certain stages in an individual life, makes links between them, and defines, implicitly or explicitly, a certain consistency of relationship between the self and outside world." This coherence assumes a narrative stance on the part of the teller; she narrates from the moment at which she reviews and interprets her life. It is the present that allows the narrator to see her life as one that has an inherent order she recognizes and conveys or one on which she imposes order and meaning. The process of autobiography "means, therefore, discrimination and selection of facts, distribution of emphasis, choice of expression." The process, of course, is heavily dependent on memory, which interrelates the narrator and the facts of events, leading to "facts in the making," a decidedly creative process, "not just reconstruction of the past, but interpretation."[21] The narrative contains an element of developing self-knowledge, and it follows that the closer she is to the reality of her culture, the more accurately her "discourse ought to become a language that directly reflects that society." The narrator's reality is in large measure predetermined by her beliefs about her life and circumstances, however, so her narration may not, in fact, mirror the objective world. "The speaker is unable to establish any diversity of viewpoints" and thus creates a wholly personal interpretation of events.[22] The events are symbolic, a way of knowing life through imagination. The symbols are not imagined, as in fiction, but instead are chosen and arranged. Autobiography is, in fact, "a judgment on the past within the framework of the present."[23] These qualities of personal narrative are not set out to question the reliability of the narrator—that is the job of the recorder-editor—but to facilitate competent critical attention to the work as aesthetic expression rather than as sociological case history.

American Indian women's autobiographies tend to be retrospective rather than introspective, and thus may seem understated to those unaccustomed to the emotional reserve of Indian people. There is little self-indulgence on the part of Indian women narrators; events occur and are articulated in words conservative in emotional connotation. Even moments of crisis are likely to be described without much intensity of language, or emotional pitch may be implied or stated metaphorically rather than directly. Such understatement is not an indication of repression or absence of emotional states but often evidence that the narrator simply takes that state for granted. Where articulation of feelings does enter the work, it may well be that the recorder-editor has asked for amplification of the narrator's feelings, and in such cases, the response is often vivid. The Indian autobiography tends to look outward, which has an effect beyond understated expression of feeling that may be equally puzzling to non-Indian readers—the apparent lack of motivation in the characters in the narrative.

In the narratives, the relationship of events is sometimes only implied, primarily because the tribal consciousness of the narrator and her comprehensive understanding of her own cultural traditions and values makes expression of the rationale for specific actions unnecessary. In the best examples of the genre, motivation is discernible, perhaps because of the narrator's consciousness of a nontribal audience or because the recorder-editor has solicited amplification. In some cases, motivational information is added to the narrative in the form of informational notes and appendices. Integrating such information into the text of the narrative is desirable, however, because it supplies a continuity and depth to the portrait without distracting from the flow of the narration.

Obviously not all women from American tribes are alike. The autobiographies addressed in this study are proof of the individuality of Indian women, but there are some characteristics that stand out as central to the identity of Indian women. In a 1981 interview, Sioux spokesman Vine Deloria, Sr., placed modesty above all other qualities that characterize Indian women—not simply modesty in dress, but in demeanor and attitude, in a bearing that is self-respectful and brings honor to the individual and her family. While it must be recognized that Deloria speaks from a specific tribal perspective and that generalizations about qualities and the character of Indian women are always speculative, it is nonetheless clear that the quality of modesty has a direct bearing on Indian women's autobiography, since it suggests that those women willing to put themselves forward in order to record or write their narratives are atypical in calling attention to themselves. It also accounts for the frequent guardedness of narrators in focusing on their own emotions and private aspects of their lives. Countering this humility, or reserve, is what Deloria describes as the centrality of Indian women to the spiritual well-being of their tribes. He notes that they are also characterized by responsibility for the steadfastness of tribal ideals and values. Traditionally, Indian men have been expected to indulge in the pursuit of glory and the release of emotion, while Indian women have been repositories of tradition and concern for spirtual ideals, upholding the stability of the tribe through both spiritual and generative power. To say that men acted and behaved at the pleasure of Indian women is a misleading oversimplification, but as Deloria points out, Indian men did not hold office without the approval of the mature women of a tribe, and if they did not fulfill their responsibilities adequately, they were not likely to be given roles of power again. This power that women have traditionally exerted in Indian communities also has some impact on the narratives under study because it clarifies the importance of the role of the narrators in the well-being of their own families and tribes and undercuts the stereotypical notion that Indian women were simply drudges whose tasks and roles were merely supportive ones.

Deloria also points to a willingness among Indian women to sacrifice immediate goals for the well-being of family members, a willingness to defer but not to forgo personal goals, thus creating a pattern of attainment of personal satisfaction in maturity that is also characteristic of many of the narrators of autobiographies who endure considerable hardship but achieve an inner strength that leads to serenity and wisdom in later years. Deloria suggests that Indian women are especially skilled in creating a community of women—what might today be called a support network—to share both responsibility and pleasure in the day-to-day tasks of life; and lest Indian women be seen as terribly solemn, he emphasizes that humor is a central characteristic of Indian women, both traditionally and in contemporary life, and that it tempers the burden of responsibility they bear individually and collectively. These aspects of character are also revealed in autobiographies by Indian women. Although such generalizations as these are less than incisive in developing an understanding of Indian women, autobiographies portray these traits through actual events and incidents and in believable characters. Autobiographies provide perhaps the most intimate portrayal of Indian femaleness available to nontribal people and develop a realism that demands the reader abandon simpleminded stereotypes. Furthermore, the fact that Deloria sees these characteristics of Indian women as adaptable, enduring, and contemporary, and not simply as abstractions or ghosts of times past, suggests that the process of autobiography is in some measure parallel to the adaptation of Indian women's identity from traditional times into the present.[24]

In addition to the processes of Indian autobiographies already discussed, there are three thematic thrusts in American Indian women's autobiography that are roughly parallel to the progressive steps—tradition and culture contact, acculturation, and return to tradition—in the history of American Indian women. These thematic concerns are addressed in both oral and written types of autobiography.

Looking closely at the earliest autobiographies, one sometimes finds clear statements of the woman's personal thoughts and narrative purpose. Even when the statements are veiled, the impact of the thought is clear. Waheenee, telling her story to Gilbert Wilson in 1912, reveals her sadness:

> I am an old woman now. The buffalo and black-tail deer are gone and our Indian ways are almost gone. Sometimes I find it hard to believe I ever lived then. . . . I cannot forget our old ways. Often in summer I rise at daybreak and steal out to the cornfields; and as I hoe the corn I sing to it, as we did when I was young. No one cares for our corn songs now. Sometimes at evening I sit, looking out at the Big Missouri. The sun sets, and dusk steals over the water. In the shadows I seem again to see our Indian village, with smoke curling upward from the earth lodges, and in the river's roar I hear the yells of the warriors, the laughter of little children as of old. It is an old woman's dream. Again I see but shadows and hear only the roar of the river; and tears come into my eyes. Our Indian life, I know, is gone forever.[25]

Because of his nontribal perspective on the past, her editor brushes these thoughts away: "Conservative and sighing for the good old times, she is aware that the younger generation of Indians must adopt civilized ways".[26] Despite his close involvement in the recording of Waheenee's autobiography, Wilson has failed to discern the intention of the narrator, dismissing her values and emotions as quaint and ineffective because his own observations are so ethnocentric.

The intent of ethnographic narratives is to document lives of individual women within their tribal societies, usually supplementing tribal ethnographies. These works focus on women who are representative of the values and roles of the female members of their societies. However, they lay the basic premises from which the more literary works evolve. Most of them are ninteenth- and early twentieth-century narratives, though there are some works, such as *Three Pomo Women,* collected later in this century. Such works offer valuable insight into tribal structure and ways. Colson intended for the Pomo life stories to supplement the ethnographies on Pomo culture and to provide some insight into the lives of the Pomo women who had grown up during the period of acculturation. Mrs. Martinez's comments may best epitomize the pulls on women's lives during this period. When asked what she wanted for her granddaughter, she answered: "I think if she stayed home with me and made baskets that would be good. And I want her to go to school and learn something. Than would be good too."[27] The pulls toward traditions and the pushes toward acculturation are obvious themes in the autobiographies of these three women.

Those autobiographies collected earliest were solicited by historians, missionaries, and early anthropologists, and some suffer from the professional biases of the collectors. They tend to focus heavily on culture disintegration and reflect the collectors' notions of what it meant to be a "good Indian," often recording lives of women eager to acculturate or accept Christianity. In some cases, they show the influence of the theory of Social Darwinism held by some early anthropologists. One of the earliest written autobiographies, Sarah Winnemucca Hopkins's *Life among the Paiutes,* is heavily biased by her acculturated and Christianized viewpoint. Most, like Waheenee's *An Indian Girl's Story,* "Yoimut's Story, the Last Chunut," by Yoimut, or "Out of the Past" by Lucy Young, are marked by regret for the passing of traditional life or abandonment of traditions to accommodate white culture. Others, like Ruth Landes's *Ojibwa Women,* the "Personal Narrative of Mrs. Andrew Stanley," and the "Personal Narrative of Anna Price," are brief ethnographic case studies, informative but stylistically flat. Three texts collected by Truman Michelson in the early part of the twentieth century, autobiographies of Fox, Arapaho, and Cheyenne women, communicate the personalities of the narrators with considerable vitality and detail. Although the purpose of ethnographic autobiography is not literary, these narratives demonstrate specific methodology, principles of narrative structure, and themes, creating a foundation for the more fully developed as-told-to autobiography.[28]

Contiguous with autobiography collected for ethnographical study are texts by Indian women who consciously chose to write their own life stories, with an editor's aid or independently. The purpose of these autobiographers is to correct the misinformation about Indians as savages and to bring the Indian and white worlds closer together. Polingaysi Qoyawayma says that her autobiography, *No Turning Back,* is an attempt to "span the great and terrifying chasm between my Hopi world and the world of the white man." When the author decided to go to school, her mother admonished her: "You have taken a step in the wrong direction. A step away from your Hopi people. You have brought grief to us. To me, to your father, and to your grandparents. Now you must continue to go to school each day. You have brought this thing upon yourself, and there is no turning back."[29] Her grandmother warned her of the loss of Hopi beliefs and culture, but she also reminded her of her responsibility as a member of the coyote clan to provide a bond between the Bahana (white man) and the Hopi people. She does not reject her heritage, but she assumes that many of the traditional ways will indeed be lost. She recognizes that the education of the children is now in the hands of the teachers and the public schools rather than the mothers or grandmothers, and she advises the educators to "help them to realize the value of their own heritage."[30]

There were other women in this generation of writers who accepted white ways and Christianity. Helen Sekaquaptewa adopted the Mormon religion and some white attitudes, and her life story, *Me and Mine,* reflects this perspective. Anna Shaw, whose parents had converted to Christianity, and who herself was unusual among Indian women in receiving a high school diploma in 1920, is described by Edward Spicer as a "culturally assimilated Presbyterian Pima." Her own view of Indian life in *A Pima Past* is that she moved from the reservation to the white world and finally back to a blend of the two.[31]

Also flourishing as a separate thematic current are autobiographies that address the difficulties of acculturation. Recorder-editor Florence Shipek, in her introduction to Delfina Cuero's autobiography, recognizes the dilemma faced in the 1930s, 1940s, and 1950s by Indian people:

> This autobiography is typical of life stories of most of the Indians who had no place to call their own. . . . All relate the same search for a place to live and the same terrible struggle to feed and clothe the children, whom they loved dearly. . . . They hold no bitterness about the past and are only looking for the chance to work and earn enough to feed and clothe their children. They feel that they have survived through the crises and that there will be a future for their children as the children are learning the new ways.[32]

Delfina's life is described as typical of the "destruction of Indian self-sufficiency on the land, of Indian society, culture, and religion." There is bitter recognition of the loss. The lessons taught by the grandmothers and through the stories do not work in the society any more. Delfina and her children become victims of her men's anger, and the changes in the culture result in disintegration of family ties as well as the loss of the traditional ways.

In a recent, noncollaborative written autobiography, Sah-Gan-De-Oh speaks for herself and for others of her generation when she remarks that her story is similar to that of "many other American Indians of today who are completely integrated in the American way of life." Yet she sees a greater purpose in sharing her experiences: "It is my hope that those of you who read this will better understand us. We are not refugees from another world, feathered and warlike as the TV and the movies depict us, but a proud race who love our heritage and are striving to keep alive our own culture."[33] Although she wished to keep alive her culture, she had accepted the philosophy taught at the Haskell Institute, an Indian school—"They all helped us to become better citizens and adjust to a better way of life." In her own teaching she adopted the attitude of an outsider: "We had the most adorable little papooses. . . . I thought it a shame those babies had been taken away from their homes at so early an age but they didn't seem to be the least bit unhappy or homesick." She accepted the policy of termination as inevitable and ends her book with a diatribe against her own people, blaming them for whatever problems they have. She faults the parents for not making public education compulsory, blames tribal politics for internal problems, says parents use welfare checks at local bars, and says, finally, that the housing situation could be improved "with a little extra work and a few less 'six-packs' of beers." In her simplistic analysis of Indian existence she divides all Indians into three groups—professionals; those making a good living; and those addicted to "firewater."[34] Perhaps more than any other Indian woman autobiographer, Sah-Gan-De-Oh represents the accultured Indian woman who believes wholeheartedly that the only way to survive is to be completely assimilated into white society. Her analysis of the economic situation ignores the realities of prejudice and rejection Indian people have experienced. She appears to be far removed from the memories of "what used to be" and has trouble recognizing the traditional Indian values and their place in her life.

Contemporary written autobiographies, like Anna Moore Shaw's *A Pima Past* and Maria Campbell's *Halfbreed* are more concerned with a fully detailed account of life experiences, centering on the personal growth of the individual, incorporating family histories and tribal context. Although these autobiographies are written, they are similar in content to the as-told-to narratives. There are also, however, contemporary life narratives that are primarily vehicles for Indian spokeswomen to bring to the reader an understanding of the difficulties of being an Indian woman in a modern world. *Bobbi Lee: Indian Rebel* and Lucille Winnie's *Sah-Gan-De-Oh: The Chief's Daughter* are two narratives in this mode.[35] Their intent is not so much literary as social, but these narratives are, nonetheless, structured and styled as literary works.

In all of the autobiographies mentioned, a similar emphasis in theme is shared; they are narratives of women born into traditional tribal societies who must come to terms with the impact of white culture on their people and their own lives. They reflect the strength and endurance of American Indian women as they face drastic changes in their own cultures and work to preserve traditional values and ways in themselves and pass them on to their children. They are women who have considered their lives and made difficult decisions, sometimes struggling to survive great hardships or identity disorientation, who have recalled their experiences in order to communicate them without bitterness or sentimentality, and with considerable spirit. They are women in transition, and the collaborative form of autobiography mirrors the coming together of two cultures in the lives of the narrators. Their lives convey the drama of the conflict of cultures. Their autobiographies attest to the endurance of the tradition of Indian storytelling as it is transformed into a new literary form.

In American Indian women's autobiographies types and trends intersect and overlap—a frustrating maze that confounds the orderly instincts of the mind. However, close examination of individual texts allows one to penetrate the maze and discern the thematic patterns and the types discussed earlier in this chapter.

It is clear that the autobiographies of American Indian women have undergone changes in several significant ways during the last century. Most obvious is a change of attitude on the part of the subject. The self-effacement that is apparent in early life stories told by an often anonymous informant through a translator changed as women became more aware of their non-Indian audience and societal pressures toward acculturation. As Indian people became more active in the dominant society, the autobiographies reflected this movement toward acculturation and integration. Recent autobiographies reflect a much more conscious attempt to present a story of an individual Indian woman and her relationships to the tribe, to other native people, and to the non-Indian world.

The subsequent chapters of this work focus on a selection of American Indian autobiographies that represents the variety of methods and types which contribute to the vitality of this form of literature. The next chapter analyzes the ethnographic approach to personal narrative by Indian women; although data are obviously the primary concern of these works, elements of the narrator's personality and personal viewpoint emerge in spite of the emphasis on collection rather than collaboration. The third chapter is a study of a Papago narrator born in the mid-nineteenth century who offers a much more complex autobiography than the ethnographic narratives, but it too was collected and prepared for publication by an anthropologist. This chapter, however, demonstrates the creative literary success of an autobiography that is the combined effort of an accomplished Indian storyteller and an anthropologist with literary sensitivity and imagination. The fourth chapter focuses on still another autobiography collected by an anthropologist, but one that differs from those preceding it in that it records the life of a twentieth-century woman faced with drastic changes in her culture and concentrates on her ability to adapt without losing her identity as a Winnebago woman. Furthermore, the narrative is compiled from taped interviews, and the degree of editorial involvement by the subject is significantly greater than in the works discussed in the two previous chapters.

The next chapter analyzes the autobiographies of two women from the Southwest, one Pima and one Hopi, who were born in the same year and attended school for a short time together, both coping with the intrusion of whites into their culture, but each adapting and adjusting in different ways. Moreover, the methodologies of the two narratives are distinct; one is a written autobiography, the other a contemporary example of the as-told-to method. The sixth chapter brings the discussion of American Indian women's autobiography into the contemporary period as it focuses on the life history of a Canadian mixed-blood woman who has written her life story without collaboration with a non-Indian editor. Finally, the last chapter addresses the future potential for American Indian women's autobiography as Indian women begin experimenting with new literary forms based on autobiographical models.

While this series of essays on individual Indian women's personal narratives cannot possibly represent the variety and scope of work in this emerging genre, it does indicate the movement from oral toward written autobiography and demonstrates the growing sophistication in methodology and literary expression within the genre. Like American Indian women's autobiography itself, the essays do not reflect consistently linear movement: similarities in subjects' experiences are abundant; oral and written autobiographies exist in each time period addressed; variation in literary quality is evident and not linked to movement through time periods. It is the very nature of autobiography to be unique; inevitably autobiography defies simple patterns. There are, however, certain obvious trends: a growing assertion of editorial control on the part of the narrators; greater sensitivity and professionalism on the part of recorder-editors; broadening ranges of experiences in the lives of the narrators along with a consistent concern for the preservation and communication of traditional values in their lives. The complexities of American Indian women's autobiography are best addressed in individual works where the reader may come to know intimately both the narrator's experiences and the process of bringing those experiences into autobiographical form.

# 2

# The Ethnographic Perspective: Early Recorders

To fail to understand another person's life story is, in general, to reject one's own humanity. Whether recorded in the extremity of personal or cultural annihilation, or in the midst of joy and productivity, the anthropological life history offers a positive moral opportunity to pass on stories that might otherwise never be told. For those who are bearers of a tradition, the opportunity to tell their story can be a gift; reassurance that they are indeed still alive, that their voices will be heard, and that their cultures can survive. It is a gift of equal importance for those generations to come who will take up that tradition and shape it to their own needs as the future unfolds.

L.L. Langness and Gelya Frank, *Lives: An Anthropological Approach to Biography*

In *Lives: An Anthropological Approach to Biography,* L. L. Langness and Gelya Frank discuss the life-history method in anthropology that emerged primarily out of research on American Indians.[1] It is this pioneering effort of recording life stories that is examined in this chapter, particularly as these works have illustrated women's views of their lives and cultures. Although the early ethnographic autobiographies do not approach the literary quality of those life stories that came later, they did serve as models for subsequent works and suggested that the lives of Indian women deserved examination within the context of tribe and culture.

At the end of the nineteenth century and early in the twentieth century a rising interest in native customs and an increasing desire "to salvage the remains of a culture" prompted anthropologists and ethnologists to begin recording life stories. The purpose was not to focus on an individual life, but rather to use a single life to illuminate a culture. The women whose lives were recorded during that period were the mothers and wives of the tribe, revealing the day-to-day events of their lives. Their stories differ from the stories of their male contemporaries in that they do not tell of war but rather of the gathering of herbs. They focus on preparing buffalo rather than hunting it, and they tell of raising children rather than of racing horses. These differences reflect the division of roles in the cultures. More than anything else, these stories reflect the relationships of women and men within a tribe.

As these life stories moved from the traditional oral mode to the recorded written form, much of the element of storytelling was inevitably lost. When the stories were written down, facial expressions, hand movements, and pauses were lost on the printed page. Editors decided what elements were significant to a woman's life or, more often, significant to field research on a given tribe. Indian women recognized that the essence of their lives could not always be communicated in a "foreign" language and that events which they thought significant might be considered naive or unimportant by their white interviewers. Taboos were broken: to tell the story of the family, women were often forced to speak the names of the dead.

Ethnographers had a distinct purpose for wanting to hear the stories; they were after linguistic or anthropological data to round out field reports. The material chosen for inclusion by these editors represented what they thought was significant. Many of the earliest collectors perceived themselves as necessary to salvage what would soon be lost: "It is evident that aboriginal manners and customs are rapidly disappearing, but notwithstanding that disappearance much remains unknown, and there has come a more urgent necessity to preserve for posterity by adequate record the many survivals before they disappear forever."[2]

The attitude of the "white man's burden" predominated in the earliest recorded autobiographies. Early ethnologists regarded the life stories as only a small part of the total field report on a given group, however. Often these narratives were published as miscellaneous additions to a tribal study. Franz Boas described autobiographies as being "of limited value, and useful chiefly for the study of the perversion of truth by memory."[3] In an article on the use of autobiographical evidence Alfred Kroeber explains that "among nonliterate tribal folk some normal elderly persons are likely to feel their life not as something interesting in its individuation and distinctiveness, but as an exemplification of a socialization. Such a person is conscious of himself first of all as a preserver and transmitter of his culture."[4]

Paul Radin had expressed similar sentiments earlier: "A native informant is, at best, interested merely in satisfying the demands of the investigator." One of the drawbacks to acquiring accurate and complete information, Radin believed, was that most investigators do not spend enough time with the tribes or individuals. Even when recorders were conscientious, Radin postulated, the final result was completely tinged with the investigator's emotional tone and "quite unsafe to follow." Despite the drawbacks, autobiography has been viewed throughout the century as a useful tool for anthropological research: "Such personal reminiscences and impressions, inadequate as they are, are likely to throw more light on the workings of the mind and emotions of primitive man than any amount of speculation from a sophisticated ethnologist or ethnological theorist."[5] It is these various assumptions that are reflected in some of the earliest autobiographies, particularly those discussed in this chapter.

One of the earliest recorders of information about North American Indian tribes was Truman Michelson. Among his published studies of tribes in the Midwest are recordings of ceremonies, descriptions of the contents of sacred bundles, accounts of funerals, and brief autobiographies. Through three narratives of American Indian women, Truman Michelson provides a generalized view of the lives of Indian women in traditional societies during a period of transition. "The Autobiography of a Fox Indian Woman," obtained in 1918, tells the story of a Mesquakie (Fox) woman who had been born in the late 1800s and who had had several children and three husbands. "Narrative of an Arapaho Woman" was obtained in 1932 from an informant born in 1855 and thus much older than the Fox woman—seventy-seven years old—when she told her story. The exact age of the Cheyenne woman in "The Narrative of a Southern Cheyenne Woman" is not indicated. The story was obtained in 1931, however, and the informant says that her mother is eighty years old, thus the narrator had also experienced the changes wrought upon American Indian tribes at the turn of the century.[6]

Much of Michelson's work was published in the volumes of the Bureau of American Ethnology, and in each case he prefaces his reports with the required introduction. This introductory material is useful, for it makes clear that Michelson relied heavily on tribal members to help him secure informants, dictate, and translate the information. In his work with the Mesquakies (Foxes) of Iowa, several tribal names appear repeatedly. It is also obvious that Michelson trusted those who were recording for him, and that he perceived his job to be the final ordering and structuring of both the original and the translation. It is useful to the linguistic scholar that Michelson frequently published both the native and English texts, making comparisons possible. The emphasis on linguistics suggests, however, that Michelson may have been less interested in the particular content and cultural information contained in the personal narratives and more interested in the linguistic patterns and variations in usage. He does not place emphasis on the informants as individual human beings; they are subjects expected to provide information, usually in a relatively short time. They are rarely named—often at their own request, because they were divulging information about the tribe or ceremonies which should have remained secret.

Despite some of these flaws, Michelson's accounts provide three early autobiographies in which American Indian women recorded their own impressions of their lives without editorial pressures: "No attempt was made to influence the informant in any way; so that the contents are the things which seem of importance to herself."[7] Michelson did serve as editor, however, and writes in the introduction to "The Autobiography of a Fox Woman," "It may be noted that at times the original autobiography was too naive and frank for European taste, and so a few sentences have been deleted."[8]

The three narratives tell of common experiences. All three women recall learning their roles from their mothers or other female relatives. Their stories dwell on their marriages, their children, and the roles other family members played in arranging marriages and caring for the children. All three emphasize the nature of proper behavior: they were concerned about what others might think of them should they talk to boys, remain out after dark, fail to protect their virtue, or become the object of community gossip. They had learned their lessons well and strove to be model women in their communities. Even after her marriage, the Southern Cheyenne woman was concerned about what others might think of her: "After I was married I thought I would have more freedom in going about with my girlfriends, but my mother watched me more closely. . . . This was done to prevent any gossip from my husband's people."[9]

None of the three narratives was recorded as literary autobiography. They appear as incidental records that were part of collections of ethnographic data on particular tribes. The exclusion of significant information, such as ages of the informants, and the emphasis on linguistic notes suggest that the collection of life stories was not the primary objective of Michelson's work. Michelson's admission that portions of the Fox autobiography which he felt were "too naive and frank for European taste" were omitted suggests further that the study had strictly defined parameters. Despite his interest in all facets of Fox life, Michelson recognized that explicit accounts of menstruation and childbirth would have to be omitted. His interest in the individual lives of these women was secondary to his interest in the languages, the tribes, and the general cultures, so he could justify omission of detailed information given by the informant.

Michelson's earliest recorded autobiography and longest narrative was obtained from a Fox (Mesquakie) woman in Tama, Iowa. The Fox woman was born many years after the Mesquakie Indians had returned to their "home" along the Iowa River. Her autobiography makes no reference to the politics involved in that move, nor does it deal with factionalism or clan differences within the tribe, yet the period at the turn of the century was a difficult time internally for the Mesquakies. There was controversy over the position of chief and continuing strife between the conservatives and progressives. The federal government had opened an Indian boarding school in 1898, but the Mesquakies refused to send their children, and the school was forced to close by 1911. In 1913 the Mesquakies performed the first public powwow, inviting the people of Tama to observe. Mesquakie history shows that the first two decades of the twentieth century were years of change for the people and a time of increasing contact with the government and their white neighbors.[10] Yet none of this is reflected in the collected life story.

The Fox woman's autobiography is the story of one woman growing up in this culture which, despite the intrusions of the outside, yet today maintains many of the traditions of the past. Her life story focuses on her tribal education and integration into the ways of her people, what she was expected to know in order to take her place within that society. She tells of "growing up"—making dolls, planting, weaving belts, and learning the many necessary tasks which would be hers as a woman. Her concern is personal—her education, marriage, and children. She is seen as a somewhat isolated figure; the important relationships are with family members, and there are only vague allusions to friends and others in the community. Tribal connections seem important only for ceremonial needs, like adoptions, giveaways, and funerals. Her strength is derived from the extended family, first her mother and uncles, later her own children. Much of the material in the Fox woman's narrative appears in a slightly different form in the information dictated to Michelson by Harry Lincoln, which appeared as "How Meskwaki Children Should

Be Brought Up" in *American Indian Life*,[11] which suggests that the narrative presents fairly typical behavior.

The events leading up to the time of recording help explain both the history of the Mesquakies and why some tribal members were eager to cooperate with Michelson in recording their customs. In 1840 Governor Robert Lucas of the Iowa Territory reported, "The Sac and Fox Indians . . . are fast progressing toward extermination."[12] Over fifty years later, E. Sidney Hartland, in the preface to Mary Alicia Owen's book *Folklore of the Musquakie Indians of North America*, wrote, "They have been beaten; and they are now a dying people. Their blood may be mingled with that of their conquerors and thus their life may in some measure be perpetuated. But their ancient beliefs and institutions are passing away forever."[13] Most observers had written the Mesquakies off by 1900, but these predictions did not come true. The Mesquakie Indians today live on the Mesquaki Settlement near Tama, Iowa. The story of their removal to Kansas in 1846 as a result of the Treaty of 1842 and their subsequent return in 1856 to purchase land is unique in American Indian history. The Mesquakies today are still traditional people who have maintained their tribal ways and preserved their stories.

Despite the constancy in Mesquakie behavior, much of what has been written by outsiders has been inaccurate. Michelson, relying on some of the earlier published reports on the Mesquakies, perpetuated the inaccurate tribal designation. The name *Fox* (*Renard*) was given to a group of people encountered by French trader-explorers early in the nineteenth century and designated clan identity of that group rather than tribal affiliation. The name, once assigned, remained, although the designation the people have for themselves is *Mesquakie*, "The Red Earth People." Michelson knew this and referred to it in published reports, but he chose the government's label to designate the tribe for this autobiography. In Parson's *American Indian Life*, however, he used the tribal name Mesquakie (Meskwaki).

Michelson was not the first to do field research on the Mesquakies. One of the earliest writers to discuss Mesquakie customs was Mary Alicia Owen. Her limited vision is obvious in several areas, and her accounts of Mesquakie life are contradicted in the Fox woman's autobiography and by Michelson in other publications. In discussing clan affiliation, Owen states that women belong to their father's totem, but that if the father dies or the parents are divorced the woman goes to her mother's totem. She states further that a woman belongs to her husband's totem when she marries.[14] This is clearly not the case. The Mesquakies are patrilineal, and children always belong to their father's clan even though they may at times participate in the activities of other clans.[15] The Fox woman made no reference to her clan membership, perhaps because she took it for granted.

The Fox woman discusses mourning in her account, and her experiences are quite different from the customs Owen describes. Owen recounts the "cries and shrieks" of women in mourning; but Mesquakie women act more in the manner described in the Fox woman's narrative: "I undid my hair and loosened it. For several nights I could not sleep as I was sorrowful. . . . I wore black clothing. . . . I was fasting. . . . Soon I would walk far off to cry, it was far off so that it would not be known."[16]

The description of the Fox woman's behavior after the death of her second husband appears consistent with Mesquakie practice then and now. Even today public emotions are deemed a "show" and only a pretense of grieving. William Jones, an anthropologist of Fox descent, confirmed that stoic behavior was expected, pointing out that a widow was mocked and insulted if she wept for her husband.[17] After her husband's death, the Fox woman did not show her emotions openly, she participated in the traditional giveaway, and she mourned appropriately for four years. She was now a true Mesquakie woman; she had fulfilled the necessary roles expected of her, and she was sad but satisfied.

Although it is unlikely that this one woman's life is representative of all Mesquakie women, her narrative does provide an insider's perspective on the role of women within the tribe. It is possible to evaluate the narrative in several ways: comparison with available information on the Mesquakies, comparison with the perceptions of Mesquakie women today, and the study of the autobiography as literary document. In particular, how does this early ethnographic autobiography fit into the loose genre of autobiographies of American Indian women?

Michelson's means of obtaining the narrative deserves examination. The number of people through whom this story was told almost guaranteed that there would be some errors in translation that might mislead a reader. The story, told in Mesquakie to Harry Lincoln, corrected by his wife, Dalottiwa, translated by Horace Poweshiek, and finally edited and published by Truman Michelson, had been dictated only once. Two years passed between the first dictation and the final translation. Harry Lincoln was half Mesquakie and half Winnebago; his wife was Mesquakie, as is Horace Poweshiek, who is now probably the oldest Mesquakie living on the Settlement near Tama, Iowa.

Poweshiek served as a translater for many of Michelson's publications and years later emerged in Mesquakie history as one of the men appointed to draft a constitution in accordance with the Indian Reorganization Act of 1934. He was at that time a member of the Young Bear faction and a progressive. This group was pro-white and ultimately was successful in getting the new constitution approved by the tribe.[18] Because Michelson does not deal with the politics on the Settlement, we do not know if the Fox woman represented the conservative or progressive faction, nor do we know how politics may have influenced the translations. (This is not a minor point; factionalism continues to be a divisive factor on the Mesquakie Settlement.)

There are some statements in the narrative that require clarification and explanation. Because of the brevity of the narrative there often are events that are not explained. For example, the Fox woman is warned against sleeping over at the wickiups of her friends. Although this appears to be a practice that in itself is inoccuous, it is, in fact, a part of the discipline a young girl must learn lest she get into the habit of sleeping in different places. A contemporary Mesquakie woman stated the reason very succinctly: girls who don't learn this early will end up "sleeping around" when they become women.[19] During a discussion of proper behavior for young girls, Adeline Wanatee, today a Mesquakie grandmother, revealed that girls are told they should not watch dogs copulate; her own mother had taught her that.[20]

Michelson's translation dealing with menstruation says that "The state of being a young woman is evil."[21] Yet the Mesquakie word *myanetwima* means more literally *bad,* or, in this context, *unclean*. This Mesquakie attitude is a part of a lifeway that recognizes opposites as well as the reconciliation of those opposites. Although a woman during her period was isolated—another way of teaching discipline—that time was also positive in that it marked the beginning of womanhood and promised the potential of motherhood. Rather than the manitous or gods "hating" the event, they took pity on her, or felt sorry for her, knowing the loneliness of isolation and the fear associated with the first experience of womanhood. The matter-of-fact attitude of the mother contrasts with the honest fear expressed by the narrator when she first menstruates. The practice of isolation was necessary to keep the power contained. Adeline Wanatee interprets the experience simply: "Men have visions, women have children."[22] The power associated with the two acts is comparable and explains why isolation is a factor in vision seeking as well as in response to bodily changes associated with menstruation and childbirth. Michelson's translation then imposes a negative value on this event which was not, and is not, present in Mesquakie society.[23]

The Fox woman makes many references to her mother's control over her. It was her mother, not a male relative, who made the decision about whom the woman would marry. Later the narrator indicates that immorality regarding men would bring shame to her brothers or uncles, so it is clear she also considers the effects her actions might have on her male relatives. It was only after her mother's death that the Fox woman believed she was free to marry the man she had always loved, for only then was she released from the traditional obligations.

The use of terms such as *mother* and *grandmother* does not conform to non-Indian labels for relatives. The label *grandmother* was assigned to several women; in fact, almost any older woman or medicine woman is likely to be referred to as *grandmother*. The label connotes wisdom and evokes respect. One cannot be a medicine woman until after menopause, suggesting further the respect and responsibility of age. Maternal involvement in the life of a daughter is confirmed by present-day Mesquakie society. Mrs. Wanatee said that her own mother was influential in her decision not to be sterilized after she had had three children; she had five more children, the last when she was fifty-three years old.[24]

The Fox woman revealed the importance of children in her life. When her first baby died, she feared her own complicity because of the unloving relationship she had with her husband. Her mother had warned her of the evils of anger:

> "Finally you will make your son angry if you are always having trouble with each other. Babies die when they become angry," I was told.

> Soon, when our little boy nearly knew how to talk, he became ill. I felt very sorrowful. Later on, indeed, he died. It is surely very hard to have death (in the family). One cannot help feeling badly. "That is why I told you about it when you were both unfortunately frightening him," I was told. . . . I felt worse after he was buried.[25]

Never happy with this first husband, the Fox woman shows great strength and independence by leaving him and marrying her first love, a man whose attitude was completely different from that of the first husband. She loves her second husband and he is good to her, but he dies, leaving her childless. After a proper mourning period, she allows a suitor to court her and decides to marry again. She states, however, that the only reason for her remarriage was to have children: "If I had had a child I should have never married again."[26] Childbirth and children were necessary to carry out her role as a Mesquakie woman. Although the narrator recognized the pain associated with childbirth, she was also aware of the important responsibility women have in continuing the tribe.

> For we women have a hard time at childbirth. We suffer. Some are killed by the babies. But we are not afraid of it, as we have been made to be that way. That is probably the reason why we are not afraid of it. Oh, if we were all afraid of it, when we all became old, that is as far as we could go. We should not be able to branch out (to a new generation).[27]

Given the circumscribed purposes Michelson had for obtaining the Fox woman's life story, evaluation of the document as autobiography raises several issues. Certainly the narrative is valuable as ethnography, as a reflection of the day-to-day responsibilities of Mesquakie women, and as a record of the moral and domestic education of a young Indian girl. The Fox woman clearly is the central character, yet we know little of her psychological motivation or her real reactions to the many events of her life. We know her only through what she is willing to tell us through translators, some of whom were male, and through what intermediaries ultimately decided was worth preserving.

The setting, the Mesquakie Settlement outside of Tama, is not significant in the telling of the story. The location is not mentioned either in the introduction or in the body of the narrative. Presumably, those anthropologists who followed Michelson's fieldwork were aware that the Mesquakies lived in Iowa. Certainly the narrator perceived no need to describe either the landscape or her immediate physical environment.

If the story had been told when the Fox woman was older we might have expected to see a turning point in her life or a climactic moment. As it is, she has experienced a great deal—three marriages, the death of children and a loved spouse, and the birth of more children—yet she has many more years to live. Ironically, she does indeed perceive her life to have reached a climax of sorts. She has borne children and now feels her role has been played out: "After we had many children then my husband died. 'Well, I shall never marry again,' I thought, 'for now these children of mine will help me (get a living),' I thought."[28]

The narrative tells of her preparation for her role as a Fox woman, and having learned and having fulfilled that role, she can begin to prepare for that time when, past her child-bearing years, she will act in the role of teacher for younger girls, perhaps even become a medicine woman herself.

Michelson collected two additional accounts from Indian women, but both are fragmentary in comparison with the Fox woman's story. The two narratives obtained in the 1930s are brief and incomplete, resulting in interesting but stylistically flat accounts. A. L. Kroeber cites Michelson's "The Narrative of a Southern Cheyenne Woman" and "Narrative of an Arapaho Woman" as examples in which the narrator supresses individuality and personal feeling in order to express the accepted social standards of the group.[29] These two reports disclose family relationships, courtship and marriage, and some ritual, and both the informants and the editor make it clear that there are omissions.

In the summer of 1931 Mack Haag, working for Michelson, obtained the record of a Southern Cheyenne woman in Calumet, Oklahoma, which was published by Michelson. It is a brief story, one that hardly does justice to the life of its teller. The Cheyenne woman tells of childhood play, of her arranged marriage, eight children, and the death of her husband; she ends with a brief account of the Sacrifice Offering Ceremony, in which she participated to fulfill her dead husband's pledge.

The narrator tells of her instruction in the practical ways of the tribe: "My mother taught me everything connected with the tipi."[30] Her mother taught her in other "ways" as well, particularly the "way" of the oral tradition. She mentions incidents that she does not remember happening but which were passed on orally by her mother and have thus become a part of her personal history. She tells also of learning social norms: "My aunt told me not to play with young men."[31] The emphasis on morality among Cheyenne women had been confirmed earlier by George Bird Grinnell: "The women of the Cheyennes are famous among all western tribes for their chastity."[32]

She understood well her role within the family and the culture and acknowledged her position: "My parents were very proud of me. In fact they treated me as if I were a male member of the family." Her awareness of male and female roles appears frequently in the narrative. The limitations of gender are apparent in her statement about the Tipi Decorators, the woman's society to which she belonged. In speaking of the Tipi Decorators, the Southern Cheyenne woman says, "I was very carefully instructed never to disclose the ceremony in the presence of males. So I shall be obliged to discontinue the subject." Ceremonial information is generally missing from this and from the other narratives obtained by Michelson, perhaps because the narratives were brief, or because Michelson recorded ceremonial practices elsewhere. The Cheyenne woman refers to old women and "sacred ritualistic ceremonies" without explanation. She does give descriptive details of the preparation for the Sacrifice Offering and includes information about the altar, but the narrative ends abruptly with the conclusion of her description of the ceremony.[33] As readers we do not know if she ended the recording session feeling she had already shared too much, or if the recorder, perhaps anxious only for the ethnographic detail about the Sacrifice Offering, ended the session when he had obtained his information. In any case, the narrative is brief and appears unfinished. It is a sketch rather than a developed literary document.

In 1932 Jesse Rowlodge obtained a narrative from a seventy-seven-year-old Arapaho woman near Geary, Oklahoma, and it was published by Michelson as "Narrative of an Arapaho Woman." This is a short account, in part because the narrator indicates she had only a few days to provide Rowlodge with information. As had the Cheyenne informant, this narrator stressed the teachings from her mother and paternal aunts. Respect, however, was reserved for male relatives;

she does not mention private experiences "out of respect to my brothers and male cousins."[34]

Michelson's comment in the Introduction prefaces the narrative ambiguously:

> Most early writers on the Arapaho have a poor opinion of Arapaho in contrast with Cheyenne women. Were this expressed only by sensational and unreliable "authorities," I should pay no attention to it; but as sober and reliable a writer as Clark confirms this; he also condemns some other tribes and praises the Sioux and Cheyenne for the morality of their women. As far as the Arapaho are concerned, I am inclined to believe that their unfavorable reputation is due to the fact that some institutional practices recorded by other writers and myself were observed and supposed to be of every day occurrence, whereas they are strictly circumscribed and do not justify the opinions expressed.[35]

Grinnell had written earlier about the "notorious looseness of [Arapaho] women" in his work on the Cheyenne.[36] This woman does not fit the negative stereotype to which Michelson alludes, however; instead, she stresses the instruction she received, mentions that Arapaho mothers watched their daughters strictly at all times, and observes the commitment to tribal custom in respecting her brother's wishes concerning her marriage. Although she describes her pleasure at having a certain degree of freedom during her marriage, her behavior is not described as immoral or loose.

The narrator states that she left her third husband when he chose to take another wife, describes each of her four marriages, and explains why she sacrificed a finger to elicit good health for her sister. In all of the telling she is direct and explicit.

The conclusion of the narrative, however, resonates with wistfulness for the "old days," making clear again that this is a life story of a woman who has experienced profound changes in her life:

> There were no briar weeds, or stickers, or burrs; so the children as well as their parents were nearly always barefooted. All that one could see on the prairies was grass, buffalo grass and blue stem. When camps were pitched we would make our beds on the ground with grass for under cushions. The air was always fresh. We wore no head-shade; in fact we didn't mind the weather in those days.[37]

The literary value of these personal narratives recorded by Michelson lies in their representation of a particular mode of autobiography. The women whose lives are documented presumably did not initiate the activity. They were willing and perhaps paid volunteers for ethnographic fieldwork on their tribes. Kroeber reports that the Arapaho and Cheyenne narratives were recorded by younger native tribesmen, probably kinsmen, so we do not know what cultural restrictions may have been operative.[38] There is no indication that the women had an opportunity to read or correct the final versions; they may not have seen them or known the use which was made of them. The narratives were parts of much longer commissioned reports and as such were for an audience of professionals in the discipline rather than for the public at large.

It is obvious that there was no attempt to produce literary documents, even though the Fox woman's account comes close to being readable as a sustained narrative. Despite the initial purposes, these narratives are valuable today as records of these women's lives and how they perceived them. It is clear that they viewed their roles as women as tribally defined, almost rigid. Their stories are not told to glorify themselves, examine tribal politics, criticize white society, or emulate non-Indian autobiography. Instead, they forthrightly tell of the events of their lives. Although Michelson's consistent intent was to record ethnographic documents, the individuality of the narrators persists. It appears impossible to depersonalize an individual life or to reduce the drama of real life to anthropological data.

Close examination of these recorded autobiographies invites us to focus on the relationship between the narrator and recorder; however, Michelson's distance from his informants allows only speculation about what kind of interaction he had with the women whose lives he chronicled. Like several early ethnographic autobiographies, Michelson's accounts do not provide many insights into the intimate lives of these women.

Clearly, the beginning of the twentieth century was a period of experimentation in the recording of life stories. While some, such as Michelson, focused on accounts that revealed general lifeways and linguistic analyses, other recorders, such as Gilbert L. Wilson, Frank Linderman, and Ruth Bunzel, spent more time getting to know their informants as individual members of their tribes. They also provided much ethnographic information, particularly Wilson in his study of

Hidatsa agriculture and Bunzel in her study of Zuni linguistics, but their sensitivity to their narrators provided for more interesting autobiographical accounts.

In 1906 Gilbert L. Wilson and his brother Frederick went to Fort Berthold Reservation and established a friendship with the Hidatsa Indians who were living there. Wilson, an ordained Presbyterian minister, spent a considerable amount of time with the Hidatsas, first doing ethnological fieldwork for the American Museum of Natural History and later as a doctoral candidate at the University of Minnesota. He sought out a "representative agriculturalist" and in 1912 recorded the story of Buffalo Bird Woman (also known as Waheenee-wea, Maxi'diwiac, and Mahidiwia); in 1913 he recorded the life story of her son Edward Goodbird (Tsaka'Kasakic). The result of Wilson's thesis work on Hidatsa agriculture, *Agriculture of the Hidatsa Indians: An Indian Interpretation,* was published in 1917.[39] Wilson established a solid relationship with Goodbird, his translator; and Buffalo Bird Woman, Goodbird's mother, became Wilson's adopted mother and his principal informant. Her accounts of corn planting were "taken down almost literally as translated by Goodbird."[40] Wilson was determined to let Buffalo Bird Woman's words remain the focus of his research:

> The writer claims no credit beyond arranging the material and putting the interpreter's Indian-English translations into proper idiom. Bits of Indian philosophy and shrewd or humorous observations found in the narrative are not the writer's, but the informant's, and are as they fell from her lips. The writer has sincerely endeavored to add to the narrative essentially nothing of his own. . . . It is an Indian woman's interpretation of economics; the thought she gave to her fields; the philosophy of her labors.[41]

Buffalo Bird Woman's account is appropriately literary, for she begins with the Hidatsa creation myth, telling the story of the tribe's ascent up a vine from the bottom of Devil's Lake. Only half of the tribe climbed to the surface, leaving the rest still drumming beneath the water. Practically every chapter includes storytelling, accounts of social relationships, and details of her own experiences. She gives a careful account of her female lineage, including biological as well as social mothers and grandmothers, before she begins to tell of planting the gardens. Although Wilson was writing ethnography, he recognized that corn and tobacco planting among the Hidatsas could not be separated from myth and ritual.

In 1921 Wilson published the autobiography *Waheenee: An Indian Girl's Story, Told by Herself,* a book suitable for children as well as for an adult audience, incorporating much of the information he had included in his scholarly account with the addition of details about Buffalo Bird Woman's life. The book was originally intended for children, thus it focuses on the child's life, giving only brief mention of her arranged marriage to Magpie and her later marriage to Son-of-a-star, a Mandan. At the conclusion, the narrator jumps ahead from the birth of Goodbird to fifty years later when she is telling her story as an eighty-three-year-old woman. Wilson writes, "The aim has been not to give a biography of Waheenee, but a series of stories illustrating the philosophy, the Indian-thinking of her life."[42] It is clear that Wilson recognized that this was not a chronological autobiography, but rather a philosophical account written to provide young readers with an understanding of this Hidatsa woman who had experienced the forced move in 1885 from the Knife River Villages, where she had been born about 1839, to Fort Berthold Reservation and who, as an old woman, recognized how much life had changed for her people and her family. Wilson's relationship with Buffalo Bird Woman and Goodbird is close, and he is sensitive to the different perspectives of the mother and her son. Goodbird, a Christian, did not identify with his mother's views of the past, believing instead that life would be better with the new ways: "We Hidatsas know that our Indian ways will soon perish; but we feel no anger. The government has given us a good reservation, and we think the new way better for our children."[43]

The different perspectives of mother and son reflect the intrusions of missionaries, the government, and anthropologists upon Hidatsa culture. Goodbird had been sent to a mission school, and he became pastor of the Congregational Chapel at Independence. He spoke Hidatsa, Mandan, Dakota, and English and dictated his autobiography to Wilson in English. Buffalo Bird Woman, however, spoke no English, and her communication with Wilson was through her son. Wilson analyzes Buffalo Bird Woman's philosophy: "She is a conservative and sighs for the good old times, yet is aware that the younger generation of Indians must adopt civilized ways." Despite some ethnocentrism in Wilson's analysis, it is clear he was sympathetic to his narrator: "May the Indian woman's story of her toil be a plea for our better appreciation of her race."[44]

Another ethnographer who published a life story of an Indian woman was Frank Linderman. He was intimately involved with his seventy-four-year-old informant, and the life story of Pretty-shield reflects, both in content and in style, their close relationship. *Pretty-shield: Medicine Woman of the Crows* was first published (as *Red Mother*) in 1932. This account was translated from Crow to English, and Linderman is present throughout the text providing explanatory comments that another anthropologist might have relegated to notes or an appendix. We learn as part of the running commentary that Pretty-shield received four dollars for her recording session, that she shared women's jokes with her interpreter Goes-together that she would not share with Linderman, and that she irreverently spoke the names of the dead to tell a more complete story. Pretty-shield is aware of the changes that have been wrought on her life, and she shares her frustrations: "I am trying to live a life I do not understand. . . . Ours was a different world before the buffalo went away, and I belong to that other world."[45] Linderman does little restructuring of the text, allowing Pretty-shield's childhood stories to be included at the place she remembered them rather than at the chronological moment. The story is a wistful one, a story of remembering and of questioning: "How could we live in the old way when everything was gone?"[46]

In 1926 Ruth Bunzel from the Department of Anthropology at Columbia University was studying the Zuni language, and she was fortunate in having as her interpreter Flora Zuni, a thirty-six-year-old woman who spoke both English and Zuni. During her second summer with the Zuni people, Bunzel recorded the brief autobiography of Lina Zuni, Flora's seventy-year-old mother. Flora Zuni was both translator and interpreter for her mother, resulting in the unique circumstance of having a completely female "team" telling, translating, and recording a woman's life story. In the Foreword to *Zuni Texts* Bunzel credits Flora Zuni for her careful interpretation and corrections of the text. Although Bunzel's concern was with language, she apparently believed the record of Lina Zuni's life, most often described as one of poverty, was significant. She includes Lina Zuni's oft-repeated phrase "We were very poor" and retains the original sentence structure; for example, "Very terrible were the words of the old people."[47] Lina Zuni recounts "how I came to be alive, how I grew up like a poor person." In her brief account she tells of rituals and prayers, and of old animosities between the Zunis and the Navajos. She ends with her uncle's advice: "Do not think of where you have come from, but rather look forward to where you are to go."[48] By means of this brief life story Bunzel adds a human quality to the study of Zuni linguistics and in the process provides yet another glimpse into the lives of American Indian women.

All of the autobiographies discussed in this chapter were recorded as ethnographic documents, and they share some characteristics. The women told their stories through interpreters to recorders who were more interested in language and culture than in autobiography. Despite the original purposes for the publications, however, the recorders often became involved in the lives of their informants; some, such as Wilson, became adopted relatives. Those recorders who knew their subjects well were able to communicate the lives with sensitivity and insight, providing the reader with a more full account of an individual life. Upon careful examination, it is clear that these early ethnographers provided the basic patterns for life stories that were to follow.

# 3

# Maria Chona: An Independent Woman in Traditional Culture

You see, we *have* power. Men have to dream to get power from the spirits and they think of everything they can—song and speeches and marching around, hoping that the spirits will notice them and give them some power. But we *have* power . . . Children. Can any warrior make a child, no matter how brave and wonderful he is?

Marie Chona, *Papago Woman*

Maria Chona is a paradox—a woman so deeply tied to the landscape and life of traditional Papago culture that she expresses it with lyrical skill, yet so personally independent that she shatters the most firmly entrenched stereotypes applied to Indian women. She is a strong woman, sometimes appearing to be at odds with the strong culture she lives in, but ultimately in harmony with her tribal traditions because she is always at one with the land that is the sacred foundation of her culture.

Like all works of American Indian literature, Maria Chona's autobiography is permeated with a sense of place, the inextricable interweaving of language and landscape, the concept that the land is not merely setting for the story, but that the story is formed and shaped by the land, and the land is given significance and vitality in language. In the introductory chapters of *Papago Woman*,[1] narrator Maria Chona makes several statements about the landscape of the Papagoria, the traditional home of her people on the southwestern desert of Arizona and northern Sonora, Mexico. As recorder-editor Ruth Underhill describes the work she and Chona began on a long, dusty ride across the Papago reservation in the 1930s; places along the road stimulate Maria's memory and cause her to speak of remembered scenes connected to particular places. Included are places to which Elder Brother, a creator, had given names, and places given significance by legends and tales, and many places where her personal experiences invest the land with particular meaning.

Underhill reveals, through Chona's responses to the landscape during their first days together, that Chona recognizes three different kinds of places as she narrates her experiences: home, where she spent much time learning and practicing traditional Papago female skills like grinding corn and cooking beans and caring for family members; the mysterious desert beyond the village where Maria ran for water, escaped Apache raids, where her brother fell into trance-like dreams that brought him medicine power; and finally, the particular places associated with ancient stories, myths, legends, tales, places given power by language.

Though in the autobiography portion of this book Chona does not give detailed descriptions of the places that are potent with meaning, her memory is totally tied to them. In her life she knew a wide area of the vast Papago landscape; and many places that she never saw she knew intimately from the stories brought home by her brother and father from their warrior raids and their sacred journey to the California Gulf for salt. She had moved around much—to Mesquite Root, to Burnt Seed (Santa Rosa Village), to where the Rock Stands Up, to Tucson and Mexico, to the cactus fruit-harvesting camps in the mountains, to the villages of the River People (Pimas) of the north who shared their language and love of gambling. In addition, she knew many places through stories and songs recited in the winter months, each one defining an element of the Papago world. She was a woman who traveled widely and imaginatively because she listened.

However, the intimacy between story and landscape in Maria Chona's autobiography is understated by Maria herself. It is Underhill who fleshes out the story and the descriptions of the landscape in her introduction to the autobiography and in the supplementary materials that follow it. In the 1979 edition of the work originally published in the 1930s, Underhill devotes considerable space to Chona, describing her relationship to her tribe and landscape in a chapter titled "Chona: Her Land and Her Time," a section that provides context, both historical and cultural, for the autobiography that follows. While Chona, in relating her life experiences, takes the landscape for granted, concentrating instead on events and incidents, Underhill, in her introduction, provides images of the Papagoria that give texture and specific setting to Chona's life.

Underhill tells the reader that the Papagos are the Bean People, who rely on the torrential rains that pass over the desert in midsummer to nourish patches of beans, corn, melons, and squash. These rains are attracted by the ceremonies that follow the harvest of the fruit from the sahuaro cactus growing on the mountains of the eastern portion of Papago land. She gives the reader a sense of the vast distances of the desert, the scarcity of water, the hunger of the late winter, the isolation from other small villages scattered across the arroyos and trails, the enmity of the Apaches to the east, and finally the effect of the Spanish missionaries and the mission at San Xavier del Bac near Tucson. Their introduction of Christianity and livestock forever changed the lives of the people and the face of the land.

Ruth Underhill's insight into Chona, the landscape of her narrative, and the ways of the Papago people are those of an outsider, but an outsider trained to observe carefully and interpret cautiously. The result of her deliberate immersion in Papago culture is the pleasing style by which the remembered scenes of Maria's life are conveyed and the life of a woman of another time and culture made accessible. Underhill immerses the reader in the land, but Chona invests the Papago landscape with motion and meaning, vitality and value, a sense of Papago life from within the culture, as she tells the events of her life from the 1840s to the 1930s. The autobiography is a story of Maria's relationship to language and landscape. "I was born there, on the land," she begins.[2]

Of all the autobiographies of American Indian women, Maria Chona's *Papago Woman* perhaps best demonstrates the power and strength of traditional Indian women within their own society. Because Maria Chona is an "executive woman," she consistently controls her own life. "Executive" is a term her recorder-editor uses to describe her in the Introduction, a judgment resulting from an intense relationship with Chona and her life story over a long period of time. It is a role Chona seems to recognize in herself as well, one which she takes considerable care to articulate in her narrative. She tells the reader she was "different" because she had husbands who took her places and she knew cures and songs—landscape and language. She was also independent enough to leave her husband when he took a second wife. The contemporary reader must wonder at the independence and mobility that marked Maria Chona's life, especially in light of the stereotypes of Indian women as domestic drudges.

It must be granted that many Indian narrators are, indeed, atypical of their tribes in some measure. The very fact that they engage in a personal narrative sets them apart from those who do not, who are not storytellers or whose tribal values dissuade them from putting themselves forward, drawing attention to themselves. However, the assertiveness necessary for narration of a life story and the dramatic elements required for an engaging narrative are hardly eccentric or unique. The very nature of autobiography seeks to differentiate the subject from the rest of the tribal members, emphasizing elements in her character and actions that depart from, or intensify, tribal norms, but also balancing this with elements that portray the subject as a member of her society. Ruth Underhill notes in a 1981 interview that Chona was untypical of Papago women in that "she was a great leader among women," controlling and directing, but her behavior grew out of Papago culture.[3] In support of this viewpoint, Papago interpreter Ella Lopez Antone, who translated for Chona and Underhill in the summer of 1930, does not see Chona as aberrant or unique but points out, "She was a very, very—I can't say sophisticated—but she was a proud person, very strong."[4] So while Chona is clearly atypical in some ways, she is not outside the bounds of acceptable tribal patterns.

Chona tells her story at age 90, so it is possible her memory is not as sharp as it could have been, yet Maria comes across as an individual Indian woman who is aware of her personal skills and position within her tribe. She is also aware of the changes that were taking place within her society and refers to liquor and Catholicism and their influences on the people. She points out, too, that her father was buried, not put in a cave, and that they no longer slept on mats but had started using blankets and pillows.

Throughout the autobiography Maria is aware of her audience—white people—and often relates events in her life to experiences with which the audience can identify. There are elements in the work that identify Maria's life as one that certainly does not fit any stereotypes. She recognizes that as a song maker and visionary she was not typical, and she also has powers to cure and skills at basket making that set her apart from the majority of both men and women. That is not to say, however, that Chona is not in many respects representative of her time and her culture. As Underhill makes clear, Maria Chona is an exceptionally good choice for a Papago autobiography. Because she is the daughter of one of the most important chiefs in Papago tribal history, Con Quien, The Gambler, she is a witness to an unusually wide variety of village events, and she participates fully in the customs and lifeways of her people.

The variety of people she has intimate contact with during her lifetime is broad and her knowledge of the sacred aspects of tribal life thorough. While her immersion in tribal ways appears to contrast sharply with her independent nature, there is no indication of serious conflict in her personality or any rupture with tribal behavior in her life story. The latitude for self-expression by Indian women is and has been broad. Some tribes are matriarchial and matrilinial; others record stories of women warriors, medicine women, tribal elders and advisers. No single role is prescribed, though often the role of mother and spouse is emphasized in ethnographic materials. Thus, Chona, despite her apparently unusual life and considerable expression of independence, at no time acted outside the boundaries of acceptable tribal behavior and in no way threatened the well-being of her family or village. Her life is both representative and unique, and her candid narration allows intimate knowledge of her. Thus the autobiography offers perhaps the clearest and most eloquent insight extant into the life of an Indian woman of her time.

The effectiveness of her personal narrative is the result of her ability to relate her life experiences fully and well, but it is also in large measure the result of the sensitivity and insight of Underhill, who recognized Chona as an appropriate subject and effective narrator. As Underhill writes in her introduction, she hazarded auto travel from New York to Arizona in the early years of this century, not to compile an autobiography, but to gather ethnographic material on the Papago Indians of the Sonoran desert. She had no notion that a Maria Chona existed when she set out, let alone that Chona could provide the raw text of a compelling narrative from her life experiences and observations. But the meeting of these two women occurred, and as Underhill collected ethnographic material from Chona over a period of months, she began to recognize Chona as an appropriate subject for autobiography.

Maria Chona's autobiography, though it was first published in 1936, is in essence a nineteenth-century autobiography, in fact, the only complete personal narrative of a nineteenth-century Indian woman that is not romanticized, or a story of conversion to Christianity, or a case history to illustrate ethnographic data, or a plea against unjust treatment of tribal peoples. Furthermore, the uniqueness and importance of this autobiography "rests only in part on the fact that it is a woman's story. Thanks to Chona's longevity and the curious circumstances of Papago history in which intensive contact with non-Indians was considerably delayed . . . we are afforded a rare, first-hand glimpse of many aspects of truly aboriginal practices among the Papago."[5] Not only is the work unusual ethnographically, but the narrative style is recognized as literary. Clyde Kluckhohn noted shortly after the work appeared, "The story has a distinct literary flavor of its own, and is much less a stark sequence of events than most of the autobiographies published earlier."[6]

As he suggests, *Papago Woman* offers both a complete social narrative and a literary expression of the life and roles of a traditional Indian woman. It is a work that breaks through the limits of social documentation to present, not just a complete life story, but one that uses literary devices and techniques to achieve a narrative persona and dramatic impact. It is a work that pays attention to the mode of presentation as well as the content.

In many ways Maria Chona's autobiography is not unique, but is strikingly similar to other narratives by Indian women approximately her contemporaries. Like Mountain Wolf Woman,[7] her life is long and spans a period of almost complete isolation from white influences to a time of frequent contact. Also, as in the case of the Winnebago narrative, Maria Chona's recorder-editor is an outstanding anthropologist. Like *Me and Mine* and *A Pima Past,* both works by women who were born two generations later than she, Chona's work is sharply focused on tribal and family ways. Like Pretty-shield,[8] Chona is called to be a medicine woman, and as with most, her work incorporates ritual and ceremony. But several distinct elements set apart Maria Chona's life story from all those other personal narratives by Indian women: lyric prose, dramatic incident, concentration on traditional life experiences, the subject's assertion of independence, exceptional ethnographic and narrative detail, extensive use of dramatic dialogue, discussion of field and editing methods in an introduction, and its use as the basis for a fictional character in a subsequent novel (*Hawk over Whirlpools*) by the recorder-editor, whose reputation as a scholar of Papago culture is recognized in both tribal and academic circles.[9]

Maria Chona's life story is neither sentimental nor desperate. Her life is hard but not rueful. Despite the seasonal threats of famine and the harshness of the desert landscape, there is a sense of joy in her life, as in her pleasure in grinding the corn harvested painstakingly from "the fair stalks, the thick root, the broad leaves" sung over each night as the corn was growing.[10] Everything in Chona's life is intimately connected to the land and to song offering sustenance, ensuring both spiritual and physical survival.

There is a range of responses to events that elicits respect and even empathy from the reader. There is delight in becoming "beautifully" drunk at the summer rain ceremony. There is humor and laughter, and always there is song. There is tragedy in the loss of child after child, but her calm fatalism is evident in her precognition, "I always knew when my children were to die." Only at the end of her life is there sorrow, and even in her statement, "It is not good to be old, not beautiful," is implicit a richness and satisfaction in all that has gone before.[11] There is diversity of emotion and action in her brief account of her life, and there is *spirit* in Maria Chona, inherent as much in her vision of life as in the unique ambience of it.

By circumstance, this woman, born in 1845, was isolated from white contact most of her life; by her choice, or Underhill's, white influence is minimal in her story. Only rarely are we given glimpses of the influx of white settlers into the Sonoran desert, as when she laments the effect of nonceremonial liquor on her brother-in-law and later when she records her recollections of going with her second husband to work in Tucson and her purchase of shawls, staples, and a sewing machine in the white man's store. The impact of white culture on her life is not strong, and characteristic of her approach to all things, Chona selects from it only that which is useful or acceptable to her. She is a woman immersed in the memory of traditional life and events, apparently little concerned with the conflicts caused by the collision of two cultures. It is probable that her isolation from extensive white contact affects not only the content of the narrative but the prose style as well. She did not speak English, so she narrated her story to Underhill through a translator because Underhill's Papago language skills were not adequate for recording in the native language.

A complex process of translation to make the Indian language of the narration accessible to an English-speaking audience was unavoidable. This process required three people. This system is the usual one for collection of material by English speakers from tribal language speakers and would also be employed with an English-speaking tribal informant if the subject's dignity prevented narration in her second language.[12] In either case a translator is required to give English equivalents (as nearly as possible since languages are seldom genuinely equivalent in vocabulary) as the narrator speaks. The contributions of the three people involved cannot be analyzed with precision without tape-recorded data. But obviously the collector is not a neutral party in this process because on this member of the translation team rests the editorial task of making an unfamiliar mode of expression accessible in English. The editing usually camouflages the original significantly, though at times there are clues.

In the case of this autobiography one interpreter who participated in the process has recorded her memories of those interviews, offering some insight into the process. Ella Lopez Antone was only fourteen when she was asked by Underhill to aid her in translating Chona's life story. Home on summer vacation from the Phoenix Indian School, Ella accompanied Underhill on her visits with Chona and worked intensively with them when Chona came to stay with Crecencia, her only surviving child, by then a married woman living at Santa Rose Village, also Ella's residence.[13] Antone recalls that Underhill had been working with Chona for some time when she was asked to become translator. She remembers that Underhill was thorough and careful in recording Chona's words, and that if she didn't understand something, "she'd keep on until she really got what she's satisfied with," a word, information, or whatever she wanted to know. She recalls, "If she didn't understand a certain word, I mean that she didn't think it fit what she was going to write about, she'd say to me, 'Is this what she [Chona] means?' or 'What does she mean by that?' " Antone would explain and Underhill would understand and say, " 'Now I've got it,' and write it down." Though Antone remembers Chona as a very pleasant woman, she does recall that Chona would "yell at Ruth sometimes when she'd keep asking a question over and over and Chona got aggravated." She would say, 'You *mil-gahn* [American], you're so dumb, you don't know anything,' and Ruth would laugh and be asking what Chona said, and when I told her, she would laugh more and say, 'Well, I just didn't quite understand, but I've got it now.' "[14]

Antone also points out that Underhill was not without some skill in Papago language. She says Underhill's speaking ability "was not too good," but that she could follow a conversation in Papago accurately, which Ella illustrates with incidents she recalls from her own household when Underhill responded appropriately to Papago conversation, demonstrating her comprehension. "She got quite a bit," Ella says, and "it helped her a lot with Chona because sometimes when I didn't go with her, she'd go by herself, and then she'd listen because she understood."[15]

Despite Underhill's care in translation, Antone does find some inaccuracies in the autobiography, which she interprets as misunderstandings on Underhill's part. When Underhill describes Chona's puberty ceremony as lasting a full month with dancing all night every night, Ella says she is wrong, that Chona said it lasted four days. She remembers she was bothered by this inaccuracy even at the time, so she went to her own grandmother to check and again was told only four days. She points out that sometimes Underhill was stubborn and that this may have led to inaccuracy, but she marvels at how all but a few details of Chona's life are presented correctly.[16]

On-the-spot translation undoubtedly led to some garbling and changes in Chona's story, yet the narrative has an attention to detail and a dignity consistent with the Papago respect for language. Maria recalls, "Prickly pear grew so thick that in summer, when you picked the fruit, it was only four steps from one bush to the next."[17] The language of this quotation, and of the whole narrative, has, however, gone through a complex process of translation and editing to reach an English-speaking nontribal audience; hence, its lyricism must be examined with some concern for authenticity. The degree of influence Underhill exerts on Chona's prose cannot be precisely calculated from the published text, but incidents that Chona recalls in her narrative do indicate a deep concern for language and for her ability to convey experience with precision and vitality. Unlike some early oral narrators, Chona is engaged in the narrative for the purpose of relating a complete life story, not simply ethnographic data, and in the course of the narrative, she articulates concern that her experiences be conveyed with clarity. Her relationship to Underhill is one of collaborator, not merely informant. The strength of her character, the range of her experiences, and her commitment to communicating to a wide audience the details of her life in precise and lively language set this narrative apart as one which surpasses social documentary because it integrates literary intention and technique with ethnographic data and demonstrates the ability of a native narrator to participate as a full partner in the autobiography process.

Economy of language and pleasure in words and rhythm are Chona's family heritage, which is clearly shown as she savors her memory of childhood awakening:

> Early in the morning, in the month of Pleasant Cold, when we had all slept in the house to keep warm, we would wake in the dark to hear my father speaking. "Open your ears, for I am telling you a good thing. Wake up and listen. Open your ears. Let my words enter them." He spoke in a low voice, so quiet in the dark. Always our father spoke to us like that, so low that you thought you were dreaming.[18]

Pleasure in her father's soft tone and gentle words is obvious. Her love of Papago language and song is transmitted into the highly personal English prose style of the narrative. Undoubtedly, Ruth Underhill's literary talent contributes to the lyric quality of the autobiography; the partnership between the two suggests such influence from Underhill. For instance, Underhill's fondness for slightly archaic, full, rich prose is evident in syntax and turn of phrase.[19] She herself says that she put things into her own words but tried to keep the prose "vivid" like Old Testament writing, perhaps her way of suggesting the dignity and complexity of the original oral form—a compromise between the two languages based on mutual literary sensitivities.[20]

The vitality and resonance of the prose are perhaps most easily described through examples of Chona's narrative. Her choice of words is deliberate; she is conscious of the importance of language itself when she points out, "We have a word that means thirst-enduring."[21] Syntax obviously not common in the English language appears in several places: for example, she says, "Fine nets we used to have in those days, all dyed with red and blue. Shaped like a cone they were, with tall red sticks to keep them in shape."[22] The grammatical structure of these sentences reflects traditional oratorical Papago word order,[23] suggesting that Underhill has translated with some concern for retaining Papago sentence form. Occasional inversions of normal English syntax also serve to elevate the style and give the text an archaic quality. While Underhill's freedom with Chona's language is disturbing in respect to accuracy and authenticity, its effect on the literary quality of the work is generally positive, since it contributes to the development of a Papago narrative voice, demonstrating the concern of both narrator and editor for the literary quality of the autobiography, a concern not shown in ethnographic narratives.

The oral quality of the narrative is reinforced by use of direct address to the audience. The reader is drawn into participation in dramatic events and empathizes with the narrator, as in the following passage describing her response to her husband's death: "His brother came to tell me. I cried. I used to go behind a hill, away from the house, and cry half the day. He almost took me with him. Does this happen to the whites?"[24] First, the reader is given information about Papago response to death that is very foreign—suggested is the danger of grief as a possible threat to the mourner's life—then the reader is involved in this dilemma by a direct question. The sense of grief is intense, and the depth of emotional expression bridges the cultural differences between Papago and white, creating a bond between reader and narrator. This passage also demonstrates Chona's consciousness of her audience as white. She takes care to clarify material that would be common knowledge to a Papago audience, urged to do so by Underhill during the interviews. To what degree this clarity and detail is Chona's effort to communicate to a white audience is, unfortunately, not possible to determine, since complete discussion of the editing process is not provided in the text. Perhaps her immediate audience, Underhill, is the sole impetus for her care in detailing Papago customs and attitudes, or perhaps she is responding directly to queries.

Chona also reminds us of the oral nature of her narrative through frequent use of dramatic dialogue. The voices of her family and herself are heard as well as described. After the birth of her first child, which came unexpectedly, her sister-in-law asked why she had not warned them: "Why didn't you tell us? We didn't know you were suffering in there. We heard you laughing." She responds, "Well it wasn't my mouth that hurt. It was my middle."[25]

The vitality of the narrative never falters because of the economical and vigorous telling, the detailed ethnographic data, and the respect for language, combined with the personal content of the narrative.

The past comes alive in her narrative, but it is controlled and evaluated from the present, as she demonstrates when she says, "That is what they said. When I sing that song it makes me dance."[26] The sense of retrospection is made explicit throughout the narrative, but the emphasis is usually on preservation of the traditions. "I am a woman to whom a man can tell solemn words and she will remember them well," she says.[27] Here is a woman who listens, considers, and actively engages in memory. The present is recognized, but the past is the focus of her devotion. She sees herself as a woman who carries the deepest traditional Papago responsibilities well. She understands the power of words and through them preserves and revitalizes the most significant Papago lifeways.

Despite the seemingly artless narration of her experiences and her place in society, like many autobiographers, Chona is extremely aware both of the significance of the events in her life and of the importance of the words that convey them. She is frequently conscious of her family's and tribe's expectations of her, which leads to self-analysis and evaluation. In Papago society the greatest gift and power is that of creating songs, which often come in the form of dreams or through medicine power. In the following passage Chona relates herself to both esteemed abilities:

> I could not go into the desert like my brother, I had no time. I had to work. But in those days I used to see things around me that no one else saw. Once a song came to me. I cannot tell you when it came, but I think it was when I was very little. You see, I come of a singing family. It is natural for us to see strange things and to make a song.[28]

Like many autobiographers, she sees herself throughout her life as someone special among her people, as coming from a gifted family. Unlike many autobiographers, she finds herself blessed rather than burdened by her selection, but she also feels some pressure from it because it is not acceptable for her to pursue the role of medicine practitioner, especially in her youth.

When these powers were first recognized in her as a child, she was put through a curing ritual to neutralize them, partly because such powers would bring fearful danger to her and her family wished to protect her, and partly because her brother was already in the process of becoming a medicine man, and her father had plans to marry her into another medicine family where her understanding of such power would aid her. While her gift of medicine power was both frustrating and frustrated in her youth, it led to a satisfying marital role, and in her old age she was ultimately able to fulfill her deep sense of calling as a curer of infants, a skill she had observed in her father during her childhood. "She was a very decided woman," Underhill notes in a recent interview, and Chona "was very definitely a leader," and might have been a medicine woman had she wished to, but she rejected that position in Papago society because "she did not want to isolate herself."[29]

Chona sees herself as one who *knows*, and while that gift was suppressed in her early life, it was nurtured in her observation of her father, brother, and husbands, and in her continuous participation in ceremonial events, so that later it reemerged. By the time of her work with Underhill, it is reevaluated and sometimes even articulated as a justification and rationale for her narration. In this way, she reminds the reader that she is all that a traditional Papago woman should be—dutiful daughter, responsible household manager and wife, ceremonial participant, reservoir of traditional knowledge and words—a Papago who lives harmoniously in the social and physical landscapes that nurture her development as an individual. She is, in the long run, more than an ordinary Papago woman because she takes control of her life and, despite delay, brings the vision of her youth to successful fruition in her maturity.

The concentration on the expression of traditional values through the careful use of word power is the crucial element of the narration, one that Kluckhohn first recognized in his appraisal of its literary as well as social merit. In Papago life, and all Indian life, words and action are one, the mode of telling the event as important as the event itself. The emphasis placed on the careful selection of words maintains the concentration on traditional Papago ways that distinguishes the narrative. The work has enormous value as an ethnographic document. As an autobiography, the traditional focus enriches the text because of the descriptive detail and the incorporation of ritual events, ceremonial practices, song, medicine visions, and social traditions. The rain festival is vivid as she remembers:

> Once I fell asleep. My father-in-law was one of the medicine men standing in the center of the ring, turning his eagle feathers this way and that to catch the wind that was bringing rain, because it was dry yet, no rain had fallen. My father-in-law shook his eagle feather over me and drops of rain fell in my ear. Then I woke and sang again.[30]

In another instance, Chona's puberty rite compels the audience to sympathize with her when she exclaims:

> Oh, I got thin at that time! We girls are like strips of yucca fiber after our coming of age is over. Always running, and mostly gruel and ash bread to eat, with no salt. And dancing every night from the time the sun sets until morning-stand-ups. I used to go to sleep on Luis' arm and he pinched my nose to wake me.[31]

Her recollections are filled with motion, gesture, fine detail, and metaphor and are thus more immediate and comprehensible than any textbook description of ritual. Interpreter Ella Antone recalls that Chona narrated with considerable expression of feeling in her voice and face: "She was a proud type, and whatever she told us, she really told it in a way with feeling from deep down. When she came to a part where there was pleasure, her eyes would just be laughing, but she was a very serious person. She had her heart in what she told about her past. At certain parts you could see that sad look in her eyes."[32] Her pain when she learns her husband has taken another wife is felt keenly when she says simply:

> Most men did not take two wives with us then, but the medicine men always did. In fact, they took four. But I had never thought my husband would do it. You see, we married so young, even before I had really become a maiden. It was as if we had been children in the same house. I had grown fond of him. We had starved so much together.[33]

Her understated yet clear emotion has strong impact because it is expressed descriptively, and the marriage custom described becomes vitalized because it is related in terms of the life and land that generates it. But Chona's grief at her husband's taking another wife is not only expressed eloquently, it is acted upon. The above passage is a prelude to a critical moment of self-assertion, a turning point in her vision of herself and her role in her society. Though she admits that the taking of four wives is common, even expected of a medicine man, she will not acquiesce in the practice. The rejection of her marriage as it is depicted in the autobiography, however, is considerably abridged. According to both Underhill's and Antone's recollections, Chona actually told them that she returned to her husband's home and saw another young woman working in the fields. She asked the woman why she was there and was told that her husband had taken the woman as a second wife because there was too much work for one woman. As Chona narrated it, the scene was dramatic and contained dialogue, but Underhill condensed it. Ella Antone says, "I interpreted it exactly. I remember. She really had an angry look on her face when she was talking about that other woman." Underhill notes that she was forced to condense much of the material Chona gave her because her publisher was not particularly supportive of the idea of an individual life story—collection of individual narratives was considered poor anthropological methodology in the 1930s and is only recently beginning to gain acceptance—so she was restricted to producing a "slim volume."[34]

Although the episode regarding the coming of the second wife is brief, the scene is still dramatic and provides a pivotal point in the narrative because, despite her grief and pain, she leaves this man and returns to her own village and family house. This is not the action of a submissive, repressed woman suddenly finding herself forced to act in a crisis. It is the logical outcome of her sense of herself as someone who understands her culture fully, as someone special within that culture, too special to share her role as medicine man's wife with another woman. She is not simply throwing a petulant tantrum in the hope of getting her way. She knows that once the woman has been accepted into the house, the new marriage is irrevocable. Renouncing her husband is Chona's way of asserting control over her life, and she does so in a traditional way by returning to her family home. There she is soon offered again in marriage, this time to an older man who had sponsored her during her puberty ritual, again a medicine man. Though a painful event, it leads directly to her development as a curer. In the company of her aging second husband she learns songs, and as his strength declines, hers rises, so that she becomes more forceful, a tribal matriarch, a woman who shapes her life and compensates in some measure for her infant children's deaths through her powers with words and hand manipulations applied to infants of others. She gains the status of a curer.

When Underhill was asked whether Chona was satisfied with her life, she emphatically replied, "Absolutely, or she would have done something about it."[35]

Maria Chona's autobiography is the accumulation of the events of her life: her active participation in all aspects of her tribal activity, her consciousness of herself as a knowledgeable woman, and her understanding of the power of language and the importance of an intimate relationship with the land. Without Ruth Underhill, Chona's story probably would never have reached a wide audience, and without Underhill's particular cultural and literary sensitivities, Chona's narration would not be as effectively presented. As recorder-editor, Ruth Underhill's part in the success of the presentation of the autobiography cannot be overlooked, and the information she gives us concerning the process and methodology of the autobiography, though limited, is of value, because it allows us to begin to comprehend the dynamics of as-told-to autobiography and provides the reader with information essential to comprehending Chona in her society. *Papago Woman* is actually two personal narratives. The central narrative is, of course, the autobiography, told without interruption or interpretation from Underhill, though obviously shaped and edited by her. The secondary narrative, however, is Underhill's. In her chapter preceding the autobiography, Underhill writes as much about herself as she does about Chona. She details early incidents of their meeting and the course of their collaboration that expanded as Chona made the transition from informant to autobiographer. In a 1981 interview, Underhill comments, "We were two of a kind."[36] This description of the relationship between the two women suggests a genuine compatibility and negates suspicion of a manipulative intent on the editor's part. Underhill notes in her original introduction that the story of Chona's life was the Papago woman's "constant preoccupation, and snatches of it were narrated at every opportunity."[37] Elsewhere, Underhill recalls that Chona narrated her story as she worked, making baskets or performing household chores, and that she talked incessantly, often telling one incident, then skipping thirty years forward, then twenty years back, in a rambling way.[38] Underhill's comments establish in some detail the circumstances and ways in which the story was collected and demonstrate her reasons for recognizing her ethnographic informant as a gifted narrator willing to entrust her story to an outsider.

Biographical evidence further establishes Underhill as an exceptionally competent and sensitive recorder-editor for a Papago autobiography. She is no dilettante in the exotica of "primitive" peoples. Her extensive canon of anthropological works on the Papago tribe demonstrates her credentials.[39] But as Joyce Herold, who has collected Underhill's memoirs over a two-year period, points out, "Underhill is really a poet. Lives and language are her passion."[40] Her anthropological credentials are equaled by her literary sensitivity. She is educated in language and literature and is a novelist as well as scholar. Her novel *Hawk over Whirlpools,* in which she fictionally creates a character similar to Chona as the mother of the protagonist, verifies her aesthetic sensibilities both by the similarity in character portrait and the difference in presentation and style between Chona's narrative and her own.[41] The narrative style of Chona's autobiography would have distorted modern fiction prose style, so the narrator of the autobiography is redefined and expressed in a wholly separate literary style. Thus, the uniqueness of Chona's narration is verified by Underhill's fictional interpretation as the anthropologist establishes her competence in two distinctly different forms.

Unfortunately, Underhill's editorial process is not fully documented. In discussing her structuring of Chona's narrative she says:

> Chona is ninety years old and her memory works with the fitfulness of age, presenting incidents in repetitious confusion. The only possible system was to write each one separately, add to it all the amendments which occurred to her during the years of our acquaintance, and then to question her patiently about the chronology until the correct order was worked out. She repeated each episode so often, however, that there was finally no question as to their sequence. Indian narrative style involves a repetition and a dwelling on unimportant details which confuse the white reader and make it hard for him to follow the story. Motives are never explained and the writer has found even Indians at a loss to interpret them in older myths. Emotional states are summed up in such colorless phrases as "I liked it," "I did not like it." For one not deeply immersed in the cultures the real significance escapes.[42]

Her comments on "unimportant details" and "colorless" phrases, plus her admission that she omitted repetitions and emphasized points Chona had not, verify the ability of the editor to change the story. But implicit in Underhill's analysis in her prefatory statement is recognition that American Indian personal narration technique is significantly different from the sequential form we assume of Euro-American autobiography. First, it is usually, as in this case, oral, and, furthermore, it is not necessarily delivered chronologically. Some comprehension of this difference may be posited in terms of cultural difference. The oral nature of American Indian autobiography relates loosely to the tradition of Indian storytelling in which each incident is a coherent whole and tales in a cycle are complete in themselves and often are not told in a given order. The sequence may be rearranged, or at least the tales that are not core elements of the cycle may be reordered at the teller's discretion. As Nancy Lurie points out, "Purists might argue that Underhill should not have led Chona with questions and should have published an untouched, verbatim text of everything, but it would have made tedious reading."[43] Indian autobiography is directed toward a non-Indian audience, so Underhill modified the native spontaneous structuring to suit white tastes:

> The writer felt most deeply the objections to distorting Chona's narrative. Yet if it had been written down exactly as she herself emitted it, there would have been immense emphasis on matters strange to her but commonplace to whites and complete omission of some of the most interesting phases in her development. Therefore, a pattern was followed. While the essentials of the narratives were retained, it is hoped, at every point many of the repetitions were excised.[44]

Underhill's use of the word *pattern* assumes a consistent methodology, a systematic uniform treatment of every incident included in the finalized text. Unfortunately, the consistency and appropriateness of her "pattern" is not accessible and her criteria for inclusion or omission obscure. Her comment on Chona's dwelling on things commonplace to whites may simply indicate a preoccupation with rather tedious day-to-day details of life or with a slighting of important events easily understood within Papago culture, such as ceremonial events, that are obscure and exotic to outsiders. In either case, some license in selection is obvious and, in light of the end result, can hardly be condemned; however, a sampling of the raw text would allow the reader fuller insight into the process of the work and would be particularly valuable, since the end product is exemplary and compelling.

Underhill's discussion of collection problems does offer some insight into the structure of the work that allows Chona's narrative to emerge in a form comprehensible and satisfying to a non-Papago audience. This assessment of Underhill's competence is supported by

Lurie who says, "Underhill's handling of Chona's story is quite defensible as a responsible effort in cross-cultural communication for a broad spectrum of non-Indian readers while also providing substantive data for the scholar engaged in comparative research or the Indian reader seeking information about an older way of life."[45] However limited the data on editing, the reader is left with admiration for the complete work.

While the autobiography is not exclusively Chona's, it seems essentially so because it is molded from her experience, her sense of self, and her skill with language. Whether the acuteness of observation and skill in narration is really Chona's or, in fact, elicited from Chona by skillful questioning by Underhill, is ambiguous. Whatever the balance of influence, the result is engaging.

Considering the range and depth of its content, Chona's narrative is short, but its brevity is perhaps its greatest strength; the reader craves more of the rich and subtle prose, is driven back to reread and thus become reimmersed in the order and security of the Papago village world. Finally, the reader must succumb to the effectiveness of the selection of events and the economy of presentation, as the following selection demonstrates:

> Once I was digging roots like that and I got very tired. I made a pile of earth with my digging stick, put my head on it and lay down. In front of me was a hole in the earth made by the rains, and there hung a gray spider, going up and down, up and down, on its long thread. I began to go to sleep and I said to it: 'Won't you fall?" Then the spider sang to me.[46]

The fusion of action, landscape, dialogue, and vision are seductive, and there is no need for interpretation or analysis. The traditions and perceptions of the Papago way are revived through Chona's memory. The result is a richly colored fabric of daily occurrences, as well as significant tribal events, that is woven so that each episode flows almost imperceptibly into the next. The continuity of the Papago vision and of Chona's participation in tribal life is fully illustrated and interpreted.

Chona's vision is that of a woman who is wholly engaged in tribal life, family relationships, and aware of herself in her various roles throughout the years of her long life. Her autobiography is the story of a woman who has grasped the potential for full life within the context of her society and environment and who, through independent decisions and actions, has brought it to a satisfying conclusion for herself and for her readers. The collaboration of Chona and Underhill has produced a unified vision, a literary whole, formed by narrative content and editorial technique that merge gracefully.

# 4
# Culture Change and Continuity: A Winnebago Life

"Respect those old people," mother and father used to say to us. That is what we used to do. We respected the old people, but today they do not respect the old people.

Mountain Wolf Woman,
*Mountain Wolf Woman*

Although many of the autobiographies collected by anthropologists were published early in the twentieth century, the practice of interviewing informants for life histories continues to be a standard anthropological technique. Both Nancy O. Lurie and David Jones have published autobiographies of American Indian women, but the works differ considerably in intent and style as well as in literary qualities. The patterns followed by Jones resemble the ethnographies collected early in the century. Jones worked with Sanapia, a Comanche medicine woman, and published her autobiography to be used primarily as a textbook and casebook providing ethnographic detail about the woman's life and her role as a Comanche Eagle doctor.[1] During her lifetime, Sanapia adjusted to pressures caused by contact with Christianity and peyotism, both challenges to her traditional Plains religion, but it was a conflict she was able to resolve. Jones provides extensive historical background and is an ever-present editor throughout the book, introducing Sanapia's comments about her life and explaining the contexts. Although the character of Sanapia comes through, the narrative is not sustained; there is no attempt to present a cohesive literary autobiography. Jones, as the adopted son of Sanapia, was entitled to much information that she might not otherwise have passed on; however, he notes in the introduction that "females who interviewed Sanapia were able to gather information of a much different nature than I was able to obtain."[2] Sanapia's purpose was to share her knowledge of medicines to ensure the survival of the healing tradition for the next generation, and Jones was her means of accomplishing that goal.

On the surface, the relationship between Nancy Oestriech Lurie and Mountain Wolf Woman, the narrator of *Mountain Wolf Woman*, may appear quite similar to that established between Jones and Sanapia.[3] Nancy Lurie was an adopted relative and an anthropologist at the University of Wisconsin; Mountain Wolf Woman was an aging Indian woman, seventy-five years old, with some knowledge of healing and storytelling. But there are some striking differences. First, Mountain Wolf Woman used her own name; Sanapia's life story depended upon a pseudonym, a characteristic of much earlier recorded life histories. Mountain Wolf Woman's story of her life makes up the bulk of the book; Jones's book is more concerned with medicines and ethnographic information. Although Jones observed that Sanapia revealed information "of a different nature" to female interviewers, Lurie doubts that the gender of the interpreter would have made a difference to Mountain Wolf Woman. She writes:

> Aunt Stella was a gregarious, generally open person and I think anyone familiar with the background of Winnebago culture who took the time to know her and demonstrate sincerity could have collected her story. The reasons might be different—other adoptive kin ties, a sense of obligation for favors received or whatever. I really don't know if the story would have been slanted differently with a male recorder. I like to think anthropologists are anthropologists and that the niceties of empathy and rapport transcend sex. Aunt Stella was a thoroughly likeable person and a good judge of character. She would be in charge with whomever might seek her story.[4]

Two anthropologists, two different views of their subjects, and both recorded life histories that legitimately can be called autobiographies, demonstrating again the flexibility of the genre and the variety of narratives that are called by that name. Although Lurie had done previous fieldwork with the Winnebagos, she does not attempt to turn her book or the autobiography into an anthropological text. Admittedly there are extensive explanatory notes and Lurie fills in gaps for the reader, but she does so, not as an intrusive editor, but rather as a helpful guide, explaining in notes the obscure references that a non-Winnebago reader may not understand.

The purpose for the writing of *Mountain Wolf Woman* is different from almost all other ethnographic autobiographies. Where other recorder-editors often recorded women's stories as an incidental part of fieldwork, Nancy Lurie specifically requested the story and did so as an adopted niece of Mountain Wolf Woman. With Mountain Wolf Woman in the position of aunt, and with the power of age and wisdom such a position connotes, it was both appropriate and necessary that she instruct her niece in the ways of the tribe. The association was one of long duration, for Nancy Lurie and Mountain Wolf Woman had met in 1945 in Black River Falls, Wisconsin. It was not until 1958 that recording actually began, allowing thirteen years of friendship and kinship to have developed.

Unlike the field methods used earlier, Lurie used a tape recorder and made a record of the life story both in Winnebago and in English. This, of course, allowed Mountain Wolf Woman to do some degree of immediate editing as she translated her own material. Lurie also notes that passages were omitted from the final manuscript at the request of the narrator. "She told me a number of things that happened, particularly when she went to get her grandchildren in the state of Washington, that she didn't want in the book. I respected her wishes. They were interesting but not all that vital to the completeness of her story."[5]

Obviously the element of selection was still in operation, but the decision here had been given to the informant and was not assumed by the recorder. Lurie describes the story as being "told *to,* not *through*," her. Of the recording sessions, Lurie comments:

> My Winnebago isn't all that good, so often I wasn't sure of what she was saying until we replayed and she told her story in English, and then I went over the Winnebago tapes with a highly competent bilingual woman, Frances Thundercloud Wentz. . . . There was probably less editing than Michelson did and certainly a lot less than Underhill did.[6]

Of the final published autobiography, Lurie says, "It was her story as she wanted to tell it. I had some reservations about her comments about the traditional religion, but she did not, so they stayed in as she told them. She got to hear herself exactly as she told her story on tape before it was committed to paper or published."[7]

Ruth Underhill, in the Foreword to the narrative of Mountain Wolf Woman, makes comparisons with Paul Radin's autobiography of Mountain Wolf Woman's brother, Crashing Thunder, describing

Radin's book as more dramatic, more artistic; in short, she sees it as more "literary." Comparing herself with Radin, Lurie noted that she was not collecting data in the field; Mountain Wolf Woman stayed at her home. She asked few questions during the narration, checking with Frances Wentz about translation details later, after Wentz had worked through the Winnebago tapes. She notes that "Michelson and Underhill could pursue things at the moment—we know Underhill did but know little of how Michelson worked."[8] Of Radin's work she wrote:

> Sam's story, Crashing Thunder, was written in the Winnebago syllabary by Sam himself for Radin. In the D. Appleton Century version Radin added other data he had collected from Sam and his brother Jasper to fill out the story. . . . I don't know if Sam was aware of the additional material before the book came out. But, unlike Underhill's and Michelson's subjects, Sam and Stella could review what they said, and had the opportunity to edit before publication if they wished.[9]

Lurie sees the two Winnebago autobiographies as reflecting fundamental differences between males and females. She writes, "Mountain Wolf Woman's autobiography is a predictable reflection of the greater self-confidence enjoyed by women in comparison to men in a culture undergoing rapid and destructive changes."[10] Women's tasks of caring for children and family did not change despite acculturation. Reflecting her own self-confidence, Mountain Wolf Woman does not tell a story of self-aggrandizement. Although she is aware of her strengths, she sees herself more as a transmitter of culture, one who is a link between the historical life of her people and the future generations. Indeed, it is her female roles of mother, wife, grandmother, and provider that concern her most.

Lurie describes Mountain Wolf Woman as "witty, empathic, intelligent, and forthright," and it is this personality that comes through in the narrative. Lurie's comments in the preface are instrumental in preparing the reader to like the narrator before reading the autobiography. It is clear that the relationship that had been established between Lurie and her narrator provided the best possible means of recording a life story with an editor. Lurie is careful to point out her methodology and to indicate where she has supplemented the narrative with her own materials.

Mountain Wolf Woman provides only superficial information on Winnebago history, information that is supplemented by Lurie in the notes. The Winnebagos were subject to many removals, causing one writer to refer to them as the "Wandering Winnebago."[11] Although contemporary American Indians reject the labels "nomadic," "transient," and "roaming" to describe travel to follow game or to find new and better locations to live, the term "wandering" perhaps aptly describes the aimless movements to which the Winnebagos were subject at the whim of the United States government.

Before 1864 the Winnebagos had been forced to move several times over a thirty-two-year period. From the Green Bay area, the Winnebagos had settled in southern Wisconsin by 1832, but after the Black Hawk War, the Winnebagos were resettled by the government in northeastern Iowa near the present city of Decorah. By 1848 there was an increasing number of white settlers in Iowa, and the Winnebagos were once again moved, this time to Todd County in north-central Minnesota. By 1855 the tribe had negotiated a move to southern Minnesota to avoid having to move west of the Missouri River; but in 1863 the Winnebagos were loaded on boats and sent down the Minnesota River to their next home, Crow Creek, in the Dakota Territory. This proved to be a disastrous move and, reacting to the desperate starvation conditions of Crow Creek, Winnebago leaders led the people to Nebraska to seek help from the Omaha Indians. Finally, after years of moving and being moved, the Winnebagos were settled in Thurston County, Nebraska. This final move was the only one initiated by the Indians themselves rather than the government. Although attention has usually focused on those Winnebagos who were moving, one group remained in Wisconsin, near Black River Falls, the entire time. Today the Winnebago tribe remains divided: one group lives on a reservation in Nebraska and the other group lives as nonreservation Indians in Wisconsin.

This history of movement and forced migration is part of Mountain Wolf Woman's tribal history. The influence of this past on her life is clear; she found moving around not a chore, or a burden, but an accepted element of her life. In her life story, Mountain Wolf Woman recalls the many journeys she made—journeys to find work, to be with her husband, or to care for children or grandchildren.

Mountain Wolf Woman begins her narrative by relating the events before her birth, referring particularly to the history of Winnebago removals. From the beginning it appears that Mountain Wolf Woman was aware of the way the Winnebagos had been treated, and she wished to place herself within this context of tribal history.

Born in 1884 in East Fork River, Wisconsin, Mountain Wolf Woman soon moved to Black River Falls. As a child she attended school for two years in Tomah, Wisconsin, but when her family moved to Wittenberg she had to change schools, remaining there only a short time before she married. Her first marriage, arranged by her brother, ended, and she remained in Black River Falls until her marriage to Bad Soldier. Her itinerary after that marriage included moves from Hatfield, Wisconsin, to Wakefield, Nebraska, on to South Dakota, back to Nebraska, and finally a return to Black River Falls. During this time there were shorter trips to trap muskrats, to dig yellow water-lily roots, to hunt deer, or to pick cranberries. She once journeyed as far as the Northwest because of her concern about her grandchildren. This acceptance of family responsibility is not surprising, for, as Winnebago educator Woesha Cloud North writes of the Winnebagos, "It is a practice . . . for a grandmother to take on the responsibility of her children's children where there is no longer parental supervision or because of death or other reasons."[12] Clearly Mountain Wolf Woman viewed this as a normal responsibility. In all of her moves Mountain Wolf Woman seemed keenly aware of the necessity of the travel and moved with ease. She was not tied down to a specific geographical location; even near the end of her life she moved her house itself from one location to another. The experiencing of many locales is an outward manifestation of the explorative nature of the narrator, a nature that prompted her to try peyote as well as to participate in traditional Winnebago ceremonies, to believe in a Christian god in the heavens with the same faith that allowed her to believe the Winnebago story of Sheiganikah living on the moon. That she went to live with an anthropology professor and her husband and became a part of the routine of yet a different environment further attests to Mountain Wolf Woman's adaptability.

Adaptability to cultural change as well as geographical change is suggested in other ways. Throughout the narrative Mountain Wolf Woman refers to changes she has observed during her lifetime. The relative ease with which she discusses or sometimes casually mentions certain events or different ways of doing things belies the profound transformations in Winnebago culture during Mountain Wolf Woman's lifetime. Cloud North summarizes some of the effects of these changes, particularly on the Nebraska Winnebagos, but also on the Wisconsin group:

> Traditional informal education or cultural transmission was to assist the boy or girl to grow as a responsible person and social being into adulthood of the Winnebago society. The conquest of the Winnebago people, their forced removals, and later a reservation existence in which their lives were taken over by the paternalistic system of the Bureau of American Indian Affairs and other outside influences, both moral and religious, made serious inroads on these educational practices.[13]

There were changes in the material culture, changes symbolized by "metal teaspoons for clam shells to scrape the corn off the cobs." Long ago the metal teaspoons of the Europeans had been substituted for the sharpened clam shells that had traditionally been used to prepare corn, but the use of clam shells had persisted as well. Mountain Wolf Woman appears comfortable with both the old and the new. She values the continuities in the culture, but readily adapts to necessary changes. She realizes that long ago her father did not need a license to hunt deer, but that adherence to a different legal system had become necessary. After recounting the entire fasting ritual of her brother Hagaga, Mountain Wolf Woman says, "Today they do not do that any more."[14]

Mountain Wolf Woman writes openly about her first menstrual period, recreating for the reader the fears she had as she fled into the woods alone. The tradition of isolation, common in many tribes, was also one which would ultimately be dropped. Irma Bizzett, a Winnebago woman and now a student at Iowa State University, said her mother told her she had been put in an isolation lodge during her first period and after giving birth to her first three children, but by the time Irma was born in 1949, this custom was no longer practiced.[15]

In the shorter version of her life story that is published as an appendix to the longer autobiography, Mountain Wolf Woman is philosophical about the past and all of the changes that she has observed, changes that are made manifest through the relationships within the tribe:

> In the beginning people loved each other. They even would all live in one house, never disagreeing. We too used to live this way. . . . We were never at odds with one another, nor quarrelling nor scolding one another. Mother and father never scolded any of us; however, we were probably well behaved. They never used to scold me. Now children are not like that. They are even against their own parents. . . . That is how it is today.[16]

The complete narrative of *Mountain Wolf Woman* is a chronological and factual account of its narrator's life. There are dramatic moments—her unwanted first marriage and the journey to Washington to retrieve her grandchildren, for example—but these events are handled so matter-of-factly by Mountain Wolf Woman that the reader doesn't always appreciate the anxiety which must surely have accompanied the moments. Literary conventions are not ignored, however. Lurie admits to making some changes in tenses, clarifying idiomatic expressions, and inserting words necessary for clarification. But the wording and tone of the original Winnebago is retained, rendering the text closer to Winnebago expression than conventional English, but making it no less literary.[17]

Because Mountain Wolf Woman's life spanned much of the twentieth century, one can note her changing attitudes toward the institutions around her. In particular, she had experience with formal education, the organized church, and the United States and local governments. Unlike Helen Sekaquaptewa or Anna Shaw (see Chapter 5), Mountain Wolf Woman did not attend school for very long or in a consistent fashion. But she did attend school, first at Tomah and later at Wittenberg, leaving to get married. She realizes that a casual attitude toward school education no longer prevails, however, noting that the Indians of the past would not have stayed home just so the children could attend school. She recognizes that "they can no longer act in this way."[18] She herself was disappointed at having to leave school, but she accepted the necessity of marriage according to tribal custom. She adhered to tradition, but she was grateful that her mother offered her an acceptable way out by telling her that when she was older she could do as she wished.

Traditional Winnebago education included naming ceremonies to teach a child to recognize clan and family relationships, story telling, fasting and vision quests for boys, fasting associated with menstruation for girls, curing and healing, and preparations for a vocation within the tribal structure.[19] Mountain Wolf Woman had received this education, and, although she was an eager learner when she was in school, she was pleased that she had not missed out on traditional Winnebago tutoring. For a time, when Winnebago families stayed close together, such informal education could continue alongside public education. Irma Bizzett recalls being given a name by her grandfather (during a story-telling session) when she was a child. Her daughter, fourteen years old in 1981, also received a name from her grandfather as they sat around on a Sunday afternoon telling traditional stories after returning from Christian church services.[20] Geographical distance from family and tribe, however, makes weekly story-telling sessions and ceremonies less likely to be experienced by children. But the Winnebagos, like other tribes, have learned to adapt to change.

Mountain Wolf Woman's funeral epitomized her allegiance to three religions, an amalgamation which she apparently did not find difficult to handle. Raised as a traditional Winnebago, Mountain Wolf Woman participated faithfully in Winnebago ceremonies, including the scalp dance and the medicine dance. She was also a practicing Christian, but the religion that made her faith whole was the Native American Church and her participation in peyote meetings: "I joined the medicine lodge. I was once a Christian. Then, when we went to Nebraska I ate peyote which is even a Christian way. Three things I did. But peyote alone is the best."[21]

Minnie Littlebear was born in 1898 and lives in Nebraska. When she was interviewed by Woesha Cloud North and asked if a Christian prayer is said at the Naming Ceremony, she answered, "It's all the same to the Winnebago. It's all the same god, Ma-una."[22] Paul Radin has pointed out similarities to Christianity in traditional Winnebago religion, and his description of the Medicine Dance—"the whole ceremony is the reiteration of one basic theme, the proper method of passing through life in order to be reborn again"—suggests why Mountain Wolf Woman and other Winnebagos may so readily have incorporated both religions into their belief system.[23]

Mountain Wolf Woman relates two important visions: one that occurred as a result of two nights of traditional dancing; and the other a vision of Jesus she had after participating in a peyote ceremony. She attributes both visions to her faithfulness to the necessary rituals of the ceremonies. Her account of these visions further suggests that she believes it is possible, perhaps even desirable, to participate fully in more than one religion. This may have been a way of answering those critics within the tribe who condemned the peyote eaters. In fact, one of the most negative responses from the Winnebago community was that the book and, by extension Lurie and Mountain Wolf Woman, were seen as promoting the Native American Church. The traditional Winnebagos resented Mountain Wolf Woman's comments on the Medicine Lodge. Asked about negative reactions, Lurie wrote, "YOU BET! It has only been since my return for extended work the last three summers that I've overcome the image as a promoter of the Native American Church."[24] Such factionalism is not unusual, however, and clearly demonstrates that the narrative is the life of one Winnebago woman and cannot be seen as necessarily representative of all Winnebagos.

The narrator was aware of the Winnebago removals and the allocation of parcels of land that had occurred before her birth. She learned to skillfully manipulate government agencies to obtain necessary help: first, for some of the old people; secondly, in arranging to get her grandchildren back to Wisconsin; and, finally, in getting her own house moved when it became necessary. The government intruded upon the lives of the Winnebagos during World War II. The narrator's most intimate comments reflect her emotions at the time her son was wounded; that event produced her strongest outpouring of grief:

> It was early in the morning when they brought the telegram. I was the first one to go to the berry place. I thought to myself, I will go before the white people arrive. I went to where they had finished picking and when I got there I wept. I prayed to God and I cried as hard as I could cry. I was crying quite a distance from the other people. I cried as loud as I could and cried as much as I wanted to. That is the way I cried. Then when I got enough crying, I stopped crying. When I stopped crying my anxiety seemed to be relieved. Then, after I cried it out, this pain in my heart, I felt better.[25]

The repetition of the words *cry, cried,* and *crying* emphasizes her grief, and through repetition in the narrative itself, she purges herself of tears.

Mountain Wolf Woman describes her emotions at other times—

her reluctance to marry, the pain of leaving her daughter in Washington, and her sorrow at her husband's death—but most of her feelings are discussed with the resigned acceptance of one who has experienced much of life's sorrows and joys and has learned to accept both as a part of the natural order of things. She sees herself as separate from white people and accepts the Winnebago position in relation to the rest of society in the same unemotional and flat manner: "I do not know why, but whatever the white people say, that is the way it has to be. I guess it must be that way."[26]

Although Mountain Wolf Woman became experienced with the institutions of white society, she held tenaciously to the traditions of her people. Religion was just one aspect of her adherence to traditional ways; she also expected proper behavior at the dances, she recognized the value of old age, and she perpetuated the oral tradition in her own way. Speaking of old age, she said, "The old people were supposed to be respected. 'Respect those old people,' mother and father used to say to us. That is what we used to do. We respected the old people, but today they do not respect the old people."[27]

Fred Rice, a Winnebago from Nebraska, expresses similar dismay: "Nowadays the kids laugh at the old people when they speak Winnebago."[28] Later in the book, Mountain Wolf Woman explains the power of age: "If you give food to an old person and he really likes it, that is very good. The thinking powers of old people are strong and if one of them thinks good things for you, whatever he wishes for you, you will obtain that good fortune."[29]

She participates in the transmission of tales early in the narrative when she tells the story about stealing beans from mice; but she admits the difficulty of remembering the oral stories, recalling the story-telling sessions with her father:

> Then father used to say, "All right, prepare your bedding and go to bed and I will tell you some stories." I really enjoyed listening to my father tell stories. Everybody, the entire household, was very quiet and in this atmosphere my father used to tell stories. He used to tell myths, the sacred stories, and that is why I also know some myths. I do not know all of them anymore, I just remember parts of stories.[30]

Her greatest tribute to the oral tradition is the narrative of her own life. Her autobiography is a collection of stories that are linked by the journeys and adventures of the central character, Mountain

Wolf Woman. She describes herself as a trickster of myth, remembering events before her birth, later "always the one who is spoiling things," the one who sees visions, and who has bridged the gap between myth and reality, having now ridden through the sky, albeit in an airplane, to bring her life story together with the life of Nancy Lurie. The final tale ties the narrative together, gives it purpose, and provides a conclusion that is appropriately literary:

> Once when I came back from Nebraska one of my relatives had died. His name was Fish Back. Mitchell Redcloud, Sr. He had three sons. One time he had told me a young white girl was going to come to Black River Falls and that she was his daughter. He even gave her a Winnebago name. Therefore, she was my niece. All of our relatives liked her very much. That is how it was. She thought a lot of us too and she liked Indians. She was an only child. When the Indians talked about their affairs, whatever they knew she knew more. She helped the Indians. She wanted me to do her a favor. "Auntie," she said, "if you come and visit me we will write down Indian stories in a book." That is why I am here, saying this at her home. I even rode in an airplane, and I came here. And here I am, telling in Winnebago how I lived my life. This I have written.[31]

The autobiography of Mountain Wolf Woman, ethnographic to be sure, much more closely approaches literature than do most of the life stories collected by anthropologists. When Paul Radin first published *The Autobiography of a Winnebago Indian* in 1920, he was pessimistic about the abilities of outside investigators to get much accurate information about a culture. He wrote that it was only "on rare occasions" that they were successful.[32] The autobiography of Mountain Wolf Woman presents one such "rare occasion," for, by letting Mountain Wolf Woman tell her own story, Lurie was able to publish a life narrative with very little editing. The bonus is that Lurie, as an anthropologist, was able to anticipate what might be confusing to readers and add that information in the notes and appendices. *Mountain Wolf Woman* serves as a model of an autobiography that combines an individual narrative told by the subject with ethnographic detail supplied by a recorder-editor.

# 5
# Two Women in Transition: Separate Perspectives

Ours was the first to be educated in two cultures, the Pima and the white. Sometimes the values of the two were in conflict, but we were learning to put them together to make a way of life different from anything the early Pimas ever dreamed of.

Anna Moore Shaw, *A Pima Past*

The dynamic processes of Indian women's lives and of the modes of telling those lives are nowhere more clearly demonstrated than in the autobiographies of Anna Moore Shaw and Helen Sekaquaptewa, two Arizona Indian women—one Hopi and the other Pima—who shared living quarters for three years during boarding school. They respected one another but were never intimate friends. They separated easily and rarely renewed contact during their lives, yet each one in later life came to stand as a model of womanhood for her tribe. Each recorded her life story, tracing the sometimes painful but ultimately satisfying course from traditional childhood, through the forces of acculturation, finally returning to tribal values and ways.

The lives and personal narratives of these two women, both born into traditional households in 1898, offer a unique record of similar experiences from separate perspectives, partly formed by tribal differences but in large measure the product of strong and very different personalities and goals. The methodologies and styles of their narratives, one oral and the other written, are separate as well. This combination of likenesses and disparities in both their lives and narrations is somewhat cumbersome to draw together, yet it offers intriguing insights into the individual lives and the literary tradition involved in women's autobiography. They are seldom so comprehensibly revealed.

The lives of Helen Sekaquaptewa and Anna Moore Shaw are superficially very similar, though from the beginning they were shaped by different landscapes and traditions. Chehia, Anna Moore, was born and spent her early childhood on the low desert of the Gila River reservation, which is south of Phoenix, an area that attracted white settlement by the mid-nineteenth century, coveted because of its reliable water supply and fertile soil. Known as the River People, the Pimas were surrounded by white ranchers and farmers by the time of Anna's childhood and were struggling to sustain their traditions. In prereservation times they had fought wars with the Yumas to the west and the Apaches to the east, sustaining themselves partly by hunting but primarily through subsistence farming, growing beans, corn, squash, and melons along the riverbanks and canals adjacent to their villages. The Pimas did not struggle against the white men who explored and later settled in their valley when the area came under United States jurisdiction after the Gadsen Purchase in 1853. They maintained consistently friendly relations with whites, and many tribal members were converted to Christianity during an intensive missionary campaign by the Presbyterian Church in the generations before Anna's birth. Chehia's life on the reservation was comfortable by Piman standards. The land was harsh but fertile because of the irrigation from the river, and she had a large number of kinsman and a close and loving family to sustain her physically and emotionally. As Christians, however, her family members were not active in traditional ceremonies or practices, such as warrior purification, rain ceremonies, or female puberty rituals, so Anna was not an active participant in rituals as Maria Chona, also a member of a Piman tribe, had been two generations earlier. Shaw was born into a tribe already involved in acquiring many white ways and values, a circumstance that contributed greatly to her adjustments in school and in her years of urban life.

Dowawisnima, Helen Sekaquaptewa, was born at the longest continually inhabited site in North America, Oraibi, a village on the edge of one of the three Hopi mesas in the high desert country of northern Arizona. Traditionally, the Hopis had been raided by the Navajos who surrounded them, and for protection they relied heavily on the mesa strongholds that jut out of the desert like fingers. Deeply immersed in ceremonies, perhaps the most widely known of which is the Snake Dance, they sustained their families from the harvests of the fields and orchards below the mesa plateaus. Each mesa supported several villages, each separate in its identity and workings though similar to the other city-states sharing the mesas. Their first contact with whites was with the Spanish explorers in the 1600s, but in 1680, during the Great Pueblo Revolt that swept the Rio Grande pueblos and reached west to Hopi, white culture was wiped out. Having suffered harsh treatment from the Spanish, the Hopis were hostile into the twentieth century toward white intrusions; they fostered their traditional ceremonies and practiced traditional forms of village government and were hardly noticed by the surrounding population since their land was barren and arid and their villages modest. Even at the time of Helen's birth, life in the Hopi pueblos was tenuous. Droughts were common, bringing famine to the subsistence farming communities with growing populations. They had always been factionalized by their city-state form of government, and that fragmentation was accelerated by the attempts of the United States government to set up a reservation and impose white ways on the people, demanding that all Hopi families send their children to boarding schools a considerable distance from the mesa villages. Helen was born into a community that was especially affected by the school issue, eventually dividing it into two factions that battled each other for possession of her village; she was born into conflict, a state of life she would not escape until she became elderly. The Hopis call themselves the "Peaceful People" and have been extremely reluctant to enter into wars and conflicts, but they have suffered from much internal strife and considerable tension with surrounding peoples and the United States government. They are a people whose tenacious adherence to the landscape of the mesas with its wide vistas and clear skies has made them tenacious in their independence. Like her people, Helen has been enduring in the midst of conflict.

For the women in these two narratives, the landscape and tribal circumstances during their respective childhoods have been critical elements, informing the consciousness of each and ultimately affecting the life each has chosen and the mode of expression for each life story.

The responses to white culture by the families of each of the narrators give the clearest sense of the differences between Pimas and Hopis in the first decade of the twentieth century. For Pimas, school was an extension of the household—close, filled with friends and kin, approved of by tribal members. Having watched her older brother trudge off to the day school nearby, Anna was eager to attend school, and she soon followed him and proved a bright student. For

Hopis avoiding school was an exhausting game. Parents of the families hostile to government interference in their ways hid their children from officials as long as possible, reluctant to expose them to non-Hopi influences and to the separation from family necessitated by sending them to Keams Canyon several miles away. Helen hid from the truant officers, but once caught, she, like Anna, was a successful student. It is in their school years that the lives of these women are most truly parallel in circumstances and experiences, particularly during the period they attended the Phoenix Indian School and actually came to know each other and compete for honors.

In 1918 their lives diverged when Anna went to the Phoenix Union High School and became the first Indian woman to graduate in the state, and Helen returned to the reservation. At the boarding school, each woman had committed herself to her future husband, and in their respective marriages they turned their energies toward family responsibilities, Helen taking up the role of a rural Hopi wife, while Anna set up housekeeping in a multiethnic neighborhood in Phoenix where her husband worked for the Sante Fe Railroad. In time, they met again in Phoenix when Helen set up a temporary household so her children could attend urban high school. By this time, both women were Christians.

Each had come to maturity, combining the most useful elements of her native and acquired cultures. Anna was determined to see her children educated away from the reservation and making their way in the white world. Helen was content to remain primarily a reservation Indian but was determined to make use of the knowledge she had acquired during her school years, and she gave her children a wide range of opportunities.

The Arizona landscapes that had nurtured them physically and psychologically in their youth never gave up a hold. Helen returned to Hopi often during her stay in Phoenix and permanently when her children graduated. Anna frequently visited her parents and in-laws on the reservation and, upon her husband's retirement, moved to the Pima reservation and became instrumental in revitaliizing traditional basket-making skills. The two women were shaped by tribal identity and sense of place, yet each adapted her childhood training and intuitions to a changing world that demanded flexibility and deft application of acquired knowledge. Immediately, the similarities are striking, but perhaps more important are differences in attitudes and objectives that are revealed in the course of their separate narratives.

Anna Shaw's autobiography, *A Pima Past,* is compiled from a series of episodic recollections she wrote down over a long period of time. Shaw's daughter Adeline recalls that her mother always carried a pad and kept notes wherever she went, an informal journal, and she loved to gather material and write.[1] Ross Shaw remembers that his late wife was determined to learn how to write and went to night classes after they were married to improve her skills. Her first published work was a collection of Pima legends gleaned from her own recollections and from the storytelling sessions they attended when she took her children to visit their maternal grandfather.[2] As she notes in her autobiography, she felt it was important to pass on these stories to her children and to those interested in Indian ways. After her success with the legends, she began to record memories of her family and her own experiences, sitting in a comfortable chair in her living room late in the night when she was unable to sleep because of health problems. According to Karen Thure, who worked as her editor at the University of Arizona Press, the manuscript was not publishable as submitted; it had no narrative structure or chronology, but because *Pima Legends*[3] had been successful, and because Shaw had recorded interesting and important experiences in her episodes, the manuscript was accepted, and the author and editor set to work to overcome the "gaps and confusion" in the text. The two of them worked together at Shaw's home, retaining all the original material and shaping it into a coherent whole by adding and reordering information. Thure recalls that she taped three or four interviews to fill in the gaps and expand the manuscript to a complete autobiography, imposing a structure but keeping Shaw's wording, working constantly with Shaw's advice and consent to changes. Thure points out that great care was taken to preserve the tone and style of Shaw's writing. As they sorted out the chronology, they found that there were descriptions of, and tributes to, various of Shaw's friends and relatives that were intrusive in the narration, so they gathered them into a separate section at the end of the book and Shaw titled them "My Indian Hall of Fame."[4] A general discussion of tribal history and customs was added to the text as an introduction, and the work was published a year before Shaw's death in 1975.

The text of *A Pima Past* differs from most other Indian autobiographies in that it does not begin with the birth of the subject but with a dramatized narration of tribal and family events that create a historical context for her life story. Shaw displays considerable poetic license and literary consciousness in her preliminary chapters. She makes no claim to ethnographic or historical research or to sophisticated interpretation of events. She tells her family's story, as she does her traditional tales, at a level comprehensible to young readers. This serves as a contrast to Sekaquaptewa's much more complicated approach to the history of her village conflicts wherein researched materials are woven into her personal recollections and a sense of first hand observation is clearly demonstrated. In Shaw's narrative, the first birth recorded is that of her father, Red Arrow, later known as Joshiah Moore, shortly after the last battle the Pimas fought with their traditional enemies the Yumas who lived to the west along the Colorado River.

Shaw makes use of techniques more often employed by fiction writers as she develops her narrative, carefully detailing Piman customs, as in her description of the ceremonial naming of her father:

> Early the next morning the parents of little Red Arrow took him from his cradleboard. When the first rays of the sun appeared over the eastern hills, handsome Woodpecker proudly held his baby up to the Sun God. Beautiful Yellow Leaves stood by his side. Woodpecker prayed: "Sun God, here is our little son Red Arrow. Let your rays fall on him. Give him a healthy body, just as your rays help our crops to grow. Let him grow and become a strong warrior to help defend his people."[5]

The dialogue gives the narration a sense of immediacy and reality, though it is obviously compiled from family stories and tribal history and embellished with simulated quotations. The traditional life she describes seems rather too idealistic; even tragedies lack the intensity that actual experience of them impresses on direct autobiographical writing, as in Sekaquaptewa's description of the expulsion of her family from their home and village. When Shaw describes the epidemic that killed many Pimas, including Red Arrow's mother, she says:

> The leaders of the village believed the calamity was brought to them by some of the medicine men. "Just look at this sorrow

> all around us," said one of them. "The medicine men must be showing off their powers again."
>
> "They want to punish us for the disrespect shown them by the young braves," said another.
>
> "Then let us stop the sickness by getting rid of the medicine men!" shouted the chief of the village.
>
> Three medicine men who had been heard boast about bringing on the Black Vomit were rounded up and slain. The sickness strangely stopped.[6]

Shaw's depiction of the moment with dialogue, while dramatic, is too simplistic to be convincing because it does not penetrate to the conflict that leads to the deliberate and brutal slaying of the medicine men. The reader wonders whether the slaying is a resolution of a political conflict in the village, or even a struggle between generations regarding the effects of acculturation. Why, after all, are the young men disrespectful? The episode raises questions that are simply ignored. The anguish and fear that provide the motivation for the event are glossed over. Such unprepared-for action as the slaying of the medicine men takes the reader by surprise, leaving unexplained the arbitrary "justice" meted out by tribal elders. None of the complexity of Piman attitudes toward witchcraft or sickness is even hinted at. A complicated problem is simply resolved by quick and final action. Re-creating such episodes, does, however, allow the author to describe in some detail traditional customs, as in this segment on the Black Vomit epidemic, where a discussion of burial customs is made concrete and comprehensible in the context of the narrative form. This retracing of events that involved her family also benefits the reader by establishing a clear geneology and supplies the reader with a means of understanding the narrator's motivations for some of her actions and attitudes in the autobiography proper.

In spite of these advantages, however, there is a lingering suspicion that much of the subject matter of the autobiography has been selected in order to leave a very comprehensive and positive impression of Pima life, putting Shaw's reliability into question.

This may be the inevitable mode of expression of a woman who, as her survivors point out, was very positive in her approach to life and motivated in all her activities by a sense of affirmation and acceptance. At any rate, the first hundred pages of her life story are simplistic and romanticized, partly because of the fictional technique she employs and partly because of her selection of events. Even her own introduction to the text is in this form, as she writes, "Little Chehia looked up at the sun for the twentieth time that afternoon. How slowly it moved across the blue desert sky! Surely it would be forever before brother Willie came home from the Gila Crossing Day School."[7] Several pages later the reader learns that Chehia is Annie Moore. As unusual as this introduction of the subject of the text is, it is appropriate because she is first presented yearning to follow her older brother to school, a desire that was fulfilled and that shaped the remainder of her life. At this point, the autobiography shifts into the first person and becomes a more conventionally written life story.

Shaw's naive view of her family history carries over into her narration of her own experiences. In part, her lack of attention to negative emotions may be attributed to Piman reluctance to express intensity of emotion; there is more concern for event and incident than response to it in traditional Piman storytelling.[8] Her approach appears also to have been influenced by her Christian training and by her inherently optimistic nature.[9] Shaw's education in white and Piman ways is simultaneous as she attends the Christian Church and the day school and also learns cooking and basket weaving at home, often also caring for her older siblings' babies and listening to her grandmother's traditional stories. Her narration describes a sense of integration of cultural elements within her kin group; culture conflict either escapes her early observation, or is easing by her generation, or perhaps is simply accepted by a child as the natural state of things. Her narration does not attempt to interpret events in retrospect but to capture them as they occurred, and the innocence of her depiction in the episodes of her childhood effectively creates a sense of a child's observations. Shaw is full of eagerness to attend school, and the willingness of her parents to send her contrasts sharply with Sekaquaptewa's family's resistance to sending their children to the agency school. Obviously Shaw's family, Christianized and much more exposed to white culture, was willing to acculturate and passed these values on to young Anna. She was again eager to follow her older brother when he went to boarding school and, at age eight, ventured with apparently no hesitancy to the mission school in Tucson.

Her characteristic acceptance of new circumstances and her ease in adapting to white ways is demonstrated when she says:

> I never climbed a stairway before. In the dorm a row of single beds stood side by side. "Oh, this is going to be fun!" I thought. "Imagine sleeping on a real bed with other girls my age!" At home we had lived too far from my schoolmates for me to play with them every day. Now I would have friends around me all the time![10]

She gives no indication of fear or homesickness, and even the harsh treatment that is so often the subject of Indian school recollection is accepted and rationalized when she continues, "We were not allowed to speak the Pima tongue at school. Some students would report on those who spoke in Indian and as a punishment our mouths would be taped. We did not mind, for the matron, teachers, and other employees were good to us, despite our naughty ways."[11] Shaw accepts without apparent rancour the punishment that induced many students to become bitter or run away. The cultural suppression that led Helen Sekaquaptewa to suffer from stomach cramps for months when she began to attend school is totally absent in her recollections. Resentment and fear of the matrons is missing too. But unlike Helen, Anna had had the experience of the reservation day school to prepare her for the boarding-school discipline.

As one acquaintance has pointed out, Anna Shaw was forward without being aggressive,[13] so perhaps this early confidence she displays accounts for the ability to consistently sustain a positive attitude toward life even under unfamiliar and difficult circumstances, or perhaps memory has simply ameliorated the situation, or her positive attitude has been applied in retrospect. Perhaps also, as she points out later in her narrative, she did not really appreciate her home then. Only later, when she began to understand how important her family was, did she become homesick at the Phoenix Indian School, which she notes was very strict.

Adaptation to the demands of boarding school was difficult for most Indian students, as was recognized even by the educational division of the Bureau of Indian Affairs. In a pamphlet prepared for the Bureau in the 1930s, experts in Indian education note:

> Poverty, isolation, and the nomadic life of many Indian families have made it difficult for them to give their children those minimum essentials of nurture, health and education which they will need as they grow up to face life in the United States today.

> Attendance at the public and day schools is more and more possible for Indians, especially for those whose homes are stable and located near a school. Fortunately this number is increasing rapidly, but there is still a considerable number of Indian young people attending boarding schools.
>
> Unfortunately many of these children have been taken from their homes at an early age and placed in these boarding schools far from familiar scenes and faces. For them the large institutional school building becomes, for a period of years, their home; the busy matron, a substitute for mother, is shared with many others.[14]

Despite its ethnocentric view of Indian culture, this report recognizes the difficulties students faced in being removed from family and tribal life and placed in a foreign environment that burdened them with rapid change in unfamiliar surroundings. Shaw adjusts easily, however, and is successful in her studies.

Also of interest is the fact that her long periods away from home and her education in white ways do not appear to disrupt her relationships with her family, as was so often the case with boarding-school students. This may be accounted for by her family's active participation in Christian practices, which may have created a neutral ground to bridge the disparities in experiences. Also, Pimas had fairly regular contact with white settlers and even occasionally did wage work for them or made shopping excursions into Phoenix. The hardest adjustment perhaps had come in their generation, as Shaw notes when she says, "I never thought of it then, but giving up the tribal ways must have been even harder for my parents, who had been raised in the old traditions."[15] This is confirmed when she says of her mother, "She was torn between two worlds."[16] When compared to Sekaquaptewa, whose educational experiences were much more anxiety ridden, it becomes clear that despite their identical ages, they are actually of two different generations. The adjustments required of Helen are actually more similar to those required of Anna's mother than of those made by Anna herself. Helen's mother was totally traditional all her life, so it is Helen who must make the first accommodations to white culture, adjustments already made within Anna's family. Like Anna's mother, Helen is "torn between two worlds," absorbed throughout her life in resolving the conflicts created by cultural tensions experienced both at school and at home. Anna, of course, is not totally without those conflicts, but because of the groundwork laid in her mother's generation, she is burdened with few extremes in cross-cultural experience. She notes in her mature years that both she and her husband "had been educated in the white man's ways, but we were still traditional Pimas with strong feelings of duty to our families and an intense love of our land."[17] Those feelings, however, do not lead to a return to the reservation on an extended basis. After her graduation from Phoenix High School and Ross's return from battle in World War I (ironically still not a citizen), the young people lived briefly with his parents, but soon left. Shaw explains:

> Our hearts ached for them in their difficult existence, but both Ross and I knew that laboring beside his parents in the fields each day was not the best way to help. The educations they had strived so hard to give us had prepared us to bring in money from the white man's work; it would be wrong to waste all those years of schooling on a life of primitive farming.[18]

Her use of the word "primitive" is revealing of the depth of her acculturation. In spite of her statements that she is a traditional Pima, her views are those of an outsider. In many respects she is the ideal product of the acculturation process advocated in the Indian school system. In a report to the commissioner of Indian Affairs, Indian educators query, "What are we educating the Indian girl for?" The authors' answer to this question in many ways describes Shaw and gives insight into her attitude toward her husband's family and her role in the white world.

> In large numbers the young people of the tribes are leaving the reservations, many of them never to return. Even where tribal life remains, white civilization is pressing close. Whether Indians wish it or not they must become a part of the life around them. . . . It is our task then to help the Indian girl equip herself to meet the demands of modern living—vocationally, spiritually and socially. . . . We must help her to fit herself, and the gifts she brings out of her own rich heritage into the communities of which she is to be a part.[19]

As a product of the policy of Indian education, Anna Shaw is a model graduate; while not alienated from her tribe, she is removed physically, and, to some degree, emotionally and spiritually, from her culture. Her motives are not, however, born or nurtured by a sense of superiority to her people, but by a desire to contribute to the welfare of her family and by a further urge to give her children the benefit of urban schooling. As her daughter relates, she didn't want them to be timid or scared of whites as she had been as a child. She felt backward on the reservation and didn't want to raise her children there, though they often visited to attend celebrations, sometimes for fairly lengthy periods of time, and she did teach her daughter traditional cooking.[20]

What becomes apparent in the early chapters of Shaw's life is that there is an eagerness to participate in white culture that is modulated by a desire to retain identity as an Indian. She does not repudiate her tribal identity, but neither does she return to it. Despite the apparent ease of her adjustment to life in two cultures, there is an underlying ambivalance that shows through in subtle ways in her narrative.

Much of the body of Shaw's narrative is taken up with the everyday activities of raising her family in an urban environment, and, while there are few incidents revealing outright bigotry suffered by the family, there are some indications that there was at least occasional prejudice against them. For instance, as her husband advanced from freight wagon driver to receiving clerk for the railroad, she notes uncomfortable moments for him: "Sometimes a customer would actually insist that a white man wait on him. But the company would not put up with such insults to its employees, and such people were always sent back to Ross's counter. In the end, their prejudice only succeeded in losing them considerable time."[21] Shaw's tone indicates a certain satisfaction in the outcome of this incident that makes it clear such bigotry was painful to her and that adjustments to white urban life were not always easy. Her narrative recognizes the impediments to Indian families sharing fully and without opposition the benefits of white society promised to her in her education, but she is consistently willing to face down the barriers and to see her family as "A Unit in the Family of America," as the title of one of her chapters indicates. She emphasizes this when she says, "That anyone could be prejudiced against Ross seemed strange to me, for I found no such attitudes in the multiracial neighborhood we lived in."[22] Protected by the unique character of her multiethnic neighborhood, she created a middle ground based on the integration of cultures rather than the adherence to a single way of life; physical circumstances mirror her attitudes.

Her concern for making a place for herself and her family in the white world while retaining Indian pride and even educating white people about Indians was given strong impetus by a visit from Dr. Carlos Montezuma, a well-known Indian spokesman, just before his death in 1922. He advised her:

> "To tackle prejudice, it is better to do it face to face in the busy world. To play the same card as the other fellow, we must know him. . . . To think of one's self as different from the mass is unhealthy. Push forward as one of them, be congenial and be in harmony with your environment and make yourselves feel at home as one of the units in the big family of America."[23]

These were ideas already compatible with Shaw's attitudes, ideas that sustained and directed her life as she became active in a parent organization and activities related to her children's interests, as well as the church activities that she had always participated in. When the family moved into an all-white neighborhood, a petition to evict them was circulated, but it failed.

Her editor Karen Thure states that Shaw's idealism about overcoming prejudice toward Indians was stubborn—she really believed that if she played by the rules, "baked enough cupcakes for the boy scouts," as Thure puts it, she would overcome bigotry. Her success in winning the support of her white neighbors attests to the effectiveness of her campaign and the viability of her ideals, at least on a limited scale. Sekaquaptewa, on the other hand, pursued the sanitary practices, vocational skills, and intellectual goals she came to value from her education, not with any notion that they would help in integrating into either Hopi or white culture, but because she found them an expression of her own values as a woman and an effective though quiet protest against prejudices she felt keenly from both cultures. Both women were self-conscious about their Indian identity, but seldom did Shaw feel compelled to articulate it publicly until late in her life. According to her daughter, though, she does remember with some humor one incident in which her mother openly challenged prejudiced whites. During a train trip to Chicago to visit Anna's brother Bill, a musician, passengers nearby called them "dirty Mexicans." Shaw immediately turned to them and retorted, "We are true American Indians."[24]

As her children grew older, Shaw began to regret the loss of traditional stories and to compile her own versions of stories she remembered and heard, leading to the publication of her *Pima Legends*, directed as much toward non-Indians as Indian audiences. Countering her desire to blend into white society was a growing need to preserve her traditional culture as she witnessed the passing of the older generations. She was not yet ready to return to the reservation, because "the white man's world taught us to appreciate civilized comforts,"[25] but she did feel a need to bridge her two ways of life, and writing became the fulfilling vehicle. Though at one point she openly opposed and successfully thwarted her husband's desire to move back to the Gila River Reservation on which she was born, they did finally move to the Salt River Pima Reservation adjacent to Scottsdale after his retirement from the railroad.[26] She admits that she still had doubts about going back to the rural life of her husband's family, but she soon realized, "We weren't going back to the blanket but back to nature."[27] After fifty years of acculturation, it is not surprising that Shaw had become accustomed to white ways and attitudes and was resistant to the move, as her denigrating phrase "back to the blanket" so clearly reveals. But once there, she devoted her vast energies to reviving traditional Pima skills, teaching basket weaving to younger women in the tribe during a period when the techniques had all but died out. She also edited the reservation newspaper and was instrumental in setting up a museum of Pima culture.

Toward the end of her narrative, Shaw looks back over her life on the date of her fiftieth wedding anniversary, still viewing the world with the optimism that characterized her first ventures into it, saying:

> What a variety of friends we had been blessed with! They represented all races and creeds, all classes and educational levels. Upon seeing them enjoy each other together at our party, one would feel that prejudice had surely been conquered. I know that this was not yet so, but my husband and I had seen great progress in the course of our lifetimes.[28]

In a didactic strain, she continues, "Let us once and for all tear down the barriers that keep people from truly knowing their neighbors."[29] Shaw ends her narrative with a direct assessment of her life, satisfied with both her traditional and acquired cultures, urging her readers to level cultural barriers. The fact that in 1981 Anna Moore Shaw was posthumously elected to the Arizona Hall of Fame, publicly acclaimed for her work in creating interracial harmony, attests to her impact on the cultures she dwelt within.

Shaw's autobiography offers a record of unusually smooth adjustment to rapid culture changes in the first half of the twentieth century. Her constant concern for overcoming prejudice indicates that she is aware of the difficulties of adapting to a new way of life, and that because she has made that adaptation, her experiences are worth sharing with both Indians and whites. The conflicts of her adjustments are hidden by her simple way of telling her life story and by her obvious desire to make the disclosure of it a vehicle for intercultural understanding.

The narrative of Helen Sekaquaptewa, which in many ways parallels Shaw's, does not record a parallel ease in adjustment. Sekaquaptewa's adjustments to the changes in her life create conflict for her, conflict that is alleviated only with strong resolve and growing maturity. The structure of *Me and Mine* is one not of fluid progress, but of conflict and resolution, perhaps because she was born into a period of Hopi history in which the intrusion of white culture created severe disruption among her people and led to great stress in her village and eventually in her own family.

Sekaquaptewa's autobiography is an oral narrative. As she recalls, she first met Louise Udall, her recorder-editor, at a church relief society meeting in the 1950s when she was temporarily in Phoenix to make a home for her children attending school there. She notes that Udall actually sought her out and that their relationship developed over a period of time when they were driving to the Maricopa Indian Reservation on a weekly basis to society meetings. As they drove, Udall questioned Helen, curious about Hopi customs and Helen's life, and later offered to record her life history for Helen's children. Only after several years of working with growing intensity did they agree that the life story they had compiled might be of interest to an audience outside the family.

Sekaquaptewa recalls that Udall took lengthy notes on their conversations, sometimes stopping the car to record an incident immediately upon hearing it. They also continued their work at Udall's home, where Helen went weekly to do housework to help support her urban household, work she recalls as being slight, more an excuse for conversation than a job. Udall also became a frequent visitor at the Sekaquaptewa home and at their ranch on the Hopi reservation, where Helen's husband, Emory, and their children also participated in the storytelling sessions. Together, as a family, they agreed that the narrative should be published. By this time Helen and Louise Udall had been working almost ten years on the material, and Helen felt that it was worth sharing, that it would allow people to learn more about Hopis. She felt that she had "told her life honestly" and represented her participation in "Hopi life honestly,"[30] though the process was frequently difficult. Helen remembers that Louise often didn't understand fully what she was told of Hopi customs; sometimes Helen had to demonstrate how traditional clothing was worn or how food was prepared.[31] Helen herself edited the recorded materials as they were completed, changing phrasing that didn't sound like her own, making additions and clarifying passages. Sekaquaptewa actually wrote two chapters, one on bartering with their Navajo neighbors and the one on her own marriage, because Udall didn't fully understand the material. She notes with some amusement that it came to her then that she probably could have written the whole thing herself, but quickly confirms that her relationship with Udall and the editor's help, as well, were invaluable in developing a coherent and polished narrative. It was not until 1968 that they determined to publish and the manuscript was accepted by the University of Arizona Press.

Sekaquaptewa recalls that it was she who set up the sequence of the narrative, which is not completely chronological, and the controlling premise, to tell only about her own experiences—leading to the very personal title of the book. She did not want to discuss Hopi life in general or anyone else's experiences because she did not want to be criticized for being too outspoken on Hopi ways. Hence, she left out a chapter they had originally included on a Navajo raid on her village before her birth, and a story of the kidnapping and rescue of her grandfather's bride, along with some material supplied by her husband. This determination to avoid any speculation on areas of Hopi culture or history is in direct contrast to Shaw's free use of events beyond her own observation. Sekaquaptewa did not see herself as a spokeswoman for Hopi culture, nor did she have any desire to introduce didactic elements into her narrative. She is self-conscious of her role as an educated Hopi woman and as a narrator and strict in her definition of what an autobiography should be—one person telling his or her own life.[32]

She notes that she and Udall had no real conflicts over the compiling of the work, and though many people tried to influence Udall, she listened only to Helen and gave her final editorial control. The only apparent hitch in this arrangement was the epilogue, which consists of brief vignettes on each of Helen's children. Though the children objected, Udall thought the family was extraordinary and insisted; and though Helen was reluctant, she finally agreed to the format.

Sekaquaptewa's only regret about the autobiography as it was published is the absence of more material concerning her mother's admonitions to guard herself sexually from men both within and outside her household and how she successfully acted on her mother's instructions when she was lured into a threatening situation in her youth. She speculates that Udall's deletion of that experience may have been the result of personal distaste or the fear of offending readers. She chuckles when she notes that whites are often much less comfortable about discussing bodily functions than Indians, and says she did not press Udall because she felt her experience might not be understood by her non-Indian readers. She also notes she left out most detailed information on food preparation because she thought readers would either not understand it or would not be able to make use of it, or find it repugnant since some traditional Hopi food preparation employs methods that would be considered unsanitary by whites. She said there was a time when she was ashamed of some Hopi ways, but she now wishes she had been more forceful and confident about including them.[33] At the time, she didn't want to include anything that would be "too strange" to non-Hopi readers or anything that she had not directly experienced, although it was she who advocated the inclusion of additional information on the traditionalist-progressive split that disrupted her village in her childhood. She encouraged Udall to research this event in the Indian archives in Washington, D.C., because her own childhood perspective on the event, which occurred when she was only eight years old, was incomplete and she felt thorough records were critical to comprehension of it.

Sekaquaptewa begins her narrative with a sense of immediacy that bridges the time from her birth to her late life by introducing the landscape that has been a molding and enduring influence. She uses the first person from the beginning, saying: "My homeland is the arid, sandy, plateau country of northeastern Arizona, where dwell the Hopi people in eleven villages, each with similar characteristics and mores, yet each a separate city-state, and not always on friendly terms with the neighbors."[34] Her attention to her family background centers exclusively on her own parents, and her birth is introduced early in the narrative followed by the statement, "There was love in my home, and I felt happy and secure during my childhood."[35] The narrative does not sustain chronological sequence for long, however, as Sekaquaptewa devotes a considerable portion of the introductory chapters to description of typical Hopi customs experienced in her childhood, such as collecting water at a communal well, initiation of youngsters into the ceremonial life of the village kiva and plaza, games and everyday activities typical of her youth. While much of this material is reported in the third person, it is carefully and fully detailed, and she continually associates herself with these activities by such phrases as: "Some of the earliest of my childhood memories center about . . . , "[36] or "My people took what was at hand and made the best of it to provide the necessities of life, and I was a participant and beneficiary during my childhood."[37]

The structure of her narrative is quite sophisticated as it also employs flashback technique and historical documentation that lends an authoritative tone to the events described. Her discussion of everyday Hopi life at the turn of the century is interrupted by the interjection of a brief background of her future husband's childhood, which sets up the inevitability of their marriage, and the chapter titled "The Line," which describes driving out of the village of Oraibi the "Hostiles," the faction of the village resistant to schooling and other changes introduced by whites.

This event, and incidents leading up to the actual expulsion in 1906, are taken from government records, personalized, and given emotional impact from her own recollections. The confusion of being forced to leave her home is dramatically captured as she says:

> Then another man, I remember him because his neck was crooked and he was more fierce and began pushing us, and as

> he shoved me I fell and rolled down the steps. As we left the house, my mother handed each of us a bundle of food or clothing to carry. We walked into the plaza and were driven out of the village with the others.[38]

Unlike Shaw, whose early memories are of harmony in her village, Sekaquaptewa's youth is disrupted, and she and her family are actually rejected because of their traditional beliefs and practices. It is likely that this is a genuinely critical moment in the life of this young girl, one that contributes significantly to her determination to work toward reconciliation of conflict in her more mature years. It also marks the beginning of a pattern of being something of an outsider, different from other Hopi girls, other students, other Hopi families; as her life progresses, this pattern is one that is only broken in her old age when she again lives in a Hopi village and is respected and looked to as a role model for Hopi womanhood. This moment is the first of many moments when Helen felt the harsh treatment accorded an "outsider," but even the anguish of being forced into a new place is treated with some humor as she recollects that in the brutal cold of winter the exiles built Navajo-style hogans to shelter themselves but were not very adept at living in them:

> We were not accustomed to the Navajo way of cooking and heating with an open fire in the middle of the floor and the smoke going out of a hole in the center of the roof. Nearly every day a house or something in it would catch fire. Everyone kept a container with water on hand, and when the alarm was given everyone ran to help. Even I remember grabbing my little bottle of water.[39]

This first experience of harsh treatment and her sensible reactions set a pattern for recovery from repeated unkindness, demonstrated when she was finally captured by the truant officers and sent to school. In her first experiences in school she notes that there, the girls who had remained in Oraibi teased the little exile girls until they cried. She remembers: "At night when the doors were closed and locked and little girls were supposed to be in bed for the night, our tormentors would take our native clothes from the boxes and put them on and dance around making fun of us."[40] But Helen and her exile friends were not ashamed; they knew they had done no wrong in holding to their traditions. However, though she endured abuse without rancor, there is little doubt that continual rejection and abuse estranged her from her classmates. She would soon be caught in an awareness that would make her situation even more difficult. Although she was seen by her progressive peers as too traditional, her traditionalist family, particularly her older sister, who escaped white schooling, would soon see her as too progressive. For the eight-year-old child, the first months of school were filled with fear and pain. In an interview in 1981, she recalls that most of the children were sick and the food was inadequate. Some children died. During that first winter Helen had a dream that helped to calm her and keep her going. In her fear of the matrons and her fellow students, she began to pray and fell into a dream of the end of the world, where everything was in chaos and destruction, but Helen remained calm and trusted in God to protect her. A childish dream, she says in retrospect, but one that helped her during a time of real suffering.[41]

Perhaps as an escape, Helen began to excel in her schoolwork, which, of course, did nothing to alleviate the hostility she received from other students, and in fact, intensified it. But it did bring positive rewards in pride in her own abilities and turned an intolerable situation into a positive aspect of her life. As a result of the early harrassments she suffered, she adopted an attitude that was to shape her response to experiences in the future. She promised herself, "When I grow up I will be kind."[42]

The 1906 conflict begins the strictly sequential narrative in the autobiography. Although Helen's formal schooling was interrupted for a year after her first term at the Keams Canyon Agency, her education was not, for she was taught by her mother to grind corn and cook piki, a wafer-thin bread that is a traditional Hopi staple. Returning to the agency the following year, she recalls, "I enjoyed school and was eager to learn. I was a good reader. . . . I tried not to be mean to anyone but still I was not favored among the students."[43] Unlike Shaw, Sekaquaptewa does not see justice in the harsh treatment accorded the students. Her enthusiasm is much narrower than Anna's, confined exclusively to the satisfaction in learning. Nonetheless, boarding school weaned her away from home. She had lived so much at school that she chaffed at home and felt herself an outsider there, too, but she was too young to assert herself in a household that looked to the elders, not children, for guidance, to tradition, not change, for stability. Her newly acquired learning was not valued, so when she had the opportunity to go to Phoenix, she took it.

It was at the Phoenix school that Anna Moore and Helen became acquainted and shared a room in the dormitory. It was modeled on military schools, and when the Hopi girls arrived, some were given offices; Helen was made a lieutenant, Anna a captain. The privileges given the Hopi girls caused resentment and prevented a close friendship—in fact, Anna would not speak to Helen—between the two girls. Still, Helen recalls that she admired Anna's ambition, that she set a good example. There was also a more basic difference between the girls: Anna did not wish to return to the reservation, whereas Helen, despite the tension with her family, was determined to go back to Hopi at the end of her schooling, hoping to open a laundry since in the vocational-academic program at the Phoenix Indian School she had been trained as a laundress.[44] Furthermore, she wanted to live on the land of her birth. Her attachment to the freedom of the open landscape of Hopi made her feel she could live and survive there more effectively than with wage work in a town.[45] Since she had attended school without her parents' permission and could only stay three years, she returned to the reservation before she was able to graduate. Not graduating is the only regret she voices in the narrative, and the only area of her life in which she felt incomplete.

While during much of her life she had been forced to deal with the conflict between Hopi and white cultures, her return home brought to a head resentment against her educated ways. When her mother, her only advocate in the family, died in an influenza epidemic, Helen felt like an intruder in her own home. Her sister was particularly critical, mocking her for using too much water, and for reading and writing letters. Helen recalls that she was not nasty in response, but also didn't stop doing the things she had learned. She felt affection for her sister, but also felt she was disruptive. Only toward the end of her sister's life were they able to work out the problems that had erupted when Helen returned to her family home.[46]

Despite their lack of money, Helen and Emory decided it would be best if they married and set up their own household. She had decided while quite young that she wanted to marry a Hopi who had some education so that they could practice their new skills in their own home. Emory, her suitor in Phoenix, fit her desires, so they were married both in a traditional and a legal ceremony.[47] With her marriage came resolution of many of the conflicts of her youth as she was able to bring together in her own home what she saw as the best of Hopi and white ways. "Our lives were a combination of what we thought was the good of both cultures, the Hopi way and what we had learned in school. Whenever we departed from the traditions our neighbors would scorn us."[48] While the tensions caused by her sister's resentment were eased, the customary sanctions of village gossip still made her uncomfortable she recalls: "I was aware that my neighbors were talking about me, laughing at me, mimicking, and generally belittling me all the time," and "I could feel critical eyes following my every move."[49] She did not, however, confront her critics, but resolutely did the traditional things she thought she should and practiced what she had learned in school in balanced measure.[50] She worked hard, like Hopis are supposed to, and even notes with some irony that whereas her neighbors bought white flour and bread, she ground corn for bread on a stone metate, and that she had her children at home as her mother had. Looking back over her life in an interview in 1981, Helen pointed out that she did everything she could to be an exemplary Hopi woman. "I was stuck here, so I might as well learn everything," she decided when she first returned. She still feels the best place for a woman is in the home, where her skills benefit the family, and she notes that homemaking skills are the ideal for marriage and that they are taught from childhood on. She was not, however, interested in the women's ceremonial societies and made no attempt to join them. She recalls that she was initiated into her mother's society when she was about eight and found the event pleasant, but that she never really participated and never had a desire to because she did not understand the activities. On this omission she was also criticized by the traditional women in the village when she returned from school.[51]

Though she was undaunted and determined in her resolve to remain kind despite abuse, the pressure did not lessen, and she and her husband gradually came to feel that life would be better if they moved to a ranch, some miles from the village, offered by his clan. The ranch was offered to them because it was on the edge of the Hopi reservation and Navajos were encroaching on the border. It was isolated, hard land, and Helen notes that the clan expected them to fail, but they felt it would give them freedom to live as they wished, a freedom Helen consistently associated with the Hopi landscape, so they accepted the offer. The move also relieved Helen of the criticism she endured for not observing every ceremony or participating in a woman's society; they were simply too far away to travel into the village by wagon very often.[52] Again, Helen found workable solutions to the culture conflict. They prospered on the ranch, raising their children in traditional Hopi values and ways, but with the addition of the skills they had come by at school. In time, because they won respect for their productivity, and because their children did well in school, the enmity with villagers lessened. Helen again shows a glint of humor when she says, "We were as stubborn about going back to the old ways as they were about changing their ways."[53] She noted with equal humor in a 1980 interview that it was a good thing they learned the traditional ways and practiced them on the ranch because one year they were snowbound for more than a month, and the air-dropped provisions burst on impact and were destroyed, so they had to survive on traditional piki bread and other Hopi staples. "We survived on it," she says, pointing out that what might seem dull fare to outsiders was exactly the diet on which Hopis should survive and was not dull to them—it was the very sustenance of Hopi life.[54] Her resolve to remain unbitter is effectively displayed in her humor and understanding for the villagers who made her the butt of their criticisms.

One of the events most important to her at the ranch, however, does not appear in the narrative. At one point Helen took care of an old woman—she notes that people in the villages were often unkind to sick, retarded, or handicapped persons—during a time when Emory was working in the fields and was away from the house at night. The old woman provided company and advised her, "Never hate or be intolerant and you will be healthy and live long. Never repay wrongs. Control your temper and be cautious in saying things." This critical incident reconfirmed for her the appropriateness and value of the attitudes and behavior she had cultivated since childhood. It is a moment, she says, that has gained significance for her only as she has grown old and seen the prophecy of longevity come to be true.[55]

In those years on the ranch, Helen raised not only her own eight children but two foster sons as well. As the children grew ready for higher schooling than the reservation could provide, Helen sent them to her sister-in-law in Phoenix and soon followed to keep house for them. By the time of her eldest daughter's graduation from high school, Helen had been much influenced by members of the Mormon church, and she made the decision to accept baptism, becoming a Christian when she was fifty-five years old. The autobiography does not place great emphasis on this event, and her daughter suggests this is as much Udall's restraint on her personal enthusiasm for Helen's conversion as it was a personal decision by Helen.[56] Udall's restraint is to be commended since it saves the narrative from becoming simplistic or sentimentalized.

Helen's life story does not fit into the conversion-literature pattern of concentration on conversion to Christianity as a turning point or salvation; Mormonism is not seen as an answer to all life's problems. She places the event near the end of her narrative and does not indicate any drastic life change because of it. Rather, she treats it as the natural outgrowth of her lifelong experiences with religion. And although she underplays it in the narrative, she is quite willing to discuss her spiritual growth, stating firmly that she had never been opposed to any religious group, but had no urge to join a Christian group until the Mormons. "They taught what I'd heard before as a child," she says. It captured her mind, so that she slowly came to believe and then converted. Her narrative expands on the similarities of the Hopi and Mormon prophecies, but what it does not detail is her childhood disillusionment with Hopi religious practices. Growing up in a traditional Hopi family, she accepted the Hopi philosophy and beliefs fully, but she says that the ceremonial participants shattered her beliefs because they didn't perform in life consistently with ceremonial ideals and Hopi philosophy. Whether this is a genuine memory or a contemporary interpretation is not clear, but even as a recent response, it serves as a rationale and reinforces her confidence in Christianity. "It seemed faked, and I became disillusioned as a child because my beliefs were shattered. Then I didn't know what to believe."[57] Only in her maturity did she come to understand the good in the ceremonies. In her youth and young adulthood she had been unable to reconcile how things are supposed to be—the Hopi ideals of her childhood—and how they really are. Furthermore, she had learned about the Bible in school and thought Christianity was good and that she might sometime accept it, but the Hopi community was very opposed to Christianity, and Helen didn't want to further aggravate her already tenuous situation. So, while she allowed her children to attend Mennonite services and sometimes helped out Christian groups, she was not anxious to join any. Rather, she observed and was impressed with the actions of the Mormon missionaries at Hopi and took the opportunity to get more involved in their religion while she was away from the village with her children. She was not, in fact, the first of her family to convert, since one of her sons had actually introduced the Mormon church into their household.[58] Conversion, then, is not the climax or turning point of Helen's life, nor the focus of her story. It is, rather, a very gradual and natural outgrowth of both her Hopi and non-Hopi observations and experiences about religion, another resolution of the old and new in her life.

The title of the final chapter of the narrative is "Dasube," the Hopi word for the time period from the moment the sun sets until night falls, what Helen describes as a period of "rosy light that glows in the western sky."[59] In this final chapter Sekaquaptewa meditates on her life much as Anna Shaw does, with satisfaction at her accomplishments. "We chose the good from both ways of living,"[60] she says.

The effects of those choices required adjustments and compromises, but she is consistently unsentimental in recalling her life. Throughout the narrative she also resists any direct address to the audience or any direct comparison between the past and present, both common patterns in autobiography. There seems to be little sense of loss or regret. Reconciliation has been her pattern, and she puts pain and rejection behind her in every episode of the narrative, or, as the interview material makes clear, simply omits it from her story.

Like Anna Shaw, Helen came to be a highly respected member of her tribe, the matriarch of the Eagle Clan, partly, she admits, because of the autobiography. Even her late years have not always been without conflict though. When she wanted to move into her old village from the ranch, people thwarted her, but since the autobiography, especially during the 1970s, people have come to accept her and did not reject her second attempt to build a home in her village.[61]

As with many other aspects of her life, she worried at first about the effect of her writing on her life at Hopi. "It was preposterous to write, the old people thought, but they have liked it," she says. She notes that Hopis are intimately involved in the book now because everything in it touches them. They think it is a wonder that she had words to say what she did and that she could remember so much. Because of it she has become, in a way, everyone's grandmother. She knows the general public responds less intimately, but her people tell her, "It keeps me company."[62]

The lives and narratives of these two women span a period of rapid, comprehensive, and often abrasive cultural contact. Inevitably, some of the changes that occurred were critical in the forming of values and personality in each of the women presented here. Similarly, they approach life with positive sensibilities, selecting carefully the workable aspects of both cultures as circumstances presented them. Both express satisfaction with their lives and little sense of loss or sacrifice, and while Anna Shaw accepts a large measure of white culture, she does remain true to her Pima beginnings, by choice, not force. Helen Sekaquaptewa never relinquishes her Hopi identity or deep attachment to her sense of place in spite of negative experiences. In her narrative, as in her life, she develops a straightforward assessment of tribal and white ways, throwing the balance distinctly in favor of traditional values and practices without rejecting practical improvements in her life.

The lives and narratives of these women, as they parallel and diverge, enrich and enliven understanding of what it was like to grow up in a world that sometimes deliberately, and often inadvertently, makes retaining the integrity of Indian womanhood confusing and difficult but not impossible. They are stories connected intimately to place, perhaps made less complicated by the distinctiveness and unique character of the land, the natural separation of people, and a slowness to yield to change in the basic concepts of life. In both life stories there is a clarity and continuity that may in part be a response to the distance and clear light of the Arizona landscape they share.

While neither Helen Sekaquaptewa nor Anna Moore Shaw can be characterized as primarily literary in her sensibilities, in the course of their adulthoods, each of them acquired a sense of herself as a writer. Anna Shaw wrote not only her collection of legends and her autobiography, but before her death began a biography of her husband.[63] Helen Sekaquaptewa admits that writing has become an enduring part of her life, that she translates hymns and even writes poetry.[64] The impact of their published works has been important to each of these women in establishing them as respected models of womanhood within their tribes and has given breadth to each life, drawing both Indians and non-Indians to them, creating a modest fame for each woman. By narrating their lives, each gave firm substance to fleeting experiences, capturing in the timeless construct of language the convergence of cultures that created unique identities.

The autobiographies of these women have far surpassed the case-history level of early narratives, partly because each was conceived as a literary work with close attention paid to stylistic concerns and the development of strong voices. In each work, it is not simply event or incident that is of interest, but the author's response to her experiences and her methods of connecting the disparate aspects of her life to bring a sense of unity and coherence to both her life and her expression of it.

The roles of the editors of these two works seem much less influential than those in earlier autobiographies. Unfortunately the absence of any editorial statement in either work makes tracing their degree of influence difficult, and because the original manuscripts of both works are lost, research cannot uncover the details of the collaboration between editors and authors. It is clear, however, that despite the apparent absence of editorial control in either work, the respective editors did exert considerable influence on the substance and structure of both books, but more than previous editors examined in this text, their approach and control of the material of these two autobiographies was literary, employing devices and techniques to give the story audience appeal and impact. The fact that the University of Arizona Press editorial assistant was simply assigned to the Shaw text and does not receive collaboration credit in the published work indicates that this book is different from the oral autobiography process that recognizes publicly the involvement of the recorder-editor. The fact that Helen Sekaquaptewa and her family have been willing to discuss the participation of Louise Udall has also been useful in determining that her role as recorder-editor was somewhat more limited than in the cases of some of the other editor-recorders discussed in this book.

Like the women in these life stories, the stories themselves are representative of change in the process of autobiography, of the assertion of more control by narrators. In one sense they reflect the simultaneous viability of both oral and written forms of autobiography, since they both trace women born in 1898. In another sense, they demonstrate the two major modes of Indian autobiography. The oral mode used for Sekaquaptewa's life story, which begins in a deeply traditional culture and emerges in a household that uses white knowledge without violating Hopi values, accommodates the emphasis on tradition in Helen Sekaquaptewa's life. Shaw's written narrative, which traces a less violent culture change from youth to maturity, mirrors Anna Shaw's strong commitment to acquiring new approaches to life and new modes of expression for Indian women. These two life stories, with their remarkable similarities and even more startling differences, reveal the complexities and subtleties of both Indian life and Indian autobiography in a period of transition.

# 6
# The Long Road Back: Maria Campbell

The tidy cabin and the familiar
smell of herbs and roots and
wood-smoke, and the rabbit soup
simmering on the stove, all made
me feel like I had come home again.

Maria Campbell, *Halfbreed*

In an essay on anthropological life histories, anthropologist David G. Mandelbaum makes a distinction between life-passage studies and life-history studies. Life-passage (or life-cycle) studies, he says, "emphasize the requirements of society, showing how the people of a group socialize and enculturate their young in order to make them into viable members of society." Life histories, however, "emphasize the experiences and requirements of the individual—how the person copes with society rather than how society copes with the stream of individuals."[1] This distinction can clearly be seen in the autobiographies of American Indian women and may account for the literary or nonliterary qualities as well. In early recorded life stories, such as those published by Michelson and other anthropologists, the emphasis was on enculturation and socialization. The prescribed roles were stressed, and the narrator followed the patterns set by the tribe, or at least dictated the story in such a way as to reflect tribal expectations. The account revealed the desired role of all women within a given tribal culture.

The difference between the two types of studies appears to be determined by the amount of control the narrator has over the material. In some autobiographies recorded by an editor, for example, *Mountain Wolf Woman,* the narrator retained control over the material and shaped it into a life history, a story of an individual. This becomes even more true with autobiographies free of extensive editorial intrusion.

Whereas life-passage stories bring out the similarities in a culture but do not concern themselves with the individual's choices and the relationship of those decisions to the larger culture or to cultural change, life histories stress the individual's relationship to the culture, to political movements, and to the significance of personal decisions in her life. Autobiographies in which there is no recorder-editor are far more reflective of the life-history category, for there is not an outsider shaping the story to reflect preconceived notions of cultural expectations.

The last autobiography specifically addressed in this study is Maria Campbell's *Halfbreed,* a written autobiography that reflects the evolution of style and theme in life histories. Sarah Winnemucca in 1883 published the story of her life, an autobiography heavily influenced by Christianity and her involvement with the United States government. At the turn of the century Gertrude Bonnin (Zitkala Sa) published a series of magazine articles reflecting on her own dilemma as an Indian woman who was educated in white schools and yet retained a strong sense of identity as a Sioux. Maria Campbell is thus carrying on a well-established tradition with her own account of growing up as a Canadian Métis woman influenced strongly, and often negatively, by the non-Indian world around her. Not only does Campbell's work carry on traditional themes of earlier written autobiographies, it serves as further proof that the two modes of autobiography, written and oral, continue to exist simultaneously.

Maria Campbell's story is that of one individual Indian woman in Canada and, although she generalizes that she is telling "what it is like to be a Halfbreed woman," clearly her story is that of one woman who has struggled to survive the prejudice and poverty in her life. Although one learns a great deal about the life of Halfbreed women in Canada from Campbell's story, it is the individual story of her life that is at the center of the narrative. The dramatic moments, the frustrations, and the fears are clearly hers, and the concern is with her life, not with the larger group of Indian women who might share similar experiences.

Although the book has been called radical by Métis working within the government, it lacks the strident voice of *Bobbi Lee: Indian Rebel,* another book by a young Canadian Indian woman that reflects the political struggles of her people. Campbell was born in 1940 in northern Saskatchewan and grew up in western Canada somewhere west of Prince Albert National Park. The most striking aspect of this autobiography, written by the subject and not processed through a recorder-editor, is the sense of identity the author assumed. Both in the title and the text, Maria Campbell identifies herself as a Halfbreed.[2]

*Métis*, *mixed-blood*, and the more perjorative term *half-breed* have been used in the United States and Canada to define an individual of mixed Indian and white ancestry. During the nineteenth century and into the twentieth century the label *half-breed* was applied most often to those Indian males suspected of being particularly evil. The fictional figure of the half-breed mirrored society's attitude toward the group. William J. Scheick, in his study of the half-blood in fiction, writes, "By his very nature the half-blood epitomized the integration (whether successful or unsuccessful) of the red and the white races, provided a dramatic symbol of the benign possibilities or malign probabilities inherent in this encounter."[3]

Several writers discussed in this study are not full-bloods; indeed, today the number of Indians with only American Indian ancestors continues to dwindle. Identity for most American Indians is not measured by blood quantum. Gerald Vizenor, in the Preface to *Earthdivers: Tribal Narratives on Mixed Descent,* defines the mixed-blood in a way that is meaningful to many American Indians: "The words *Métis* and *mixedblood* possess no social or scientific validation, because blood mixture is not a measurement of consciousness, culture, or human experiences; but the word *Métis* is a source of notable and radical identification."[4]

Although Vizenor's definition makes good philosophical sense, in Canada, and to a lesser extent in the United States, it does not make good legal sense. Canadian law strictly defines the native population; there are registered treaty Indians and registered nontreaty Indians, classifications that depend on past legal relationships with the Crown. In another group are nonregistered Indians, persons who may be biologically and culturally Indian, but who are not legally defined as such. In this group are Indian women who have lost their Indian status by marrying non-Indians. The last major group is classified as Métis, those people and their descendants who have mixed ancestry, usually Indian and French, and who between 1870 and 1875 were given land and for whom the government set up colonies. In 1940 the Indian Affairs branch of the Canadian government refused to acknowledge the Métis as a legally defined group.[5] The Métis have continued to fight for legal recognition, and it is this struggle that provides both the frustration and the motivation for Maria Campbell's life.

The most literary of those narratives discussed in this study, this autobiography is a life story that was written by the subject for publication. Throughout the book the author is aware of her audience, and, although she is informal in her relationship with that audience, the persona remains constant. The reader is drawn into the life being narrated and becomes an intimate of the writer, sharing the pain and celebrating the small victories.

There is a circular pattern to Maria Campbell's autobiography, for it begins with her return to her childhood home. The description in the Introduction is one of desolation and of emptiness; there is little left of the physical past:

> The house where I grew up is tumbled down and overgrown with brush. The pine tree beside the east window is dried and withered. . . . The graveyard down the hill is a tangle of wild roses, tiger lilies and thistle. . . . The blacksmith shop and cheese factory across the road have long since been torn down and only an old black steam-engine and forgotten horseshoes mark the place where they once stood. . . . The French owners who came from Quebec are dead and their families have gone. It is as if they were never there. . . . The old people who were so much a part of my childhood have all died.[6]

Seventeen years have passed, and Maria Campbell has returned home; but what of those seventeen years and what of the years before that, the years she spent growing up on this land? She tells in the Introduction why she is writing her autobiography: "I write this for all of you, to tell you what it is like to be a Halfbreed woman in our country. I want to tell you about the joys and sorrows, the oppressing poverty, the frustrations and the dreams."[7]

To fulfill that purpose she must go back and record the realities and the dreams of her childhood. Her autobiography is the culmination of her personal search: "If I was to know peace I would have to search within myself," she writes.[8]

Maria Campbell's life story is one of poverty, of deprivation, of alcoholism and prostitution, and finally it is a story of the strength in knowing who she is. Through her search she came to understand the message her great-grandmother Cheechum had been trying to communicate. The autobiography of Maria Campbell is clearly a product of contemporary experience. It is frank, and the pain of Campbell's life comes through clearly. The events of her life might be unique, except that the status of Indian people in Canada has been well documented, particularly the deplorable conditions of the Métis, or Halfbreeds, who do not have treaty rights with the government.[9] Maria Campbell is a Halfbreed, and she is only too aware of what that means in her country.

The arbitrary labels of *Halfbreed, Métis, Indian, status Indian, nonstatus Indian, and Eskimo* continue to work their evil, just as Cheechum told her granddaughter they would: "The white man saw that that was a more powerful weapon than anything else with which to beat the Halfbreeds, and he used it and still does today. Already they are using it on you. They try to make you hate your people."[10] Conflict among the groups is inflamed by the different ways in which they are treated by the government and the Indian Act of 1951. Labels are legal in nature and do not reflect blood quantum, parentage, or cultural identification. An Indian woman loses her Indian status if she marries a white; a white woman can gain Indian status and a place on the reserve if she marries an Indian. Indian men do not face the same restrictions, adding another internal conflict.

Although Campbell's book is written as autobiography, it incorporates urban and rural sociology, a study of ethnic relations in Canada, and a historical account of the political situation; but primarily it is literature. She is aware of the need to develop her plot, to use suspense, and to end the narrative neatly when the protagonist is about to set out on a new and more promising venture. Having experienced the most negative aspects of life, she has rehabilitated herself, has written the story of her life up to that point, and has ended the narrative on a note of resolution and promise that allows us to speculate on her future.

Central to Campbell's development of her personal search for identity is the character of Cheechum, a guiding force in the narrator's life and a unifying force in the narrative structure of the text. It is the advice and counsel of this woman, old already when we meet her, that is important. When Campbell writes of her integration into the family and community, she says: "As far back as I can remember Daddy taught me how to set traps, shoot a rifle, and fight like a boy. Mom did her best to turn me into a lady, showing me how to cook, sew and knit, while Cheechum, my best friend and confidante, tried to teach me all she knew about living."[11]

When Cheechum dies in an accident at the age of 104, Campbell has reached a climax in her life. Will Cheechum's advice have been in vain, or will Campbell finally understand it? The story is dramatic and moving. Her Cree great-grandmother has been very important, and now that Campbell must make some crucial decisions, she will have to follow the advice of the wise old woman. Cheechum, then, is a literary device, although no less real for that fact, and she serves to direct the thoughts and actions of the narrator as she develops her story, which she tells deliberately and, at times, quite self-consciously.

Maria Campbell can speak to the reader as an intimate friend, relating the pain and misery of her life. Early in the narrative she makes an obvious reference to her audience as non-Indian, yet it is clear that the events she is about to relate are not meant as an indictment against her reader:

> I am not bitter. I have passed that stage. I only want to say: this is what it was like; this is what it is still like. I know that poverty is not ours alone. Your people have it too, but in those earlier days you at least had dreams, you had a tomorrow. My parents and I never shared any aspirations for a future.[12]

Clearly she is making an attempt to communicate to the non-Indian audience what her experiences as an Indian have been. Through the story of her family, Campbell explains how poverty and prejudice can destroy a people. It is a personal story which she has edited herself, changing some names and places to protect identities. As a narrative that reveals the essence of her life, the story meets most critical criteria for autobiography.

Life changes for everyone, but Maria Campbell knew early that for her people the future held no hope. Her worst fears were confirmed when she returned to Spring River, for the deterioration had been almost complete. Her descriptions expose her pain—lonely, dilapidated, desolate, dried-up, ruins; it was not a pretty picture. And of the people: "I saw people whom I had know as a child, now with such empty, despairing faces."[13] The changes were all negative—more drunkards, more children being neglected. Campbell's emotions are reflected in the landscape.

Despite the hopelessness of her people, there is one hope for

Maria Campbell—to hold on to the advice of her great-grandmother Cheechum, her most important teacher. Cheechum had seen the "little people" and had the gift of second sight. When Maria Campbell was rejected by white storekeepers, it was Cheechum who said, "You always walk with your head up and if anyone says something then put out your chin and hold it higher."[14] Cheechum understood the philosophy of divide and conquer that the whites had used against the native people and recognized that the enemy was greater than individuals. The government, the missionaries, and the shopkeepers had worked together to destroy the spirit of her people. As she often does in the course of her story, Campbell recalls her great-grandmother's words:

> My Cheechum used to tell me that when the government gives you something, they take all that you have in return—your pride, your dignity, all the things that make you a living soul. When they are sure they have everything they give you a blanket to cover your shame. She said that the churches with their talk about God, the Devil, heaven and hell, and schools that taught children to be ashamed, were all part of that government. . . . She used to say that all our people wore blankets, each in his own way.[15]

By the end of the narrative, Campbell proudly asserts: "I no longer need my blanket to survive." She finally learns what Cheechum meant when she told her, "The blanket only destroys, it doesn't give warmth."[16]

The blanket metaphor is effective. Indians and blankets are inextricably linked in textbooks, picture postcards, and the movies. Shedding the blanket is synonymous with throwing off an image that has fostered dependence and encouraged prejudice. Only when Campbell realizes that her warmth can come in other ways can she get rid of the heavy baggage of her youth. She is not destroying the positive parts; she is, in fact, building on the strength of that oldest and wisest family member, Cheechum. But she is getting rid of all the negative self-images that were fostered by those around her as she was growing up, images of herself and her people as they had become. Their faces had molded to fit the masks made by outsiders, and many of them no longer knew their own images. It was the false face that had to be abandoned.

One of the ways in which a people are destroyed is by their believing the labels given to them. The Halfbreeds were constant victims of labeling. "Indian," "Halfbreed," "white," "Métis," "nigger," "owl eyes," "road-allowance people," and "awp-pee-tow-kooson" ("half-people")—at one time or another Campbell and her family were called all these things. Who defines a people? That dilemma exists for many groups, but for the Halfbreeds of Canada, and Campbell in particular, it has been especially disastrous. Stereotypes abound. Even Campbell writes:

> They (the Indian relatives on the reserves) were completely different from us—quiet when we were noisy, dignified even at dances and get-togethers. Indians were very passive—they would get angry at things done to them but they would never fight back, whereas Halfbreeds were quick-tempered—quick to fight, but quick to forgive and forget.[17]

There were real differences to remind the Halfbreeds that even if they were not like the Indians, neither were they white. At school the white children brought bread, eggs, fruit, and sweets. The Halfbreed children had bannock, lard, and wild meat or cold potatoes. The whites teased them because of their gopher meat and patched clothes. Maria later was to meet Stan Daniels, president of the Alberta Métis League, who justified his involvement with the political actions of his people by his own childhood experiences, explaining that where he grew up the favorite sport was "kicking the asses of the half breeds all the way to school."[18] Because Maria had dark skin and blue eyes, she was caught even tighter in the web of identity confusion.

Maria Campbell presents a compelling picture of her own life as a Halfbreed. As a Métis woman she is subject to the general stereotypes produced by the cultural mix of Canada. She is outspoken, and this is attributed to her "white" blood by Treaty Indians: " 'It's the white in her.' Treaty Indian women don't express their opinions; Halfbreed women do."[19]

Her story is a sequence of conflicts: Indian and white, status and nonstatus Indians, males and females. After her devastating experiences with marriage and unsatisfactory relationships with men, she analyzes the attitudes of native men toward women: "The missionaries had impressed upon us the feeling that women were a source of evil. This belief, combined with the ancient Indian recognition of the power of women, is still holding back the progress of our people today."[20]

The missionaries had not been charitable. Her memories of them include the day her mother was asked to leave the church and the night the priest came to dinner and ate all the food. Her father burned the Christmas packages distributed to the "poor Indians" each year. They all resisted and resented the missionaries, but it was Cheechum who recognized clearly what the churches were doing: "Cheechum would often say scornfully of this God that he took more money from us than the Hudson's Bay store."[21] As a final irony, Campbell's mother, who died when Maria was twelve, was denied a funeral Mass because, although she had never missed church, she had not been given the Last Sacrament. The irony was not missed by Cheechum, who provided the young Maria with a different explanation of God:

> She taught me to see beauty in all things around me; that inside each thing a spirit lived, that it was vital too, regardless of whether it was only a leaf or a blade of grass, and by recognizing its life and beauty I was accepting God. She said that each time I did something it was a prayer, regardless of whether it was good or bad; that heaven and hell were man-made and here on earth; that there was no death, only that the body becomes old from life on earth and that the soul must be reborn, because it is young; that when my body became old my spirit would leave and I'd come back and live again. She said God lives in you and looks like you, and not to worry about him floating around in a beard and white cloak; that the Devil lives in you and all things, and that he looks like you and not like a cow. . . . Her explanation made much more sense than anything Christianity had ever taught me.[22]

Campbell presents the cycle of poverty, the despair generation after generation, as a downward spiral. The only escape from the dismal existence is with alcohol and fighting; violence is an outlet for the frustrations of the people. The fights were an accepted and expected part of the social scene: "We never had a dance without a good fight and we enjoyed and looked forward to it as much as the dancing."[23]

The patterns of social interaction and the reality of poverty limited severely the possibilities for escape. Although Campbell was exposed early to good literature by her mother and knew she wanted an education, she admitted that making it through high school was a "daydream." Indeed, she *was* a dreamer, but her dreams were always turning into nightmares. Her dream of Vancouver being a place of "toothbrushes and pretty dresses, oranges and apples, and a happy family sitting around the kitchen table talking about their tomorrow"[24] was destroyed by the reality of a dirty and grimy neighborhood and garbage-littered stairs in her apartment building. The urban ghetto was not any better than the rural poverty she had escaped. Her entry into the world of prostitution promised yet another dream-life—fine clothes, styled hair, and moneyed men. But this life was not to be any better than what she had left: "Something inside of me died."[25] It was only in her involvement with the political action of her people that Campbell could begin to exchange fanciful dreams for realistic expectations:

> I've stopped being the idealistic shiny eyed young woman I once was. . . . I believe that one day, very soon, people will set aside their differences and come together as one. Maybe not because we love one another, but because we will need each other to survive. Then together we will fight our common enemies. Change will come because this time we won't give up.[26]

This too is a dream, but it is a dream Campbell seems determined to translate into reality. She has come to terms with dreaming: "Dreams are so important in one's life, yet when followed blindly they can lead to the disintegration of one's soul."[27]

Throughout her life Campbell wrestled with the question of her own identity. To identify herself as Indian, or Halfbreed, meant to accept the stereotypes, to expose herself to prejudice and discrimination. To reject the label, however, meant to turn her back on the love and warmth of her family, the traditions of the culture. The conflict was always with her, and Indian men did not escape the wrath of her frustrations:

> I loved my people so much and missed them if I couldn't see them often. I felt alive when I went to their parties, and I overflowed with happiness when we would all sit down and share a

> meal, yet I hated all of it as much as I loved it. . . . The drunken Indians I saw would fill me with a blinding hatred. I blamed them for what had happened to me, to the little girl who had died from an overdose of drugs, and for all the girls who were on the city streets. If they had only fought back, instead of giving up, these things would never have happened. It's hard to explain how I felt. I hated our men, and yet I loved them.[28]

This confessional and personal account by Maria Campbell marks a dramatic change in the autobiographies of American Indian women. Her life story is more like those of other contemporary women writers than those of previous Indian writers. *Halfbreed* reflects the period in which it was written, a time of personal searching and a time of political action by Indian groups in North America. A major difference is that, whereas many contemporary women writers have found a place for themselves in feminist philosophy or the women's movement, Maria Campbell has found her niche in the politics of her people. Her struggle is a communal one. Having survived the personal struggle, she is ready to work to make life better for all her people.

Campbell has seen the worst aspects of white politics. As a child she watched her father taken to jail for hunting to feed his family, and she hid her brothers and sisters to prevent the government from taking them away. As a prostitute she had businessmen and government leaders among her clients. She is not convinced that political clout will cause positive change, for she has experienced the powerlessness of poverty:

> When I think back to that time and those people, I realize now that poor people, both white and Native, who are trapped within a certain kind of life, can never look to the business and political leaders of this country for help. Regardless of what they promise, they'll never change things, because they are involved in and perpetuate in private the very things that they condemn in public.[29]

She distrusted power and was used by the powerful, but ultimately, Campbell realized that it would be only through sharing the power that Indian people could change the laws that govern their lives. To change the laws the people must unite. Campbell and others are only too aware that "bitterness is perhaps the only bond linking the natives of Canada."[30] The law doesn't consider poverty or individual circumstances in meting out justice, and new powers in government can change the status and benefits of the natives simply by passing new laws. To be a people whose identity is defined by law rather than by themselves is to be in a hopeless struggle that can finally exhaust dreams and energy. Maria had seen these forces at work on her own family and on herself, but she is not ready to give up.

Although she does not emphasize the strength of her people, probably because she experienced the harsh results of their weaknesses, that strength is there. Cheechum is the Indian great-grandmother, the source of life and the teacher of the next generations. Indeed, it is Cheechum's advice from which Maria draws her strength and her hope. When Cheechum dies, it is as if Maria Campbell is born to carry on, to provide a model for the succeeding generations.

One generation of her people had been beaten by the Riel Rebellion, another generation had failed as farmers. Her father's entry into politics had resulted only in more poverty and ridicule for the family. Yet, at the end of her narrative Maria Campbell is taking her place in the circle, ready to carry on in a new way, a different way, but in a way which she hopes will guarantee survival.

# 7
# Traditional Values in Modern Context: The Narratives to Come

In the years since I began following the ways of my grandmothers I have come to value the teachings, stories, and daily examples of living which they shared with me. I pity the younger girls of the future who will miss out on meeting some of these fine old women.

Beverly Hungry Wolf, *The Ways of My Grandmothers*

The contemporary women's movement has focused on the role of women in society, and change has been significant in individual lives as well as in society's perception of women's roles. Family, marriage, parent-child relationships, career opportunities—all have been carefully scrutinized. The role of minority women has also been examined, and the importance of ethnicity over feminism has been debated. Indian women repeatedly deny their interest in, or need for, "liberation," saying they cannot afford the luxury of feminist goals because they must devote their energies to keeping families intact, getting jobs, and fighting the political battles of their people. This attitude does not mean that Indian women have not achieved recognition, however. Ada Deer, Bea Medicine, Annie Wauneka, LaDonna Harris, Leslie Silko, Helen Hardin, and Buffy Sainte-Marie are examples of the varieties of success Indian women have achieved in politics, education, medicine, and the arts. Throughout the country Indian women serve on tribal councils and Title IV committees. The belief that Indian women do not need the feminist movement is consistent with the role Indian women have played within their societies through the years. Recent autobiographies reaffirm this belief. The roles described by Indian women in traditional societies reveal the power that is alluded to by contemporary Indian women in their autobiographies.

Each personal narrative by an American Indian woman is unique—in content, mode of expression, and intention. Each demands to be judged on its own terms; yet collectively these autobiographies give structure to the fragmented nature of human lives in a way that is recognizable as both specifically female and specifically Indian. From these narratives can be drawn some generalizations about Indian women's lives over the past 150 years and how changes in life have wrought changes in the literary tradition. American Indian women's autobiographies probe identity, as all life stories do. In many of the early narratives the probing is shallow because the intent of the work is ethnographic rather than deeply personal. Yet even these personal histories reveal personality to some degree, and through the selection and omission of events reveal the intention of the teller, which is often to preserve the passing customs of her people.

As the purpose of the editor-collector shifted from the desire to preserve a record of "vanishing Americans" toward a more specific interest in the individual narrator and her experiences, Indian women's autobiographies have portrayed fuller and more detailed histories of personality and conscious narrative technique. Most of these narratives focus on the everyday aspects of life, family, social interaction, feelings and responses to experience, and record tribal customs and traditions as well. As Indian women have become more self-conscious about their changing roles and the effect of acculturation on their lives, their narratives have begun to reflect concern for mediating the influences of traditional Indian life and white ways, leading to themes of conflict and resolution in their narratives. In contemporary works, the effect of urban society, often disruptive and disorienting, has become a major theme, with resolution coming through reassertion of traditional tribal identity and values.

The narratives of Indian women throughout the years might be best described as stories of adaptability. Like all women in all times, Indian women have been forced to be flexible, resourceful, and tenacious in facing struggles for survival and growth in constantly shifting circumstances. They have drawn on the past for traditional values and spiritual stability. They have guarded the customs and ways of their ancestors and have passed them on to their children in measure they deemed appropriate in a changing society. They have spoken the anxieties of their people, and through their narratives have offered models of individual strength and action. They have evaluated their lives and their times in their stories, for the most part without using the narrative format for didactic purposes. The narrators of most of the autobiographies discussed in the foregoing chapters have seen themselves as rather ordinary, presenting records of gradual attainment of personal satisfaction rather than recountings of personal triumphs. They have revealed themselves rather quietly, but with growing recognition of the strengths of their positions in a world that has demanded adaptability. They have seen themselves, not as women on the margins of two cultures, but as women who take pride in their ability to draw effectively on traditional resources as they assert themselves in the plural society of contemporary North America.

Looking at contemporary life stories, one finds that the old methods of obtaining autobiographies still exist today. The editors' level of awareness about Indian perspectives is generally higher, however, and is reflected in the methods of presentation as well as the editorial comments. Nancy Lurie explains why Mountain Wolf Woman told her story—her niece requested it—and explains her own purposes—to provide a literary document as well as an anthropological source. She provides extensive explanatory footnotes for the reader, thus enabling Mountain Wolf Woman to tell her own story free from intrusion. Nancy Lurie focuses on the role of the Winnebago woman and compares Mountain Wolf Woman with her brother Crashing Thunder:

> Mountain Wolf Woman's autobiography is a predictable reflection of greater self-confidence enjoyed by women in comparison to men in a culture undergoing rapid and destructive changes. As was true of many American Indian groups, the roles of wife, mother, and homemaker for which the Winnebago girl was prepared could be fulfilled in adulthood despite the vagaries of acculturation. . . . Winnebago boys were prepared for traditional roles as warriors, hunters and shamans long after these roles stood little chance of effective fulfillment.[1]

Just as Mountain Wolf Woman adapted, Sanapia adjusted to Christianity and peyotism, at the same time maintaining the traditional patterns of Comanche culture. Her purpose is clearly stated—to pass down necessary information to the next Eagle doctor. Ironically, although almost a century had passed since the first recorded women's autobiographies, Jones comments, "Women occupied an inferior position in society, though they were respected for their full share in the food quest." Sanapia, however, in the narrative clearly states she considered herself equal to a male.[2] Once again the purpose here is to document a life in such a way as to illuminate a culture's history and cultural patterns. In this regard it is very similar to those stories collected by the earliest ethnographers.

In yet another recently recorded autobiography, the editor allowed the subject to record her life over a period of one and a half years. *Belle Highwalking: The Narrative of a Northern Cheyenne Woman* was published in 1979 and tells the life story of a woman who was not involved in Indian politics and who did not have any special knowledge of ceremonies or medicines. Her own purpose for the autobiography was personal; it was to record her life so her grandchildren would remember her. The book reflects the awareness of native people that their lives are worth remembering, and that the mode of written autobiography may preserve what otherwise might be lost. Born in 1892, Belle Highwalking recalls the changes that have influenced her role as a Cheyenne woman, a common theme in life stories throughout the century. She was the sister of John Stands in Timber, and her narrative provides a companion to his book, *Cheyenne Memories*. Perhaps most significant and indicative of things to come is that her autobiography was published by the Montana Council for Indian Education, a nonprofit organization interested in providing accurate reading materials for Indian education. The process of evaluation ensures that the book has been scrutinized by American Indian people before publication, an aspect of the process that has not been typical in the past for materials published about American Indians.[3]

Some recent autobiographies have a different perspective. In *Bobbi Lee: Indian Rebel*, the narrator is responding to the oppression of her people with a political perspective. She recognizes the three responses to oppression that have characterized Indian experience of this century and which are reflected in earlier autobiographies. Submission and integration led many Indian people to adopt the dominant nation's values, aspirations, and world view. Another response to oppression throughout the century has been through internalized violence, violence that is manifested through drugs, alcohol, prostitution, and physical abuse. Bobbi Lee sees a more positive response for her generation through self-determination, Red Power, and a spate of political movements and causes. The 1970s brought the confrontation at Wounded Knee, the Trail of Broken Treaties, the Longest Walk, fish-ins, and numerous other expressions of Indian power. This renewal of interest in Indian experience is reflected in the recent autobiographical works. Bobbi Lee's ancestors earlier in the century responded to oppression by submission and integration, by acceptance of an inferior status within a dominant culture. She details the violence that has often characterized Indian experience, a violence that the writers in the 1940s and 1950s sought to explain away as a result of too much "firewater." She recognizes the ambivalent roles of contemporary Indian women and men within a society still operating by traditional values:

> Most of the militants there at a demonstration in Olympia, Washington, were women and three of them did most of the speaking. . . . They were traditionalists so there was nothing unusual about women acting as spokesmen for the group. In fact, they told me they were having trouble getting the men involved. The only man who spoke was Hank Adams, who's been to university and wasn't traditional.[4]

Canadian Indian women, perhaps because of a double dilemma of identity in a country that quite arbitrarily categorizes women according to heritage as well as the husband's identity, have written about their position within society. Author Emma LaRoque, having experienced the contemporary struggle for identity, describes her and other women's dilemma—that American Indian people are faced with two choices. They may choose to remain Indian, which associates them with the reservation, or choose to join the dominant society, which is erroneously linked with being white. She is concerned because non-Indians treat Indian existence as frozen in time and assume that Indian culture cannot change.[5]

There is obvious biculturation today, but it is a biculturation that is not new, a dilemma that has existed from the moment of first contact. When the first Indian women began allowing the stories of their lives to be committed to paper, to be edited and analyzed by those from another culture who did not understand the taboos, the rituals, or the roles, the differences in culture became apparent. For a brief period midcentury, Indian women tried to fit the mold of white society, to condemn those Indians who clung to tradition, who did not accept the new ways. But even they did not stray far from their heritage, recognizing always from whence they came, and at the same time not knowing how to cope with that heritage.

The elements which appeared in the earliest recorded life stories continue to appear in autobiographies of Indian American women. Above all, the desire to preserve cultural heritage is emphasized. Such preservation continues to be accomplished in similar ways. Family ties continue to be important. Especially significant as a strong force in native cultures is the grandmother, both mythical and real. It is the grandmother who often is the storyteller, the preserver of the past, and the strength for the future. Her role as storyteller emphasizes the role of the oral tradition and the significance of the stories. This emphasis on the role of the grandmother is integrated with the emphasis on sex roles and the division of labor. In earlier autobiographies and in earlier times the division of labor was far more explicit and roles were defined and understood by the tribe and by individuals. Recent accounts, however, emphasize the disintegration that has resulted from the lack of a defined role. In contemporary accounts the woman is often responsible for holding the family together, getting jobs, and raising the next generation. The most significant transition in the autobiographies reflects this blurring of defined sex roles. Roles that once were defined by the tribe and by tradition are now being questioned by society, by those in political movements, and by the people themselves.

But the Indian woman is and has been strong within her culture. The evidence from the women themselves supports this perspective. The trappers who desired Indian women, the missionaries whose religion dictated that women be defined as inferior, the painters who saw only romantic figures—all were viewing Indian women from a decidedly ethnocentric position. The life stories of Indian women contradict these images and support the view that the role of the Indian woman was and is defined within American Indian cultures as important and essential.

But what of the autobiographies that have not yet been published and disseminated, or not yet written? The growing awareness on the part of American Indian women of the varied alternatives available to all women today is likely to create new themes and modes of expression in autobiography. On that premise a number of predictions about future personal narratives may be posited. It is likely that the narratives to come will reflect the growing self-consciousness Indian women have about their roles in contemporary society. As more and more women become intensely active in tribal politics, education, social services, and cultural revitalization, their narratives will inevitably articulate their growing assertiveness both in tribal and white society. As their experiences and criteria for judgment about life widen, their narratives are likely to become more consciously evaluative about themselves and their worlds. Sophistication and complexity will be heightened. It is also likely, as more and more Indian women acquire skills in writing, they will experiment more with style and structure, and will take fuller control of their narratives, in many cases eliminating the recorder-editor from the narrative process. Where a collaborative effort between recorder-editor and narrator is used, the power of the editor will undoubtedly be lessened and applied with more discretion. As increasingly professional and more intensive training becomes available in Indian studies, editors will be able to bring more refined skills, and certainly less culture bias, to their work on autobiographies.

One example of the growing interest of Indian women in presenting their own narratives is Woesha Cloud North's "Autobiography of a Winnebago Family."[6] As introduction to her presentation at a scholarly meeting, Cloud North said she "felt a need to write this paper" to "bring everything up to date." She describes the paper as being about "living in two worlds," and she said she was not aware of this while she was growing up, but that after sixth grade, "I questioned my own identity." Cloud North is a Winnebago woman and fondly remembers the times she spent on the Winnebago Reservation in Nebraska. In 1915 her parents founded the American Indian Institute in Wichita, Kansas, which offered Indian students a chance for education. They were adamant about education for their own children as well, and Cloud North graduated from Vassar College in 1940 and went on to teach at several Indian schools after her graduation. As an activist she participated in the occupation of Alcatraz, and now, having received her doctorate degree, she is active in scholarship about American Indians. It is entirely appropriate that one of the first tasks she undertook was to make a record of her own life.

Like all literary trends, the trends in Indian women's autobiography will undoubtedly be gradual, with many of the themes of earlier narratives continuing or receiving new emphasis. It is probable that an ongoing concern for the past, preservation of traditional ways and roles, and concern for protecting the uniqueness of Indian life will continue to be of importance. There may be changes in the expression of those concerns, but the choices and human concerns that have created the drama and structure of Indian women's narratives will remain in large measure consistent.

As scholars are trained in Indian studies programs, it is also possible that there will be more work done on autobiographies that have never been published, those stored in archives. Competent Indian women will move into the role of editor and aid in bringing to the public a wider variety of nineteenth- and twentieth-century narratives. It is also possible that Indian women will be drawn into field collection of oral autobiographies as tribes begin to recognize the importance of preserving their own histories through community and grant-sponsored projects. Those women with bilingual skills and established tribal ties will be particularly effective in collecting, translating, and editing such materials.

There is already evidence of narratives that develop overt political stances. *Bobbi Lee: Indian Rebel,* published by a Canadian Marxist press, is primarily concerned with the disruption of Indian ways and identity caused by urban problems and the break-down of traditional family life; the latter portion of the narrative devotes considerable attention to the author's participation in Indian rights protest demonstrations in the 1960s and the advocacy of sometimes radical political methods. But it and the few others similar to it do not dominate, nor are they likely to, because a very small percentage of Indian women are active in Red Power movements or willing to be spokeswomen for particular ideologies. Also, autobiography is not a particularly effective mode of writing for the promulgation of political theory or action, and hence usually not adopted by writers with pragmatic goals. It is much more likely that surviving and maturing in a modern age while retaining tribal values and ways will remain the focus of most Indian women's narratives, but that life stories will be expressed with growing stylistic sophistication, reflecting the growing leadership roles of Indian women.

One example of such a trend is Beverly Hungry Wolf's recent work, *The Ways of My Grandmothers,* which focuses on the author as a recipient of traditional knowledge useful to her in a contemporary world. The book is composed of many narratives, some written by the author from her recollections of stories and advice passed down to her from her mother, her own grandmothers, and other elderly women of the tribe; hence, the term *grandmothers* in the title, meaning those women who have preceded her in the way of the

Blood people of the Blackfoot nation. Included are stories of women warriors, women who held central ceremonial roles in tribal rituals, and women who practiced specialized household skills. She also incorporates short narratives by two other women who relate their memories. The thrust of this collection is toward the education of the author in traditional ways, and the education of other Indian women to their own traditions. It is possible that the use of many voices, as in this work, will provide an expansion of autobiography as a form, and certainly the author's direct purpose of writing for other Indian women will be a growing trend as more Indian women become concerned about participating in the continuity of traditions.[7]

Another trend that may have increasing impact on the literary tradition of Indian women's autobiography is the growing interest in autobiography expressed by those Indian women who write fiction and poetry. While it is generally accepted that there are always elements of autobiography, transmuted and reimagined, in fiction and poetry, it is only recently that some of the Indian women writers in these genres have begun to work directly in the form of autobiography or use it as a structuring device in mixed media works.

Anna Lee Walters, a Pawnee-Oto woman who resides with her Navajo husband and two children on the Navajo reservation, demonstrates in her recent writing the trained fiction writer's approach to personal narrative and the potential for stylistic creativity in autobiography. She very deliberately and pervasively establishes a theme of pride in Indian identity as she writes:

> I am a full-blood. Though I am full-blood American Indian, I am of two tribes. . . . I am an American Indian woman who married out of her tribe and into another. . . . I am an Indian woman with two children. . . . There are four in our family who actually reside in our home. But there are many, many more when grandmas, grandpas, aunts, uncles, brothers, sisters, and (always there are) cousins counted. With Indian people, I have been taught that I must always count everybody who's related to me in any way at all. Often it amounts to the whole tribe.[8]

The beginning of this narrative, with its insistant repetition of the word "Indian," is very consciously crafted to introduce the theme of identity that shapes it. Genealogy is addressed, focusing on the person of the narrator as the center of relationships presented in the work. As the life story progresses, she introduces her grandparents and parents as she recalls them directly, emphasizing their roles in shaping her sense of herself as an Indian woman. While such recollection may not seem particularly different from other such narratives, her style brings into play a new approach to this material. For instance, when she begins to describe the landscape of her birth, she says:

> The ever swollen hills in Oklahoma have given birth many times. I was born in the north central country, in what was once a part of the old Cherokee Strip. It is a land that drinks a lot of water and never seems to swallow much. The liquid sits on top of dewy grass and in dewy eyes. If that is not enough, the sun squeezes it from your insides until it sits and rolls down your forehead and falls, bright light into the whites of your eyes. That is in the summertime when the humidity drowns the land and you lose yourself in it. I was born there. I was born when the land had water on its lids and somewhere in the middle of the gulps taken in by the people I came to know too well, my father's people. Despite all the water on the land, our people had a fierce thirst which was never quenched.[9]

The poetically sustained metaphor of moisture is consciously contrived to amplify and intensify the observable landscape and give it a personalized context. The result is an impressionistic and simultaneously interpretive mental picture of a sensual place that injects longing into its people.

Not all of Walters's life is drawn with such delicacy of language. As she recalls her youth, abuses, harshness, and violence are told with contrasting and appropriately tense language:

> I have seen handsome people become ugly and disfigured. I have been close when people have been murdered and women raped and given birth. I have seen it over and over, and always it seems it happens to those same people. I am familiar with people who have given their children away for a price, cash or a drink. I grew up with children whose parents fought and maimed each other by plan, no accident. I know of men who have given away their daughters.[10]

There is no wavering in these lines. The grimness is catalogued in flat, colorless tones that contrast sharply with the sensuous quality of the previous description. The range of her style suggests an attention to language that surpasses that of most narrators, that indicates a poetical sensibility and imagination honed to meet a range of experiences and feelings, a direct concern with the literary quality of the narrative and the effect of style as well as content on the audience.

This narrative is not, however, outside the perimeters of traditional autobiography. It records childhood experiences, resistance to school, celebrations and deaths, teenage rebelliousness, accomplishments, and bonds with loved ones. It ends with an affirmation of Indian identity: "The old folks are all gone. They were tired, prepared and they went on. Life goes on. Nothing diminishes it. We have been taught also that life is a fragile thing. Grandma always said that it almost feels too good to be alive."[11] These final lines attest to the tenuousness of continuity, but also to its possibility. They also bring full circle the theme of Indian identity presented in the first lines of the work, the unifying theme which subtly but pervasively holds the narrative very tightly together and marks it as the work of a very contemporary and consciously creative narrator.

While Walters uses new stylistic techniques within a basically traditional narrative structure, Laguna Pueblo poet and fiction writer Leslie Marmon Silko utilizes fragments of autobiography as a structuring device in a mixed-media work, another inventive addition to the field of personal narrative. Her book *Storyteller* combines sections of spoken prose in the form of personal reminiscences interposed among short stories and poems and photographs taken by her father and grandfather over a period from the 1890s to the present to create an interplay between the four mediums that demonstrates "the way remembrance works."[12] She states that the people, stories, poems, and pictures are a "way of knowing" that say to the reader, "Find the relationships and the meaning yourself." Silko amplifies this: "The book shows how directly and indirectly, relying on my past and family, how much my 'autobiography' has become fiction and poetry. The stories in my family and my life are part of what's made" in the book. She notes that *Storyteller* is a result of seeing her life as a series of stories and that the purpose of using her short fiction, poetry, traditional stories, and fragments of her life with the photography is "to give the reader an idea of the relations I see and feel" and to show "how autobiography gets distilled and comes back in fiction and poetry."[13] While autobiography is not the overt content of the work, it is the controlling force and the source for imaginative interconnections between her life and creative production.

Still another use of autobiography in contemporary creative writing by Indian women is evident in Paula Gunn Allen's novel, *The Woman Who Owned the Shadows*. In describing her novel Allen says, "It leans on the tradition of autobiography." Noting that it is an experimental novel which "contains much Indian lore and legend, working toward blending them into a significance of the events that occur to the narrator," Allen indicates that the point of view is internal.[14] She describes the main character as a woman made up of qualities and characteristics drawn from her grandmother, mother, and herself,[15] as well as fictional elements—an autobiographical composite transformed into a multifaceted imagined woman. One critic describes the title character as "a woman looking for, searching for herself, her roots—that deep source from where she emerged—for answers to the genocide and maiming of her people, for a bit of reality she can anchor herself to." She goes on to ask "Is this really the story of a fictitious woman or a real woman or Allen herself?"[16] The question is legitimate, since the third-person view of the protagonist—"she" in the novel—creates an ambiguity, but Allen addresses this distancing from the usual first-person stance of autobiography by explaining that the use of "she" does not contradict the "deeply subjective account" of the main character in the novel because the third person "fits any number of as-told-to autobiographies where the story is told by an informant in the first person but reworked by a collector into 'she' or should be if it isn't."[17] Allen's consciousness of the autobiographical process and its relationship to her novel suggests that autobiography is a rich resource for Indian women engaged in testing the boundaries of fiction by developing multigenre approaches to their art.

While it is probably not reasonable to expect that there will be many works that derive from autobiography or interlace personal narrative with fiction and poetry, it is important to recognize that the influence of autobiography is wide and varied. For this reason, perhaps it is best to restrain the inclination to impose strict parameters on this rather elusive genre. It is, after all, a relatively new mode of literary expression that perhaps should be given room to grow and experiment without artificial restrictions imposed from without. As innovation and creativity are lauded in other literary areas, so too should they be accepted here as a sign of strength and a promise of endurance.

# Notes

## PREFACE

1. John C. Ewers, "Mothers of the Mixed Bloods: The Marginal Woman in the History of the Upper Missouri," in *Probing the American West,* ed. Kenneth Ross Toole (Santa Fe: Museum of New Mexico, 1962), p. 62.
2. Katherine M. Weist, "Plains Indian Women: An Assessment," in *Anthropology on the Great Plains,* ed. W. Raymond Wood and Margot Liberty (Lincoln: University of Nebraska Press, 1980), pp. 255–71.
3. Clara Sue Kidwell, review of *Bright Eyes: The Story of Susette la Flesche, an Omaha Indian,* by Dorothy Clarke Wilson, *Journal of Ethnic Studies* 2 (Winter 1975): 118, 122.

## CHAPTER 1

1. Arnold Krupat, "American Autobiography: The Western Tradition," *Georgia Review* 35, no. 2 (Summer 1981): 307.
2. Richard Slotkin, *Regeneration through Violence* (Middletown, CT: Wesleyan University Press, 1973), pp. 95, 102.
3. Krupat, "American Autobiography," pp. 311–12.
4. Frances Smith Foster, *Witnessing Slavery: The Development of Antebellum Slave Narratives* (Westport, CT: Greenwood Press, 1979), pp. 1, 5–6.
5. Ibid., p. 65.
6. Ibid., p. 2.
7. Ibid., p. 4.
8. Ibid., p. 58.
9. Roy Pascal, *Design and Truth in Autobiography* (Cambridge, MA: Harvard University Press, 1960), p. 5.
10. Estelle Jelinek, *Women's Autobiography: Essays in Criticism* (Bloomington: Indiana University Press, 1980), pp. 8, 14–15.

11. Frank B. Linderman, *Pretty-shield, Medicine Woman of the Crows* (Lincoln: University of Nebraska Press, 1972).
12. See Arnold Krupat, "The Indian Autobiography: Origins, Type, and Functions," *American Literature* 53, no. 1 (March 1981): 24.
13. Clyde Kluckhohn, "The Personal Document in Anthropological Science," *The Use of Personal Documents in History, Anthropology, and Sociology* (New York: Social Science Research Council, 1945), pp. 79–173; Lewis L. Langness, *The Life History in Anthropological Science* (New York: Holt, Rinehart and Winston, 1965), pp. 4–5; Arnold Krupat, "The Indian Autobiography," p. 240.
14. Sarah Winnemucca Hopkins, *Life among the Paiutes*, ed. Mrs. Horace Mann (New York: G. P. Putnam's Sons, 1883); Helen Sekaquaptewa, *Me and Mine: The Life Story of Helen Sekaquaptewa*, ed. Louise Udall (Tucson: University of Arizona Press, 1969).
15. Paul Radin, Ruth Benedict, Franz Boaz, Albert Kroeber, Theodora Kroeber, Truman Michelson, and scores of other anthropologists collected ethnographic narratives and, in some cases, recorded full life stories and published them as autobiographies.
16. Lynn Z. Bloom and Orlee Holder, "Anais Nin's *Diary* in Context," in *Women's Autobiography: Essays in Criticism*, ed. Estelle Jelinek (Bloomington: Indiana University Press, 1980), p. 207.
17. Maria Chona, *Papago Woman*, ed. Ruth M. Underhill (New York: Holt, Rinehart, and Winston, 1979); Linderman, *Pretty-shield;* Mountain Wolf Woman, *Mountain Wolf Woman, Sister of Crashing Thunder: The Autobiography of a Winnebago Indian*, ed. Nancy Oestreich Lurie (Ann Arbor: University of Michigan Press, 1961); Sekaquaptewa, *Me and Mine:* Annie Lowry, *Karnee: A Paiute Narrative*, ed. Lalla Scott (Reno: University of Nevada Press, 1966); Polingaysi Qoyawayma (Elizabeth Q. White), *No Turning Back: A True Account of a Hopi Girl's Struggle to Bridge the Gap between the World of Her People and the World of the White Man*, ed. Vada F. Carlson (Albuquerque: University of New Mexico Press, 1964); Delfina Cuero, *The Autobiography of Delfina Cuero*, ed. Florence Shipek (Los Angeles: Dawson's Book Shop, 1968).
18. Zitkala-Sa (Gertrude Bonnin), "Impressions of an Indian Childhood," "The School Days of an Indian Girl," "An Indian Teacher among Indians," *Atlantic Monthly* 85 (January, February, March 1900): 31–45, 185–94, 381–86; idem, "Why I Am a Pagan," *Atlantic Monthly* 90 (December 1902): 802–3.
19. Pascal, *Design and Truth*, pp. 1, 9, 181, 185.
20. James Olney, *Metaphors of Self: The Meaning of Autobiography* (Princeton: Princeton University Press, 1972), p. 31

21. Pascal, *Design and Truth*, pp. 9, 10, 19.
22. Dick Gerdes, "Monologo desde las tinieblas: Oral Tradition and Ideological Silence," *Rocky Mountain Review* 35, no. 4 (Winter 1981): 275.
23. Pascal, *Design and Truth*, p. 19.
24. Interview with Vine Deloria, Sr., Denver, Colorado, March 26, 1981. Permission for use granted by Michael Taylor, project director, "Generations," a study of five generations of Indian women.
25. Waheenee (Maxidiwiac, or Buffalo-Bird Woman), *Waheenee: An Indian Girl's Story, Told by Herself,* told to Gilbert L. Wilson (St. Paul, MN: Webb Publishing, 1921; reprint, Lincoln, University of Nebraska Press, 1981), pp. 175–76.
26. Ibid., p. 189.
27. Elizabeth Colson (Berkeley: Archaeological Research Facility, Department of Anthropology, University of California, 1974), p. 82.
28. Hopkins, *Life among the Paiutes;* Wilson, *Waheenee;* Yoimut, "Yoimut's Story, the Last Chunut," in F. F. Latta, *Handbook of the Yokut Indians* (Bakersfield: Kern County Museum, 1949). pp. 223–76; Lucy Young, "Out of the Past: A True Indian Story," ed. Edith V. A. Murphey, *California Historical Society Quarterly* 20 (December 1941): 349–64; Ruth Landes, *The Ojibwa Women* (New York: Columbia University Press, 1938; reprinted 1977), pp. 227–47; Mrs. Andrew Stanley, "Personal Narrative of Mrs. Andrew Stanley," and Anna Price, "Personal Narrative of Anna Price," *Western Apache Raiding and Warfare,* ed. Keith H. Basso (Tucson: University of Arizona Press, 1971); Truman Michelson, "The Autobiography of a Fox Indian Woman," *Fortieth Annual Report of the Bureau of American Ethnology* (1925): 291–349; idem, "Narrative of an Arapaho Woman," *American Anthropologist* 35 (October–December 1933): 595–610; idem, "The Narrative of a Southern Cheyenne Woman," *Smithsonian Miscellaneous Collections* 87 (1932): 1–13.
29. Qoyawayma, *No Turning Back,* p. 26.
30. Ibid., p. 174.
31. Sekaquaptewa, *Me and Mine;* Anna Moore Shaw, *A Pima Past* (Tucson: University of Arizona Press, 1974), p. 166.
32. Shipek, ed., *Delfina Cuero,* p. 15.
33. Lucille Winnie [Sah-Gan-De-Oh], *Sah-Gan-De-Oh: The Chief's Daughter* (New York: Vantage Press, 1969), p. 7.
34. Ibid., p. 56, 58, 185.
35. Shaw, *A Pima Past;* Maria Campbell, *Halfbreed* (1973; reprint, University of Nebraska Press, 1982); Bobbie Lee, *Bobbie Lee: Indian Rebel,* ed. Don Barnett and Rick Sterling (Richmond, B.C.: LSM Information Center, 1975); Winnie, *Sah-Gan-De-Oh.*

CHAPTER 2

1. L. L. Langness and Gelya Frank, *Lives: An Anthropological Approach to Biography* (Novato, CA: Chandler and Sharp, 1981).
2. J. Walter Fewkes, *Fortieth Annual Report of the Bureau of American Ethnology* (1925), p. 1.
3. Boas, as quoted in A. L. Kroeber, *The Nature of Culture* (Chicago: University of Chicago Press, 1952), p. 320.
4. Ibid., p. 324.
5. Paul Radin, *The Autobiography of a Winnebago Indian* (New York: Dover, 1963), pp. 1–2.
6. Michelson, "The Narrative of a Southern Cheyenne Woman," 1–13; idem, "The Autobiography of a Fox Indian Woman," pp. 291–349; idem, "Narrative of an Arapaho Woman," pp. 595–610.
7. Idem, "The Autobiography of a Fox Indian Woman," p. 295.
8. Ibid., p. 298.
9. Idem, "The Narrative of a Southern Cheyenne Woman," p. 17.
10. Richard Frank Brown, "A Social History of the Mesquakie Indians, 1800–1963" (Master's Thesis, Iowa State University, 1964), pp. 68–72.
11. Elsie Clews Parsons, American Indian Life (New York: Viking Press, 1922), pp. 81–86.
12. William T. Hagen, *The Sac and Fox Indians* (Norman: University of Oklahoma Press, 1958), p. 205.
13. Mary Alicia Owen, *Folklore of the Musquakie Indians of North America* (London: David Nutt, 1904), p. vi.
14. Ibid., p. 39.
15. Michelson, "The Autobiography of a Fox Woman," p. 341.
16. Ibid., pp. 329–31.
17. William Jones, *Ethnography of the Fox Indians*, Smithsonian Institution, BAE Bulletin 125 (Washington, D.C.: U.S. Government Printing Office, 1939), p. 69.
18. Brown, "A Social History," p. 80.
19. Interview with Priscilla Wanatee, Mesquakie Settlement, Tama, Iowa, February 28, 1980.
20. Interview with Adeline Wanatee, Mesquakie Settlement, Tama, Iowa, February 28, 1980. Adeline Wanatee, a Mesquakie woman, was eight years old when Harry Lincoln recorded the life of a Fox woman later published by Truman Michelson. Mrs. Wanatee answered questions about the manuscript and provided invaluable assistance with the Mesquakie language. Her daughter-in-law, Priscilla Wanatee, offered comments on the expected behavior patterns of young Mesquakie women today that mirror those recorded in the past.
21. Michelson, "The Autobiography of a Fox Indian Woman," p. 303.

22. Interview with Adeline Wanatee, Mesquakie Settlement, Tama, Iowa, February 28, 1980.
23. For a discussion of the derivation of the use of *unclean* to describe women during their menstrual periods, see Ruth M. Underhill, *Red Man's Religion: Beliefs and Practices of the Indians North of Mexico* (Chicago: University of Chicago Press, 1965), pp. 51–61.
24. Interview with Adeline Wanatee, Mesquakie Settlement, Tama, Iowa, February 28, 1980.
25. Michelson, "The Autobiography of a Fox Indian Woman," p. 321.
26. Ibid., p. 335.
27. Ibid., 317.
28. Ibid., p. 337.
29. Kroeber, *The Nature of Culture,* p. 324.
30. Michelson, "The Narrative of a Southern Cheyenne Woman," p. 2.
31. Ibid, p. 3.
32. George Bird Grinnell, *The Cheyenne Indians: Their History and Ways of Life* (New Haven: Yale University Press, 1923), p. 156.
33. Michelson, "The Narrative of a Southern Cheyenne Woman," pp. 2, 9.
34. Michelson, "Narrative of an Arapaho Woman," p. 609.
35. Ibid., p. 596.
36. Grinnell, *Cheyenne Indians,* p. 156.
37. "Narrative of an Arapaho Woman," p. 610.
38. Kroeber, *The Nature of Culture,* p. 325.
39. Gilbert Livingstone Wilson, *Agriculture of the Hidatsa Indians: An Indian Interpretation* (Minneapolis: University of Minnesota Studies in the Social Sciences No. 9, 1917); idem, *Goodbird the Indian: His Story Told by Himself to Gilbert L. Wilson* (New York: Fleming H. Revell Co., 1914).
40. Wilson, *Agriculture of the Hidatsa,* p. 3.
41. Ibid., p. 5.
42. Wilson, *Waheenee,* p. 189.
43. Wilson, *Goodbird the Indian,* p. 79.
44. Wilson, *Agriculture of the Hidatsa,* pp. 4–5.
45. Linderman, *Pretty-shield,* pp. 24, 70.
46. Ibid., p. 250.
47. Ruth L. Bunzel, *Zuni Texts* (New York: G. E. Stechert and Co., 1933), p. 81.
48. Ibid., p. 96.

## CHAPTER 3

1. Maria Chona, *Papago Woman,* ed. Ruth M. Underhill (New York: Holt, Rinehart and Winston, 1979). Reprinted from *Memoirs of the American*

*Anthropological Association,* number 46 (1936), under the title *The Autobiography of a Papago Woman.* The title of the original publication of the work supports the position that the narrative was told, collected, and edited as a literary, not simply ethnographic, text.

2. Ibid., p. 3.
3. Interview with Ruth M. Underhill, Denver, Colorado, November 3, 1981.
4. Interview with Ella Lopez Antone, Santa Rosa Village, Papago Reservation, Arizona, November 20, 1981.
5. Nancy Oestreich Lurie, "A Papago Woman and a Woman Anthropologist," *Reviews on Anthropology* 7 (Winter 1980): 120.
6. Clyde Kluckhohn, "The Personal Document in Anthropological Science," in *The Use of Personal Documents* (New York: Social Science Research Council, 1945), p. 90.
7. Lurie, ed., *Mountain Wolf Woman.*
8. Linderman, *Pretty-shield.*
9. In November 1979, at tribal headquarters in Sells, Arizona, Ruth Underhill was honored by the Papago tribe for her contributions, both anthropological and literary, to the understanding of Papago culture.
10. Chona, *Papago Woman,* p. 53.
11. Ibid., pp. 72, 86.
12. Donald M. Bahr, *Pima and Papago Ritual Oratory* (San Francisco: Indian Historian Press, 1975), pp. 109–11.
13. Interview with Ruth M. Underhill, Denver, Colorado, November 3, 1981. Underhill notes that Crecencia was more typically Papago; "She ran with the group," so Chona didn't pass on her independence or disrupt traditional female role adherence in her own family.
14. Interview with Ella Lopez Antone, Santa Rosa Village, Papago Reservation, Arizona, November 20, 1981.
15. Ibid.
16. Interviews with Ruth Underhill, November 3, 1981, and Ella Lopez Antone, November 20, 1981. Underhill notes that she translated loosely but worked with Papagoes of several ages to get at specific meanings, then worked them into English. Antone points out that she replaced a woman of late middle age who had been working as Underhill's translator but who was blind and could not travel or point out specific places as Antone could. Antone reports she met Underhill because she was curious about what she was talking to village elders about; she sat by observing, then introduced herself to the anthropologist.
17. Chona, *Papago Woman,* p. 34.
18. Ibid., p. 35.

19. Bahr, *Pima and Papago Ritual Oratory* p. 11, and interview, Arizona State University, Tempe, Arizona, September 3, 1981.
20. Underhill interview, Denver, Colorado, November 3, 1981.
21. Chona, *Papago Woman,* p. 56.
22. Ibid., p. 36.
23. Bahr, *Pima and Papago Ritual Oratory,* p. 23, and oratorical speeches translated throughout his text.
24. Chona, *Papago Woman,* p. 78.
25. Ibid., p. 66.
26. Ibid., p. 40.
27. Ibid., p. 46.
28. Ibid., p. 51.
29. Underhill interview, Denver, Colorado, November 3, 1981.
30. Chona, *Papago Woman,* p. 70.
31. Ibid., p. 61.
32. Antone interview, Santa Rosa Village, Arizona, November 20, 1981.
33. Chona, *Papago Woman,* p. 76.
34. Antone and Underhill interviews. Underhill says she also collected an autobiography of a Walpai Indian man but could not secure a publisher and abandoned the project. She regrets that she could not have spent a greater proportion of her career collecting and editing individual autobiographies. Underhill also says that she sometimes condensed areas of the Chona autobiography where she felt she did not have a full grasp of the material. For instance, she was hesitant to discuss Chona's suppressed visions because she was not confident she fully understood Chona's experiences in this area.
35. Underhill interview, Denver, Colorado, November 3, 1981.
36. Ibid.
37. Chona, *Papago Woman,* pp. 32–33.
38. Underhill interview, Denver, Colorado, November 3, 1981.
39. Among Underhill's works on Papago culture are: *Singing for Power* (Berkeley: University of California Press, 1938); *People of the Crimson Evening,* Education Division, U.S. Office of Indian Affairs, Indian Life and Customs Pamphlet no. 7, 1951; *Papago Indian Religion* (New York: Columbia University Press, 1946); *Social Organization of the Papago Indians* (New York: Columbia University Press, 1939); *The Papago Indians of Arizona and Their Relatives, the Pima,* Education Division, U.S. Office of Indian Affairs, Sherman Pamphlets, no. 3, 1940.
40. Interview with Joyce Herold, Anthropology Department, Denver Museum of Natural History, Denver, Colorado, November 4, 1981.
41. Underhill, *Hawk over Whirlpools* (New York: AMS Press, 1977). Underhill further attests to her own literary skill when she claims that

Papagos took the novel so seriously that they wanted to know who the protagonist was so they could chastize him. They "wouldn't believe I had invented him, so I explained I had dreamed him, and they understood," Interview, Denver, Colorado, November 3, 1981.

42. Chona, *Papago Woman,* p. 33.
43. Lurie, "A Papago Woman," p. 122.
44. Chona, *Papago Woman,* p. 33.
45. Lurie, "A Papago Woman," p. 123.
46. Chona, *Papago Woman,* p. 67

CHAPTER 4

1. Sanapia, *Sanapia, Comanche Medicine Woman,* ed. David E. Jones (New York: Holt, Rinehart and Winston, 1972).
2. Jones, ed., *Sanapia,* p. 4.
3. Lurie, ed., *Mountain Wolf Woman.*
4. Personal correspondence, Nancy Oestreich Lurie, July 30, 1980.
5. Ibid.
6. Ibid.
7. Ibid.
8. Ibid.
9. Ibid.
10. Lurie, ed., *Mountain Wolf Woman,* p. 100.
11. Ed Shannon, "The Wandering Winnebago," *Frontier Times* (August–September 1971): 30–31, 68–69.
12. Woesha Cloud North, *Informal Education in Winnebago Tribal Society with Implications for Formal Education.* (Ph. D. Diss.: University of Nebraska–Lincoln, 1978), p. 41.
13. Ibid., p. 107.
14. Lurie, ed., *Mountain Wolf Woman,* pp. 12, 15, 20.
15. Interview with Irma Bizzett, Ames, Iowa, November 17, 1981.
16. Lurie, ed., *Mountain Wolf Woman,* pp. 87–88.
17. Ibid., p. 95.
18. Ibid., pp. 21–22.
19. Cloud North, *Informal Education,* p. 11.
20. Interview with Irma Bizzett, Ames, Iowa, November 17, 1981.
21. Lurie, ed., *Mountain Wolf Woman,* p. 91.
22. Cloud North, *Informal Education,* p. 147.
23. Paul Radin, *Primitive Religion: Its Nature and Origin* (New York: Viking, 1937), p. 304.
24. Personal correspondence, Nancy O. Lurie, July 30, 1980.
25. Lurie, ed., *Mountain Wolf Woman,* p. 74.

26. Ibid., p. 60.
27. Ibid., p. 17.
28. Cloud North, *Informal Education,* p. 148.
29. Lurie, ed., *Mountain Wolf Woman,* p. 61.
30. Ibid., p. 31.
31. Ibid., pp. 82–83.
32. Paul Radin, *The Autobiography of a Winnebago Indian,* p. 1.

CHAPTER 5

1. Interview with Adeline Shaw Russell, Salt River Pima Reservation, June 16, 1980.
2. Interview with Ross Shaw, Salt River Pima Reservation, June 16, 1980.
3. Anna Moore Shaw, *Pima Legends* (Tucson: University of Arizona Press, 1968).
4. Interview with Karen Thure, Tucson, Arizona, May 22, 1980.
5. Shaw, *A Pima Past,* p. 16.
6. Ibid., p. 20.
7. Ibid., p. 101.
8. See Chona, *Papago Woman,* p. 3.
9. Interview with Karen Thure, Tucson, Arizona, May 22, 1980.
10. Shaw, *A Pima Past,* p. 126.
11. Ibid., p. 127.
12. Interview with Helen Sekaquaptewa, New Oraibi, Arizona, June 3, 1981.
13. Interview with Allison Lewis, Scottsdale, Arizona, December 20, 1979.
14. The Child Study Association of America, *The Indian Girl: Her Social Heritage, Her Needs and Her Opportunities,* Washington, D.C.: U.S. Government Printing Office.
15. Shaw, *A Pima Past,* p. 121.
16. Ibid.
17. Ibid., p. 122.
18. Ibid., p. 150.
19. Child Study Association, *The Indian Girl,* p. 17.
20. Interview with Adeline Shaw Russell, Salt River Pima Reservation, June 16, 1980.
21. Shaw, *A Pima Past,* pp. 152–53.
22. Ibid., p. 154.
23. Ibid., p. 161.
24. Interview with Adeline Shaw Russell, Salt River Pima Reservation, June 16, 1980.
25. Shaw, *A Pima Past,* p. 199.

26. Interview with Ross Shaw, Salt River Pima Reservation, June 16, 1980.
27. Shaw, *A Pima Past,* p. 201.
28. Ibid., p. 215.
29. Ibid.
30. Interview with Helen Sekaquaptewa, New Oraibi, Arizona, June 11, 1980.
31. Ibid., June 3, 1981.
32. Ibid., June 11, 1980.
33. Ibid., June 3, 1981.
34. Sekaquaptewa, *Me and Mine,* p. 3.
35. Ibid., p. 7.
36. Ibid., p. 17.
37. Ibid., p. 36.
38. Ibid., p. 77.
39. Ibid., p. 82.
40. Ibid., p. 94.
41. Interview with Helen Sekaquaptewa, New Oraibi, Arizona, June 3, 1981.
42. Sekaquaptewa, *Me and Mine,* p. 104.
43. Ibid., p. 125.
44. Interview with Helen Sekaquaptewa, New Oraibi, Arizona, June 11, 1980.
45. Ibid., June 3, 1981.
46. Ibid.
47. Ibid.
48. Sekaquaptewa, *Me and Mine,* p. 186.
49. Ibid., p. 187.
50. Interview with Helen Sekaquaptewa, New Oraibi, Arizona, June 11, 1980.
51. Ibid., June 3, 1981.
52. Ibid., June 10, 1980.
53. Sekaquaptewa, *Me and Mine,* p. 203.
54. Interview with Helen Sekaquaptewa, New Oraibi, Arizona, June 10, 1980.
55. Ibid., June 3, 1981.
56. Interview with Allison Sekaquaptewa Lewis, Scottsdale, Arizona, September 5, 1981.
57. Interview with Helen Sekaquaptewa, New Oraibi, Arizona, June 3, 1981.
58. Interview with Allison Sekaquaptewa Lewis, Scottsdale, Arizona, September 5, 1981.
59. Sekaquaptewa, *Me and Mine,* p. 245.
60. Ibid., p. 247.

61. Interview with Helen Sekaquaptewa, New Oraibi, Arizona, June 3, 1981.
62. Ibid., Scottsdale, Arizona, December 20, 1979.
63. Interview with Ross Shaw, Salt River Pima Reservation, June 16, 1980.
64. Interview with Helen Sekaquaptewa, Scottsdale, Arizona, December 20, 1979.

CHAPTER 6

1. David Mandelbaum, "The Study of Life History: Gandhi," *Current Anthropology* 14 (June 1973): 177.
2. See Valerie Miner Johnson, "Dad Was Always Drunk, Mom Always Pregnant," *Saturday Night* 88 (August 1973): 31.
3. William J. Scheick, *The Half-Blood: A Cultural Symbol in Nineteenth-Century American Fiction* (Lexington: University Press of Kentucky, 1979), p. ix.
4. Gerald Vizenor, *Earthdivers: Tribal Narratives on Mixed Descent* (Minneapolis: University of Minnesota Press, 1981), p. ix.
5. James S. Frideres, ed., *Canada's Indians: Contemporary Conflicts* (Scarborough, Ontario: Prentice-Hall of Canada, 1974), pp. 2–3.
6. Campbell, *Halfbreed,* p. 7.
7. Ibid., p. 8.
8. Ibid., pp. 7–8.
9. James A. Draper, ed., *Citizen Participation in Canada: A Book of Readings* (Toronto: New Press, 1971); James S. Frideres, *Canada's Indians: Contemporary Conflicts;* Norman Sheffe, ed., *Canada's Indians* (Toronto: McGraw Hill, 1970); John A. Price, *Indians of Canada: Cultural Dynamics* (Scarborough, Ontario: Prentice-Hall of Canada, 1979).
10. Campbell, *Halfbreed,* p. 47.
11. Ibid., p. 19.
12. Ibid., p. 157.
13. Ibid., p. 148.
14. Ibid., p. 36.
15. Ibid., p. 137.
16. Ibid., pp. 157, 150.
17. Ibid., p. 28.
18. Walter Stewart, "Red Power," in Frideres, *Canada's Indians: Contemporary Conflicts,* p. 195.
19. Campbell, *Halfbreed,* p. 27.
20. Ibid., p. 144.
21. Ibid., p. 32
22. Ibid., pp. 72–73.

23. Ibid. p. 52.
24. Ibid., p. 114.
25. Ibid., p. 116.
26. Ibid., pp. 156–57.
27. Ibid., p. 116.
28. Ibid., pp. 102, 123.
29. Ibid., p. 118.
30. Stewart, "Red Power," in Frideres, *Canada's Indians: Contemporary Conflicts,* p. 195.

CHAPTER 7

1. Lurie, *Mountain Wolf Woman,* p. 100.
2. David Jones, ed., *Sanapia,* pp. 4, 9.
3. Belle Highwalking, *Belle Highwalking: The Narrative of a Northern Cheyenne Woman,* ed. Katherine M. Weist (Billings: Montana Council for Indian Education, 1979); John Stands in Timber and Margot Liberty, *Cheyenne Memories* (New Haven: Yale University Press, 1967).
4. Barnett and Sterling, eds., *Bobbi Lee,* pp. 91–92.
5. Emma LaRoque, *Defeathering the Indian* (Agincourt, Canada: Book Society of Canada Ltd., 1975), p. 10.
6. Woesha Cloud North, "Autobiography of a Winnebago Family" (paper presented at the Midwest Modern Language Associations Meeting, Indianapolis, Indiana), November 8–10, 1979.
7. Beverly Hungry Wolf, *The Ways of My Grandmothers* (New York: William Morrow, 1980).
8. Anna Lee Walters, "Autobiography," MS, 1977, pp. 9–10.
9. Ibid., pp. 11–12.
10. Ibid., p. 30.
11. Ibid., pp. 33–34.
12. Leslie Marmon Silko, *Storyteller* (New York: Richard Seaver, Random House and Grove Books, 1981).
13. Interview with Leslie Silko, Tucson, Arizona, June 27, 1980.
14. Personal correspondence, Paula Gunn Allen, December 2, 1981.
15. Interview with Paula Gunn Allen, Tempe, Arizona, October 24, 1981.
16. Personal correspondence, Paula Gunn Allen, December 2, 1981.
17. Ibid.

# Selected Bibliography

The following bibliography is intended to provide additional sources for readers interested in the study of American Indian women. Because culture, literature, and personal life are so often inextricably linked, the division of the bibliography into sections is necessarily arbitrary. In Section I we have included those works that are primarily autobiographical, told through editors or written by American Indian women themselves. Section II includes works that are biographical, usually written by an outsider to describe the life of a historical figure such as Pocahontas, Sacajawea, or Sarah Winnemucca. This section also includes biographical reference works, often with mere sketches of lives. Section III provides a broad range of ethnographic and historical material, essays and books written to interpret various facets of Indian women's experiences. Section IV provides a listing of contemporary poetry, stories, and novels by American Indian women with a selected listing of the criticism that has been published. In Section V we have collected a number of miscellaneous publications that speak directly to issues of concern to American Indian women or that reflect in some measure native women's experiences. Some fiction by non-Indian writers is included in this section because we believe it is important to indicate the scope of the portrayal of American Indian women in the literature of this country.

There are no doubt many omissions in this bibliography, for new works appear frequently and older publications are "discovered." Furthermore, there is no attempt to evaluate the accuracy or literary value of the works cited, for to do so would require several volumes. The ultimate purpose of the bibliography is to present the variety, the scope, and the very real bulk of material that exists and that defines American Indian women's experiences.

## I. AMERICAN INDIAN WOMEN'S AUTOBIOGRAPHIES

Adams, Winona, ed. "An Indian Girl's Story of a Trading Expedition to the Southwest about 1841." *Frontier* 10 (May 1930): 338–51, 367.

Told by Catherine, daughter of a Nez Perce woman and a Mohawk and white father. The story of her trip to the mouth of the Colorado River was copied down about 1875 by her husband.

Allen, Elsie (Pomo). *Pomo Basketmaking: A Supreme Art for the Weaver.* Healdsburg, CA: Naturegraph Publishers, 1972.

Chapter One, "The Life of Elsie Allen, Pomo Basketweaver," tells of Elsie's life experiences. She was born on September 22, 1899, but didn't begin basketweaving in earnest until she was 62 years old. Most of the book describes the art of gathering materials and making baskets.

Anahareo [Gertrude Motte] (Mohawk). *Devil in Deerskins: My Life with Grey Owl.* Toronto: New Press, 1972.

Grey Owl was Archie Belamey, an Englishman who passed as an Indian and worked actively for wildlife conservation projects. The story is told by the Mohawk woman who influenced him and shared much of her life with him.

Anauta (Eskimo). *Land of Good Shadows: The Life Story of Anauta, an Eskimo Woman.* Edited by Heluiz Chandler Washburne. New York: John Day Co., 1940.

Anauta is also the author of *Children of the Blizzard,* stories about Eskimo children, and *Wild Like the Fox,* a narrative based on her mother's childhood. This autiobraphy of a Baffin Island Eskimo relates her experiences through youth, marriage, and widowhood, focusing primarily on her relationship to white society and her regret at the loss of traditional lifeways. Text includes an Eskimo alphabet and glossary.

Arnaktauyak, Germaine, illustrator. *Stories from Pangnirtung.* Edmonton: Hurtig Publishers, 1976.

Although this collection includes several stories by men, there are two pieces by women who tell stories and their childhood experiences. Katsoo Eevic and Koodloo Pitsualak tell of the changes in the Baffin Island area.

Ashley, Yvonne (Navajo). " 'That's the Way We Were Raised': An Oral Interview with Ada Damon." *Frontiers: A Journal of Women Studies* 2, no. 21 (Summer 1977): 59–62.

Ada Damon is the interviewer's great aunt who was born in 1900 south of Shiprock, New Mexico. She tells of weaving, trading on the reservation, and her experiences attending boarding school and raising her adopted children.

*Autobiographies of Three Pomo Women.* Edited by Elizabeth Colson. Berkeley: Archaeological Research Facility, Department of Anthropology, University of California, 1974.

Intended to supplement ethnographic work on Pomo culture, these three narratives are primarily concerned with the conflict of traditional and white ways in the lives of women growing up during the early twentieth century. Collected in the 1940s, the life stories reveal regret at the passing of old ways while recognizing the inevitability of the effects of white culture.

Bennett, Kay (Navajo). *Kaibah: Recollections of a Navajo Girlhood.* Los Angeles: Western Lore Press, 1964.

Covering the period 1928 to 1935, this narrative details the New Mexico childhood and girlhood of the author, including family relationships, work and play experiences, and ceremonial life. The work is a loosely connected series of vignettes with illustrations by the author.

Bighead, Kate (Cheyenne). "She Watched Custer's Last Battle: The Story of Kate Bighead." Interpreted by Thomas Bailey Marquis. Hardin, MT: Custer Battlefield Museum (?), 1933.

As a girl, Kate Bighead witnessed the battle of the Washita, and later in her young adulthood, witnessed the Battle of the Little Bighorn, where Custer died, the ensuing separation of the tribes taking part in the battle, and the final surrender of the Cheyenne people a year later. Her first-person account of the Little Bighorn battle focuses on the Cheyenne tribe as the heroes of the encounter with the Custer forces, giving details of soldiers killing themselves, which she interprets as a form of madness brought on by their attack on a peaceful tribal gathering. She captures in detail the chaos, heat, dust, smoke, and noise of the battle. Little of her personal life is revealed in the short narrative, and no interpretive material is supplied by editor Marquis, a scholar of the Little Bighorn event.

Bourguignon, Erika (Ojibwa). "A Life History of an Ojibwa Young Woman." *Primary Records in Culture and Personality,* vol. 1, no. 10. Madison, WI: Microcard Foundation, 1956.

Bourguignon records the life story, collected in 1946, of a Lac de Flambeau woman. This is a literal transcription of conversations in which the personal names have been changed.

Campbell, Maria (Métis). *Halfbreed.* Toronto, Canada: McClelland and Stewart, 1973. Reprinted Lincoln: University of Nebraska Press, 1982.

A contemporary autobiography, this narrative includes historical background on Métis in central Canada but concentrates primarily on the history of the author's family. Extreme poverty and a sense of isolation from both Indians and whites are detailed through anecdotes that range from serious to comic to bitter. The general theme is one of breakdown in government, community, schools, family, and personal life. The narrative is confessional in tone as the author describes her bad marriage, drug addiction and prostitution, and drinking problems, but there is a tenacious sense of hope in the reuniting of her family and her success in returning to a normal life.

Carius, Helen Slwooko (Eskimo). *Sevukakmet: Ways of Life on St. Lawrence Island.* Anchorage: Alaska Pacific University Press, 1979.

In this short book, which is divided into three sections, an Eskimo woman who was born on St. Lawrence Island writes about the history and traditions of her people, how those lifeways were changed by the missionaries and the traders, and how her own life was shaped by her heritage. As a child she had polio and had to learn to deal with the crippling effects of the disease. After twenty years of living in the Lower 48, Carius returned to St. Lawrence Island to live and work as a resource person for the Anchorage schools.

Chona, Maria (Papago). *Papago Woman.* Edited by Ruth M. Underhill. New York: Holt, Rinehart, and Winston, 1979.

Lyrically narrated, with detailed descriptions, dialogue and interpretation, this full life story of a Papago woman, born in 1845, incorporates song, ceremony, and curing rituals as well as day-to-day events. As the daughter of a chief, Chona is privy to, and carefully observant of, all aspects of tribal life in her youth. Married to a medicine man who takes her to tribal fiestas and ceremonies, she is constantly in the center of tribal activity. Although she was not untouched by tragedy—the deaths of most of her children, in particular—she is basically positive in her narrative. She is aware of the influence of white presence in Papago territory in her later life, but is minimally affected by it. Chona is a self-conscious narrator, aware of her role as a trusted woman to whom men can speak of serious matters, and of her own special powers in curing. The editor describes Chona as an "executive" woman in her informative discussion of their friendship and work together and of Papago culture.

Crying Wind (Kickapoo). *Crying Wind.* Chicago: Moody Press, 1977.

Artist, short-story writer, and poet, Crying Wind is active in missionary work among American Indian people. Her autobiography, written in a rather fictional style, traces her childhood and youth in a traditional household racked by poverty and dissension. Disillusioned with her life, she seeks solace in peyote ritual but quickly rejects that for conventional Christianity. Her personal narrative incorporates dramatic incidents and dialogue but places emphasis on analysis of her spiritual and emotional responses to the events in her life.

Cuero, Delfina (Diegueno). *The Autobiography of Delfina Cuero: A Diegueno Indian*. Edited by Florence Shipek. Los Angeles: Dawson's Book Shop, 1968.

The narrator, now living in Mexico, with no way to reenter the United States, records the destruction of her tribe's self-sufficiency, its culture, and religion when they were forced from their Southern California home by farmers. Because they were never given a reservation, they became nomads and squatters. The narrative includes recollections, the puberty ceremony (defunct by her time), and other remembrances passed down from her grandparents concerning childbirth, healing, and storytelling. The tone is optimistic and uncomplaining despite the concentration of the narrative on the disintegration of old ways and the focus on the tragic effects of poverty and family disintegration experienced in her three marriages. She consistently rejects government help and holds a tenacious hope for reuniting her family and returning to California. Her narration is thoughtful and interpretive and is preceded by a historical introduction.

Deer, Ada (Menominee), and R. E. Simon, Jr. *Speaking Out*. Chicago: Children's Press, 1970.

Autobiography of a contemporary Menominee woman of Wisconsin who was active in the restoration of Menominee tribal rights.

Dominguez, Chona (Cahuilla). "Bygone Days." *Cahuilla Texts*. Bloomington: Indiana University Press, Language Science Monographs 6 (1970): 148–52.

This is an extremely brief life history of a California Indian woman, which is actually a case history used to illustrate an ethnographic and linguistic study of Cahuilla Indians.

Filomena, Isidora [Princess Solano] (Churucto). "My Years with Chief Solano," Translated by Nellie Van de Grift. Edited by Hubert Howe Bancroft. *Touring Topics* 22 (February 1930): 39, 52.

Brief but colorful memoir of a northern California woman who married an important chief of the Suisun Indians, interceded for peace and decent treatment of enemies, observed traditional life, and compares it to the harsh subjection of Indians by whites.

Forbes, Jack D., ed. *Nevada Indians Speak*. Reno: University of Nevada, 1954.

Among the narratives anthologized in this work are several by Indian women who represent a fairly broad spectrum of tribal experiences. None of the narratives is long enough to be considered a full autobiography. All are concerned with first encounters with whites and the struggle to retain traditional ways.

Freeman, Minnie Avdla (Inuit). *Life among the Qallunaat*. Edmonton: Hurtig Publishers, 1978.

The writer has worked as a translator for the Canadian government since 1957. She was born at Cape Horn in 1936 and tells of her life and childhood in the North and her exposure to whites (Qallunaat), schools, Christianity, and the world outside her close-knit Inuit family.

Green, Rayna (Cherokee). "Diary of a Native American Feminist." *MS* 11 (July–August 1982), 170–72, 211–13.

Green, director of the Native American Science Resources Center at Dartmouth College, shares a journal of her experiences with Native American women covering 1977 to 1981.

Highwalking, Belle (Cheyenne). *Belle Highwalking: The Narrative of a Northern Cheyenne Woman*. Edited by Katherine M. Weist. Billings: Montana Council for Indian Education, 1979.

This is an autobiography of a woman born in 1892 who was not involved in tribal politics and who did not have any special knowledge of ceremonies or medicines. She wanted to record her life for her grandchildren, and she spoke in Cheyenne into a tape recorder. Her daughter-in-law, Helen Hiwalker, translated the narrative, and Weist arranged the material and provided notes. She tells of childhood and marriage and includes prayers, ceremonies, and stories. John Stands in Timber is Highwalking's half-brother, making possible some comparison of male and female roles within the Cheyenne culture.

Hopkins, Sarah Winnemucca (Paiute). *Life among the Paiutes: Their Wrongs and Claims*. Edited by Mrs. Horace Mann. New York: G. P. Putnam's Sons, 1883.

Though the work is a sustained first-person narrative, it incorporates oratory, history, ethnography, legend, treaty information, and Indian agent commentary. The daughter of Chief Winnemucca, Sarah Winnemucca spent a good deal of her life fighting unsuccessfully trying to get better treatment for her people. Because of her status and her skill in English, she was privy to important tribal events, and she reports them with detailed description, including dramatic dialogue. Among the most detailed incidents reported by this woman, born about 1844, is the first encounter of her tribe with whites, when she was only a child. As an adult, she taught school and later married a white man and moved to the East, giving up tribal ways for an acculturated life. The inflated Victorian prose style of the text reflects this, since it reveals no apparent mark of her first language or of traditional oral technique.

Hungry Wolf, Beverly (Blackfoot). *The Ways of My Grandmothers*. New York: William Morrow and Co., 1980.

A member of the Blood group of the Blackfoot tribe of Canada,

Beverly Hungry Wolf records the myths, legends, household practices, and customs handed down to her from her female relatives and elder women of her tribe. Although the emphasis in her work is on traditional ways, she also focuses on her own life story as it was shaped and influenced by the women of her tribe. An educated contemporary woman, she deliberately fosters traditional ways in her daily life and advocates the preservation of traditions for the benefit of future generations. Incorporated into her narrative are the life stories of the women of past generations who have contributed to her vision of Blackfoot life. Not a sequential narrative, the work is centered on various aspects of the teachings of her grandmothers, with personal anecdotes and stories interwoven with thematic material.

Johnson, Broderick H., ed. *Stories of Traditional Navajo Life and Culture by Twenty-two Navajo Men and Women*. Tsaile, Arizona: Navajo Community College Press, 1977.

Included in this collection of narratives by elderly Navajo people are four life histories by women: Myrtle Begay, Mrs. Bob Martin, Jeanette Blake, and Molly Richardson. Their accounts of traditional life on the reservation include legend, Navajo customs, and philosophy, with emphasis on childhood and boarding school recollections. All four subjects express concern about the modernization of the reservation and deterioration of family and traditional ways.

Kegg, Maude (Ojibwa). *Gabekanaansing/At the End of the Trail: Memories of Chippewa Childhood in Minnesota, with Text in Ojibwa and English*. Edited by John Nichols. Occasional Publications in Anthropology, Linguistic Series, no. 4 (1978), University of Northern Colorado Museum of Anthropology.

This narration of childhood experiences is published bilingually in English and Ojibwa with a brief introduction and linguistic study by the editor. The first chapter is inter-linear translation, which establishes the translation methodology. The narrative itself focuses on the personal and family life of a woman born in 1904 whose childhood was dominated by traditional customs and food-gathering practices of her people in the lake country of Minnesota. The text is dramatized by extensive dialogue and often made immediate by the use of the present tense in describing particular experiences, such as rice gathering and sugar making. Kinship terms are clarified by the editor, and a glossary is provided. Though episodic, the narration is lively and clear, and the involvement of Kegg in preparing the text suggests reliability.

———. *Gii-Ikwezensiwiyaan/When I Was a Little Girl*. Edited by John Nicols. Onamia, MN, 1976.

In booklet form, this brief childhood memoir (a private printing of seven of the tales from *Gabekanaansing*) is published in side-by-side Ojibwa and English. The author recalls such traditional tasks as snowshoe crafting, sap collecting and sugar making, wild rice gathering and drying, and berry picking in Minnesota. Also included are moments of childhood mischief. Dialogue with her grandparents gives the text immediacy and vitality.

Keys, Lucy L. [Wahnenauhi] (Cherokee). "The Wahnenauhi Manuscript: Historical Sketches of the Cherokees." Edited by Jack Frederick Kilpatrick. Smithsonian Institution, *Bureau of American Ethnology Bulletin 196,* Anthropological Papers, no. 77, 1966, pp. 179–213.

Written in 1889 by a woman whose mother was a full-blood and her father white, Lucy Key's narrative is a fairly comprehensive, though brief, history of her people, beginning with myths and describing the forced move to Oklahoma and the major events in the Cherokee leader Sequoyah's life, as well as the life of her white grandfather, George Lowery. As an early written text, it is of interest, particularly because of the Victorian language the author acquired while attending the Cherokee Female Seminary. As editor Kilpatrick points out, Wahnenauhi was of the mixed-blood planter class, wealthy and educated. She is surprisingly well informed about her tribal history and customs and fiercely loyal to them. Despite little personal content in the narrative, the style and topics selected give considerable insight into a highly acculturated nineteenth-century mixed-blood woman's psychological and social posture.

Kroeber, A. L. *Ethnology of the Gros Venture.* Washington, D.C.: American Museum of Natural History, 1908, pp. 216–21. Reprinted New York: AMS Press, 1978.

Includes the narrative of Watches-All as she tells of the battle with the Piegans, her capture, and eventual escape.

———. *Handbook of the Indians of California.* Washington D.C.: U.S. Government Printing Office. Bureau of American Ethnology Bulletin 78 (1925): 63–66.

Included in a short report on the stages a woman goes through to become a shaman is an anonymous personal narrative of a Yurok woman who experienced the process of purification, fasting, dreaming, dancing, and prayer to achieve curing power. The narrative is brief and used to support ethnographic analysis of Yurok religion; no literary persona is developed, since the purpose is to report representative experience.

Landes, Ruth. *The Ojibwa Woman.* New York: Columbia University Press, 1938, pp. 227–47. Reprinted 1977.

This work contains three life histories of Ojibwa women, none of which are full length narratives, though they do give a fairly complete illustration of family relationships and marriage practices in Ojibwa culture. The narratives are appended to a comprehensive ethnographic study of the role of women in Ojibwa life that also includes briefer case studies related to youth, marriage, and occupations. All three narratives are rather flat in tone with emphasis on events and responses; information useful to ethnographers is included.

Lee, Bobbie (Métis). *Bobbi Lee: Indian Rebel.* Edited by Don Barnett and Rich Sterling. Richmond, B.C., Canada: LSM Information Center, 1975.

This narrative, first of a projected two-volume life story, covers the first twenty years of a quarter-blood Métis woman reared in the Vancouver, B.C., area. Growing up in a turbulent household, Bobbi Lee leaves school and home in her teens to work in California vineyards and later to take up a hippie life-style in Toronto in the 1960s. Upon her return to British Columbia, she becomes involved in the Red Power movement, and the narration traces her growing awareness and involvement in Indian political action, including the fishing rights disputes in the Pacific Northwest during the late 1960s. The tough façade she portrays in her account is countered by a sensitivity to the difficulties of urban Indian life and a growing need to articulate and act upon her sympathies.

Leevier, Mrs. Annette (Ojibwa). *Psychic Experiences of an Indian Princess.* Los Angeles: Austin Publishers, 1920.

This autobiography of the daughter of Chief Tommyhawk tells of Leevier's experiences as a medium and healer. Her father was Ojibwa and her mother French. The life story reflects a mixture of Catholicism and belief in traditional religion.

Lindsey, Lilah Denton (Creek). "Memories of the Indian Territory Mission Field." *Chronicles of Oklahoma* 36 (Summer 1958): 181–98.

Lindsey was one-quarter Creek. She wrote her memories in 1938 of life at the mission school and her experiences as a teacher in Indian Territory.

Lone Dog, Louise (Mohawk-Delaware). *Strange Journey: The Vision Life of a Psychic Indian Woman.* Edited by Vinson Brown. Healdsburg, CA: Naturegraph Co., 1964.

*Strange Journey* is a book centered on naive spiritualism, rather than a true personal narrative. The author is highly acculturated, frequently quoting from Tennyson, Kahlil Gibran, Dryden, and the Psalms, proselytizing toward spiritual betterment through a very personalized version of vision seeking. Her pursuit of a written treatment of psychic experience is disconnected from Mohawk or Delaware tribal traditions. The quality of the writing and editing is amateurish, and the work gives a romanticized and extremely narrow view of Indian life that would mislead uninformed readers.

Lowry, Annie (Paiute). *Karnee: A Paiute Narrative.* Edited by Lalla Scott. Reno: University of Nevada Press, 1966.

The text is a composite of personal narrative supplemented by material from anthropological works, legends, and tales, but all sources are well integrated into the narrative. The focus is on the affinities toward two cultures and the decision to adapt, despite the narrator's realization she will always remain marginal. She says, "I am a half-breed. That means I live on the fringe of two races. My white friends think I am just a plain old Paiute, while Indians say I think I am better than they because my father was a white man. When the time came to make a choice between the Indians and the white race, I made up my mind to be an Indian" (p. 20). The first half of the work begins with the mother's desertion by her white father and traces the subject's life up to her marriage, using dramatic technique and flashback. The second half is more detached and objective, different in both tone and technique, perhaps because it was collected seven years after the first. It voices the subject's regret at disintegration of tribal life and values.

Manitowabi, Edna (Ojibwa). *An Indian Girl in the City.* Buffalo, NY: Friends of Malatesta, c. 1971. (Reprinted from "An Ojibwa Girl in the City," *This Magazine Is about Schools* 4, no. 4 (1970): 8–24.)

The brief autobiography traces the events in the life of a young Ojibwa woman whose life is severely disrupted when she is uprooted from the reservation to attend boarding school. The experience cuts her off from her family and leads to destructive urban incidents that culminate in a suicide attempt and months spent in a mental hospital. In time she comes to terms with her Indian identity and becomes involved in native language study and revitalization of traditions. The style is terse and self-analytical, more sociological than literary.

Michelson, Truman. "The Autobiography of a Fox Indian Woman," *Bureau of American Ethnology Fortieth Annual Report* (1925): 291–349.

Recorded in 1918, this is primarily a nineteenth-century narrative that concentrates on the teller's role as a woman in traditional culture. There is a fairly complete description of her instruction in traditional skills, behavior and virtue, her participation in puberty ceremonies, and marriage and childbirth and child-rearing experiences. The text is heavily weighted to advice she received from her elders on all aspects of her life. The tone and prose style is somewhat bland, lacking in detail and emotional description necessary for vitality. Stiff dialogue is partly responsible for this, but the subject's obvious passivity and lack of independence is the major factor. Despite the lack of spirit, she narrates a wide variety of tribal and personal events with a tone of satisfaction with her life. Good ethnological and linguistic notes accompany the narrative.

———. "Narrative of an Arapaho Woman," *American Anthropologist* 35 (October–December 1933): 595–610.

The narrator does not develop an intimate portrait of herself, but through random recollections, rather than straightforward chronology, records the events of, and her responses to, her four marriages, the final one to a chief. The lack of detail by the seventy-seven-year-old narrator is, she reports, a mark of respect for the male members of her family. Michelson's footnotes are useful and nonintrusive.

———. "The Narrative of a Southern Cheyenne Woman," *Smithsonian Miscellaneous Collections* 87 (1932): 1–13.

This brief narrative develops a characterization of an independent, confident, yet innocent and dutiful daughter much loved by her family. The narration develops a strong sense of personality, but the focus on the narrator is lost in details of ceremony and ritual in the last few pages. Ethnological footnotes are helpful in comprehending rituals and tribal ways in this narrative collected in 1931.

Modesto, Ruby (Cahuilla), and Guy Mount. *Not for Innocent Ears*. Angelus Oaks, CA: Sweetlight Books, 1980.

This collection of materials on Cahuilla curing practices contains a brief autobiographical narrative from medicine woman Ruth Modesto as well as her versions of several folktales; however, the work is heavily interpreted by Mount with the intention of advocating a "spiritual" understanding of holistic medicine and relies heavily on Mount's adherence to the tenets of Carlos Castaneda's books. What personal narrative exists is superficial because of the manipulation of the co-author and is more ethnographic than literary.

Mountain Wolf Woman (Winnebago). *Mountain Wolf Woman, Sister of Crashing Thunder: The Autobiography of a Winnebago Indian*. Edited by Nancy Oestreich Lurie. Ann Arbor: University of Michigan Press, 1961.

This narrative spans a period of traditional Winnebago life from thriving hunting and ceremonial practices to the period of dispersal and government dole, tracing the life of the narrator through childhood, marriages, and conversion to peyotism. The narrative style is rather flat, but detail is abundant and the variety of experiences broad. The work is especially valuable in relationship to her brother's autobiography, edited by Paul Radin.

Nuñez, Bonita Wa Wa Calachaw (Luiseno). *Spirit Woman*. Edited by Stan Steiner. New York: Harper and Row, 1980.

Drawn from diaries and autobiographical fragments, this work is a loose series of episodes in the life of a California Indian woman born in 1888, who was raised by a prominent New York family. She was trained in art and sciences, considered a child prodigy, and later in life became an active spokeswoman in Indian causes. The tone of the material is rather obscurely psychic, in part because of the nonstandard English usage and syntax that makes the material difficult to comprehend. The author's rather mystical approach to her experiences casts some suspicion on the reliability of the work, but the text does record the distress caused by isolation from her natural heritage, and the efforts of the author to create an Indian identity in an alien environment.

Owens, Narcissa (Cherokee). *Memoirs of Narcissa Owens.* 1907; reprinted Siloam Springs, AR: Siloam Springs Museum, 1980.

A written, nonsequential memoir, this narrative by a well-educated, genteel and scholarly Victorian woman whose grandfather was the last hereditary Cherokee war chief includes a brief history of her tribe, a family genealogy, descriptions of curing practices, vignettes of friends, family members, and important Cherokee leaders, as well as her experiences living in the South during the Civil War and later as a teacher at the Cherokee Female Seminary. The memoir is addressed to her family to preserve her knowledge of history and tribal ways and also fills her purpose to "show the world that the Cherokees were a cultured and civilized people."

Pitseolak (Eskimo). *Pitseolak: Pictures Out of My Life.* Edited by Dorothy Eber. Seattle: University of Washington Press, 1972.

This narrative with text in Eskimo as well as English, relates the story of an Eskimo artist from Cape Dorset on Baffin Island. The narrative includes drawings that relate to her telling of childhood events, her marriage and childbearing experiences, and the effect of new ways on her life and traditions in her arctic society.

Potts, Marie (Maidu). *The Northern Maidu.* Happy Camp: Naturegraph, 1977.

An eighty-one-year-old Maidu traditionalist writes of her own experiences and the life and history of her people.

Pretty-shield (Crow). *Pretty-shield, Medicine Woman of the Crows.* By Frank B. Linderman. Lincoln: University of Nebraska Press, 1972. (Originally published as *Red Mother,* 1932.)

Born in the 1850s, this Crow woman is reluctant to discuss reservation times, expressing confusion and regret over deterioration of old ways. Although there is no detailed discussion of her role as medicine woman, she is from an important Crow family and gives detailed attention to events in her childhood and early maturity, incorporating myth, legend, and historical event into her narrative. The story is roughly chronological, its order dictated by the format of a dialogue with editor-recorder Frank Linderman. Unfortunately this methodology leads to intrusion of the editor and excessive commentary by him.

Price, Anna [Her Eyes Grey] (Apache). "Personal Narrative of Anna Price." In *Western Apache Raiding and Warfare,* edited by Keith H. Basso, pp. 29–39. Tucson: University of Arizona Press, 1971.

Limited to childhood observations, this narrative actually relates the war and raiding activities of Price's father, an influential chief of the White Mountain Apache tribe, during their conflicts with Mexican and Navajo enemies. Some details of the author's childhood are related.

Qoyawayma, Polingaysi [Elizabeth Q. White] (Hopi). *No Turning Back: A True Account of a Hopi Girl's Struggle to Bridge the Gap between the World of Her People and the World of the White Man.* Edited by Vada F. Carlson. Albuquerque: University of New Mexico Press, 1964.

This full-length personal narrative by a Hopi woman born at the end of the nineteenth century focuses on the conflicts and difficulties she faced on account of her choice in early youth to live in the white world. The narrative includes legend, ceremony, and ritual, but the emphasis is on the individual process of acculturation while still preserving effective ties to tribal traditions and values.

Sanapia (Comanche). *Sanapia, Comanche Medicine Woman.* Edited by David E. Jones. New York: Holt, Rinehart and Winston, 1972.

A twentieth-century autobiography by a woman deeply affected by peyote culture and Christianity, this story is both a personal and cultural history with inclusion of detailed ethnographic material which she hopes to pass on to influential members of her tribe. The intention of the author to address information and personal narrative to her own tribal members sets this text apart from others, most of which are aimed at white audiences.

Sekaquaptewa, Helen (Hopi). *Me and Mine: The Life Story of Helen Sekaquaptewa.* Edited by Louise Udall. Tucson: University of Arizona Press, 1969.

This narrative moves from the subject's childhood in a traditional tribal family, through her schooling and marriage, to an acceptance of white influence without hostility toward traditions or loss of Indian identity or attachment to the land. It covers all aspects of Hopi culture, both traditional and modern, but the personal and family narrative dominates. Though she is a Mormon, little emphasis is placed on Christianity other than details of her conversion. She dwells most on traditional ceremony, boarding school experiences, family life, farming and ranching. The narrative posits attitudes of adjustment and flexibility, a sense of control and contentment with life, despite hardships in raising a family and struggling for existence in a harsh landscape. Stylistically, the narrative is modestly related and well detailed.

Shaw, Anna Moore (Pima). *A Pima Past*. Tucson: University of Arizona Press, 1974.

This personal narrative and cultural memoir is written in fictional third-person style when discussing family history and first person in telling her own story from youth through her education, marriage, move to Phoenix for employment, and eventual return to the reservation. The author places heavy emphasis on the effects of Christianity. Shaw expresses regret over lost traditions but desires to function effectively in the white world, returning to the reservation to regain contact with the land, but especially to engage in community service and church work. The narrative offers good detail, but it is somewhat simplistic.

Simpson, Richard, ed. *Ooti: A Maidu Legacy*. Millbrae, CA: Celestial Arts, 1977.

This short book is a record of Maidu life as told by Lizzie Enos, an eighty-seven-year-old woman from northern California. Lizzie Enos's comments are interspersed with explanatory notes by the editor. She tells of the mythology of the people and of the importance of the ooti, the acorn, to Maidu culture. Photographs show the gathering, grinding, and preparation of the acorns.

Speare, Jean E., ed. *The Days of Augusta*. Vancouver: J. J. Douglas Ltd., 1973.

A Canadian Indian woman's story is told. She was born in 1888 at Soda Creek in British Columbia as Mary Augusta Tappage and lost her Indian status when she married a white. The book includes memories, poems, and pictures.

Stanley, Mrs. Andrew (Apache). "Personal Narrative of Mrs. Andrew Stanley." In *Western Apache Raiding and Warfare,* edited by Keith H. Basso, pp. 205–19. Tucson: University of Arizona Press, 1971.

The author briefly records her daring escape from Fort Apache in the Arizona territory in the late nineteenth century and the hardships of her journey to rejoin her people in a renegade Apache band.

Stewart, Irene (Navajo). *A Voice in Her Tribe: A Navaho Woman's Own Story*. Edited by Doris Ostrander Dawdy and Mary Shepardson. Socorro, NM: Ballena Press Anthropological Papers No. 17, 1980.

More an oral memoir than a chronological autobiography, the work includes versions of traditional Navajo stories, discussion of tribal politics, Navajo social behavior, as well as incidents from the life of the author. Stewart was Christianized in her youth, but she still holds to belief in traditional healing practices and lifestyle with no apparent conflict. She describes the hardships of raising children from a brief early marriage and the satisfactions of a happy marriage in her later years when she became active in the Chinle chapter of the Navajo Tribal Council as secretary and arbiter of disputes. Much of her knowledge of traditional ways comes from her father and from her second husband's stories, some of which are included in the text. The narrative style lacks vitality, but there is value in her valuation of Navajo life-ways and politics from her perspective of age and intense involvement.

Ticasuk [Emily Ivanoff Brown] (Eskimo). *The Roots of Ticasuk: An Eskimo Woman's Family Story*. Anchorage: Alaska Northwest Publishing, 1981.

The narrator of this memoir is the surviving daughter in the line of an Eskimo leader of legendary fame. Taken from oral tradition and recollections of other people, the narrative is actually a dramatized genealogy, primarily anecdotal and episodic, including character vignettes, some ethnographic material, but little actual autobiographical information.

Velarde, Pablita (Santa Clara Pueblo). *Old Father the Story Teller*. Globe, AZ: D. S. King, 1960.

A major painter of pueblo life, whose murals can be seen in public buildings in New Mexico, Velarde relates stories and legends heard from her grandfather and great grandfather, weaving them into the narrative of her family history and own personal narrative.

Waheenee [Maxi'diwiac, Buffalo-Bird Woman] (Hidatsa). *Waheenee: An Indian Girl's Story, Told by Herself.* Told to Gilbert L. Wilson. St. Paul, MN: Webb Publishing, 1921. Reprinted in *North Dakota History* 38 (Winter-Spring 1971): 7–176. Also published as an Occasional Publication no. 4, Bismarck: State Historical Society of North of North Dakota, 1981. Also reprinted Lincoln: University of Nebraska Press, 1981.

Although told in 1921, this is essentially a nineteenth-century narrative by Maxi'diwiac and is characterized by an attitude of regret at the passing of the old ways and the necessity for modern Indians to accommodate white ways. Little attention is paid to reservation times other than to lament the breakdown of traditional ways.

Wanatee, Adeline (Mesquakie). "Education, the Family, and the Schools." In *The Worlds Between Two Rivers: Perspectives on American Indians in Iowa,* edited by Gretchen M. Bataille, David M. Gradwohl, and Charles L. P. Silet, pp. 100–103. Ames: Iowa State University Press, 1978.

Wanatee writes of the super-imposition of white culture on Mesquakie education. She is concerned about Indian students losing both their native language and their culture through education.

Waseskuk, Bertha (Mesquakie). "Mesquakie History—As We Know It." In *The Worlds between Two Rivers: Perspectives on American Indians in Iowa,* edited by Gretchen M. Bataille, David M. Gradwohl, and Charles L. P. Silet, pp. 54–61. Ames: Iowa State University Press, 1978.

Bertha Waseskuk writes history from the point of view of a Mesquakie woman who has lived on the Settlement near Tama, Iowa. It is based on accounts by Mesquakie historians.

Wilson, Gilbert Livingston. *Agriculture of the Hidatsa Indians: An Indian Interpretation*. Minneapolis: University of Minnesota Studies in the Social Sciences no. 9, 1917.

Maxi'diwiac (Buffalo-Bird Woman, or Waheenee) is the principal informant. The interpreter is her son Edward Goodbird. The account is described as an Indian woman's interpretation of economics. Focusing on Maxi'diwiac's sense of her people's relationship to the land and practices of raising crops, this collection of material includes creation stories, legends, and day-to-day agriculture practices, but it is autobiographical in nature because it is based on her recollections of family attitudes, customs, and practices and develops a clear personality and narrative style and relates personal information in a discernible chronology. The nurturing of growing things and the narrator's sense of the sacredness of the earth create a unifying thread.

Willis, Jane (Cree). *Genieish: An Indian Girlhood*. Toronto: New Press, 1973.

Story of mixed-blood Cree girl in Canada. She was born in 1940 and raised by her Indian grandparents. She tells of her involvement with the Indian agency.

Winnie, Lucille (Seneca-Cayuga). *Sah-Gan-De-Oh: The Chief's Daughter*. New York: Vantage Press, 1969.

A twentieth-century woman who has lived on reservations in Oklahoma, Montana, and Kansas, Winnie is representative of modern acculturation and its effect on Indian women. There is little attention or concern for traditional ways; rather, she accepts white domination and blames her own people, particularly tribal politics, for poverty and other reservation problems.

Yoimut (Chunut). "Yoimut's Story, the Last Chunut." In *Handbook of the Yokut Indians* by F. F. Latta, pp. 223–76. Bakersfield, CA: Kern County Museum, 1949.

This narrative by the last full-blood Chunut woman, who died in 1933, concentrates heavily on descriptions of childhood recollections, particularly ceremonies; however, discussion of family life, hunting and fishing, and relationship to white settlers in northern California is included. The subject, who is fluent in Spanish and English as well as in four dialects of her native language, includes ceremonial songs and translations. Though she records the struggle for survival of her people who are without a reservation and continually forced to abandon their settlements as they are taken over by settlers, her tone is regretful rather than bitter.

Young, Lucy (Wailaki). "Out of the Past: A True Indian Story." Edited by Edith V. A. Murphey. *California Historical Society Quarterly* 20 (December 1941): 349–64.

The narrative is a brief record of a Wailaki woman writing in her nineties about her first encounter with whites in her childhood in which her father was killed and about the subsequent persecutions and survival of her family in the wilderness. The story is one of acculturation in her adulthood, through her marriages to two white men. The narrative is without substantial detail, includes no tribal context, and is too brief to be adequately developed; however, stylistically it is interesting because it is written in nonstandard English.

Zitkala-Sa [Gertrude Bonnin] (Sioux).

"Impressions of an Indian Childhood." *Atlantic Monthly* 85 (January 1900): 37–47.

"The School Days of an Indian Girl." *Atlantic Monthly* 85 (February 1900): 185–94.

"An Indian Teacher among Indians." *Atlantic Monthly* 85 (March 1900): 381–86.

"Why I Am a Pagan." *Atlantic Monthly* 90 (December 1902): 802–3.

This collection of stories about Sioux Indians in the late nineteenth and early twentieth centuries centers on personal experiences and ends with an explanation of the author's adherence to old beliefs and ways.

Zuni, Lina (Zuni). "An Autobiography." In *Zuni Texts* by Ruth L. Bunzel, pp. 74–96. New York: G. E. Stechert and Co., 1933, Publications of the American Ethnological Society.

Lina Zuni was seventy years old when Ruth Bunzel recorded her autobiography as part of her fieldwork on Zuni culture and language in 1926–27. Lina's daughter Flora Zuni translated the material for Bunzel.

*MANUSCRIPTS*

Arizona State Museum, Tucson

Doris Duke Collection

This collection includes oral histories taken among Apaches, Navajos, Pimas, Mojaves, Hualapais, and Yavapais during the 1960s, including women, though only one of the narratives is lengthy or complete enough to be considered autobiographical, and even that is more ethnographic than autobiographical in intention. The narrative is told by Nellie Quail, born in 1882 to a Yavapai family, though her grandfather was Apache. She narrates recollections of her parents, including her father's capture and forced residence at San Carlos, Arizona, where Nellie was born. The interviews, which are not chronologically narrated, include: family history; migrations from place to place in central Arizona; puberty, marriage, and childbirth customs; discussion of boarding school experiences; origin myths and animal legends; dress and food customs; experience working for white families; and a discussion of her refusal to become Christianized.

Ella Rumley Collection

This collection is a series of interviews done in the 1960s with urban Papago Indians living in the Tucson area. Among them are a number of transcripts of interviews with women, though none is a full autobiography. Autobiographical material is restricted to brief family and personal histories.

Bancroft Library, University of California, Berkeley

Valory Guide, CU23.1 Collection

Item 87-A. Autobiography of Mary Cornwell, a ninety-one-year-old Bishop Paiute woman, as told to F. J. Essene.

Item 93. Autobiography of Mary Rooker, a seventy-three-year-old Independence Paiute, as told to F. S. Hulse in 1935.

Item 91. Autobiographies from Rose Wayland, Jennie Cashbaugh, and Mattie Bulpitt, all Bishop Paiute women, compiled by F. S. Hulse in 1935.

These narratives were collected under a State Employment Relief Administration program that employed Indians to interview older Indians. Only those on relief were eligible. Emphasis is on traditional life and customs in an autobiographical context.

Minnesota Historical Society, St. Paul

*Chippewa and Dakota Indians: A Subject Catalog of Books, Pamphlets, Periodical Articles, and Manuscripts, 1969.*

While there are no full length autobiographies in the archive, there are short personal narratives by women and some short family histories.

Nebraska State Historical Society, Lincoln

Autobiography of Susan Bordeaux Bettelyoun, a Story of the Ogallala and Brulé Sioux. Edited by Walter Mahlen Herbert. MS185, series 2, box 1, folders 1 and 2, 366 pages.

The manuscript records the history of the Bordeaux family, Fort Laramie, Crazy Horse, the Battle of Ash Hollow, the fur trade, the Crow Butte legend, and Sioux history from 1840 to 1877. The narrator gives a fairly full account of her youth and adulthood as a teacher at Fort Laramie on the Rosebud Sioux Reservation. Though a mixed-blood, she identifies strongly with her mother's Sioux traditions. The autobiography was told to Josephine Waggoner.

Western History Collections Library, University of Oklahoma
Indian Pioneer Papers

This 112-volume set of manuscripts and materials collected from WPA interviews during the 1930s contains some personal narratives by Indian women. Materials are edited by Grant Foreman.

W. H. Over Museum, University of South Dakota, Vermillion
Ella Deloria Research Project. Ed. Agnes Picotte.

A brief autobiography is on file in the Institute of Indian Studies.

## II. BIOGRAPHIES OF AMERICAN INDIAN WOMEN

Anderson, Owanah (Choctaw). *Ohoyo One Thousand: A Resource Guide of American Indian/Alaska Native Women, 1982*. Wichita Falls, TX: Ohoyo Resource Center, 1982.

Biographical sketches of 1,004 American Indian/Alaska native women indexed according to area of expertise.

Anderson, Rufus. *Memoir of Catherine Brown: A Christian Indian of the Cherokee Nation*. Philadelphia: American Sunday School Union, 1931.

Anderson relates the story of an Indian woman born about 1800 in Alabama who attended missionary school at Brainerd, was converted to Christianity, and then worked to convert other Indians. Excerpts from the diary are included.

Axford, Roger W. *Native Americans: Twenty-three Indian Biographies*. Indiana, PA: A. G. Halldin Publishing, 1980.

Although the format for these biographical sketches is mixed, Axford provides information on a number of American Indian women: Ida Carmen, Betsy Kellas, Clara Sue Kidwell, Veronica L. Murdock, Joanne Linder, Vivian Ayoungman, Yvonne Talachy, Gay Lawrence, Carol Allen Weston, and Roxie Woods.

Barnouw, Victor. "The Phantasy World of the Chippewa Woman." *Psychiatry: Journal for the Study of Interpersonal Relations* 12 (February 1949): 67–76.

This comparison of the life histories of Tom Badger and his wife, Julia, emphasizes the fantasies of Julia, especially those with the guardian spirit Beoukowe and her visions.

Bennett, Kay (Navajo), and Bennett, Ross. *A Navajo Saga*. San Antonio: The Naylor Co., 1969.

The text is a family chronicle from 1845 to 1868 using fictional form with dialogue, incorporating family events with emphasis on hardships and the resiliency and loyalty of family members. The central figure in the narrative is Shebah, who is based on the author's grandmother. The focus is on the Bosque Redondo experience and "The Long Walk" back.

Brand, Johanna. *The Life and Death of Anna Mae Aquash*. Toronto: James Lorimer, 1978.

This is a thorough study of Anna Mae Aquash, AIM organizer and activist, and her death near Wanblee on the Pine Ridge Reservation in South Dakota. Includes reports published by the FBI related to AIM and Wounded Knee.

Brimlow, George F. "The Life of Sarah Winnemucca: The Formative Years." *Oregon Historical Quarterly* 53 (June 1952): 103–34.

In this account of Thoc-me-to-ny (Sarah Winnemucca) Brimlow writes of her childhood, school years, marriage to Lieutenant Barlett, and her struggles to aid her people.

Buehrle, Marie Cecilia. *Kateri of the Mohawks*. Milwaukee: Bruce Publishing, 1954.

Biography of Mohawk woman who was scarred by smallpox, never married, was converted by the Jesuits, and ministered to her people.

Clough, Wilson D. "Mini-Aku, Daughter of Spotted Tail." *Annals of Wyoming* 39 (1967): 187–216.

Biography of a young Indian woman who died in 1866 at the age of seventeen. Her story was popularized in Wyoming as the story of Falling Leaf.

Coulter, E. Merton. "Mary Musgrove, 'Queen of the Creeks': A Chapter of Early Georgia Troubles." *Georgia Historical Quarterly* 1 (March 1927): 1–30.

Cousaponakeesa, daughter of a white trader, married John Musgrove, ran a trading house, and served as an interpreter in 1700s.

Cowan, Susan, ed. *We Don't Live in Snow Houses Now: Reflections of Arctic Bay*. Ottawa: Canadian Arctic Producers, 1976.

This book includes a series of interviews with Arctic Bay residents, several of whom are women. There are photographs, English translations, and Inuktitut text. The interviews chronicle the changes in means of subsistance, housing, education, and society in general. One informant comments, "I still remember it all clearly and if I were to go back to that life I could do it all exactly as I was taught. It's just that we don't live in snow houses now."

Cruikshank, Julie. *Athapaskan Women: Lives and Legends*. Canadian Ethnology Service Paper No. 57. Ottawa: National Museums of Canada, 1979.

Report of a project of interviewing and recording biographies of Athapaskan women between the ages of 40 and 85 in the Yukon Territory. Includes excerpts from the biographies and versions of some Athapaskan legends.

Defenbach, Byron. *Red Heroines of the Northwest*. Caldwell, ID: Caxton Printers, 1929.

Stories of Sacajawea, the Dorian woman, and Jane Silcott.

Finney, Frank F., Sr. "Maria Tallchief in History: Oklahoma's Own Ballerina." *Chronicles of Oklahoma* 38 (Spring 1960): 8–11.

This is a brief biographical account of ballerina Maria Tallchief with historical references to her family.

Foreman, Carolyn Thomas. "Aunt Eliza of Tahlequah." *Chronicles of Oklahoma* 9 (1931): 43–55.

A tribute to Eliza Missouri Busyhead, the daughter of a half-blood Cherokee and a missionary.

———. "A Cherokee Pioneer, Ella Flora Coodey Robinson." *Chronicles of Oklahoma* 7 (1929): 364–74.

Biography of a Cherokee woman born in 1847.

———. "A Creek Pioneer: Notes Concerning 'Aunt Sue' Rogers and Her Family." *Chronicles of Oklahoma* 21 (1943): 271–79.

Biographical account of a Creek woman, Mrs. Susannah Drew Rogers.

———. *Indian Women Chiefs*. 1954; reprinted Washington, D.C.: Zenger Publishing, 1976.

Foreman records customs of women and accounts of women rulers. She discusses some well-known women such as Nancy Ward and Sarah Winnemucca as well as lesser-known figures.

———. "Two Notable Women of the Creek Nation." *Chronicles of Oklahoma* 35 (Autumn 1957): 315–37.

This is a biographical sketch of Mary Lewis Herrod (born 1840s), who was a teacher of Indian children for fifty years, and of her niece Kate Shawahrens (born 1864), who was also a teacher among the Indians.

Foster, Mrs. W. Garland. *The Mohawk Princess: Being Some Account of the Life of Tekahion-Wake* [E. Pauline Johnson]. Vancouver: Lions' Gate Publishing, 1931.

This is a biography of the Canadian Mohawk poet and includes a bibliography.

Garbarino. Merwyn S. "Seminole Girl." *Trans-Action* 7 (February 1970): 40–46.

This is the story of "Nellie Green," a Seminole woman who was raised in a chickee, graduated from college, went back to the reservation, and had to deal with the frustration of living in two different worlds.

Gehm, Katherine. *Sarah Winnemucca*. Phoenix: O'Sullivan, Woodside, 1975.

A biography of Sarah Winnemucca (1843–91) which focuses on her achievements and importance to Indian people.

Gerson, Noel B. *First Lady of America: A Romanticized Biography of Pocahontas*. Richmond, VA: Westover Publishers, 1973.

This is another view of the life of Pocahontas.

Green, Norma Kidd. *Iron Eye's Family: The Children of Joseph La Flesche*. Lincoln, NE: Johnson Publishing, 1969.

Study of the La Flesche family traced in letters and historical documents. Several chapters focus on Suzette and Rosalie La Flesche. The lives of the less well-known daughters, Marguerite and Susan, are also examined.

Gridley, Marion E. *American Indian Women*. New York: Hawthorn Books, 1974.

Eighteen American Indian women are featured. The introductory chapter provides information about the tribal status of Indian women.

Hebard, Grace Raymond. *Sacajawea: Guide and Interpreter of the Lewis and Clark Expedition*. Glendale, CA: Arthur H. Clark, 1933.

This is a researched account of the life of Sacajawea with an extensive bibliography.

Heizer, Robert, and Albert B. Elsasser. *Original Accounts of the Lone Woman of San Nicholas Island*. Ramona, CA: Ballena, 1973.

Heizer and Elsasser collected accounts of Juana Maria (subject of Scott O'Dell's *Island of the Blue Dolphins*), who spent eighteen years alone on an island off the coast of southern California.

Howard, Harold P. *Sacajawea*. Norman: University of Oklahoma Press, 1971.

Howard has researched Sacajawea's experiences with the Lewis and Clark expedition and presents what is known of her later life.

Johnson, Emily Pauline (Mohawk). *The Moccasin Maker*. Toronto: Ryerson, 1913.

This Canadian Iroquois poet compiled a personal anthology made up of short stories about Indian women, several legends and tales and fictional character sketches, and a fairly lengthy reminisence about her mother's life. Though several of the sketches are based on real incidents, the material is not directly autobiographical. Her writing style is somewhat picturesque, though she is adroit at capturing salient incident. She is also the author of *Legends of Vancouver*, myths and traditions from Canadian coastal tribes.

Katz, Jane B. *This Song Remembers: Self-Portraits of Native Americans in the Arts*. Boston: Houghton Mifflin, 1980.

In part biography and in part personal narrative, Katz relates the lives of several American Indian women who are active in the visual or performing arts: Pitseolak, Pearl Sunrise, Mary Morez, Grace Medicine Flower, Helen Hardin, Cecilia White, and Leslie Silko.

Kelley, Jane Holden. *Yaqui Women: Contemporary Life Histories*. Lincoln: University of Nebraska Press, 1978.

Narratives of Dominga Tava, Chepa Moreno, Dominga Ramirez, and Antonia Valenzuela with an introduction focusing on the editor's methodology and the background of the Yaqui people.

Knudtson, Peter N. "Flora, Shaman of the Wintu." *Natural History* 84 (May 1975): 6–17.

Biographical account of Flora Jones, a practicing shaman in northern California. She tells of her helping spirits and doctoring.

Lane, Sheryl. " 'We Don't Make Baskets Any More.' " *Salt: Journal of Northeast Culture* 4 (1979): 4–16.

Interesting interview with Madasa Sapiel, a seventy-five-year-old woman who is half Penobscot and half Passamoquoddy and who lives on "Indian Island" in the midsection of Maine. She tells of the old days and how things have changed. She also tells of the power of Indian women: "As I said, the man walked ahead and the woman walked behind. But she was the law."

Liberty, Margot, ed. *American Indian Intellectuals*. St. Paul: West Publishing, 1978.

Liberty includes chapters on Sarah Winnemucca and Flora Zuni.

Little Bear, Mary (Cheyenne). *Dance Around the Sun*. Edited by Alice Marriot and Carol K. Rachlin. New York: Crowell Publishing, 1977.

This work combines both autobiographical and biographical techniques in relating the life story of Mary Little Bear, a mixed-blood Cheyenne woman. Born in a tipi in the Oklahoma Indian Territory in 1875, Little Bear participated in traditional Sun Dance ceremonies and learned the traditional crafts, particularly beadwork. She was educated in a white boarding school where she met and married a Caddo Indian. Her narrative traces her marriage and the raising of six children during a period of drastic change from traditional life to acculturation. Little Bear is both representative of her tribal ways and highly individual. The latter part of the work concentrates on her craftsmanship and relationship to Alice Marriot and Carol Rachlin, who become her "daughters." Presented primarily in a third person, biographical manner, the narrative is based on recollections told to Marriot and Rachlin over a period of several years before her death in the mid-1960s. The text is enlivened by detailed descriptions of incidents and dramatic dialogue.

McClary, Ben. "Nancy Ward, the Last Beloved Woman of the Cherokees." *Tennessee Historical Quarterly* 21 (December 1962): 352–64.

Life story of Nancy Ward, a mother image for Cherokees since 1755.

McRaye, Walter. *Pauline Johnson and her Friends*. Toronto: Ryerson Press, 1974.

McRaye provides a biography of Tekahionwake, Pauline Johnson, a Mohawk poet of Canada. Her mother was English and her father was Indian. She was born in 1862.

Mariott, Alice. *Maria, the Potter of San Ildefonso*. Norman: University of Oklahoma Press, 1945.

This is the story of the famous Pueblo potter who developed the traditional black pottery of her tribe.

Meachum, A. B. *Wi-ne-ma (The Woman Chief) and Her People*. Hartford: American Publishing, 1876.

This story of the woman who sought to save the Peace Commission to the Modoc in 1873 was written to tell the Indian side of Modoc-White relations.

Nelson, Mary Carroll. *Annie Wauneka*. Minneapolis: Dillon Press, 1972.

This is a biography of the first woman elected to the Navajo Tribal Council and winner of the Medal of Freedom in 1963. Wauneka has been a crusader for improved health care for the Navajo.

———. *Maria Martinez*. Minneapolis: Dillon Press, 1974.

Maria Martinez is famous among Southwest Indian potters as the woman who rediscovered the traditional black-on-black technique that had been lost for generations. The story, however, does more than trace the complex search for the exact process of the old technique. Martinez's narrative details the relationship of herself and her art to her family, personal loss and tragedy, and the passing on of her art to her family and tribe. Because the impact of her pottery raised the standard of life for the whole village, she was called the Mother of the Pueblo.

———. *Pablita Velarde*. Minneapolis: Dillon Press, 1971.

This is a biography of the Tewa artist Pablita Velarde, born in 1918 at Santa Clara Pueblo. Velarde used the traditional art forms of her people; the book discusses the conflicts between the artist's Indian heritage and the Anglo world.

Pence, Mary Lou. "Ellen Hereford Washakie of the Shoshones." *Annals of Wyoming* 22 (1950): 3–11.

This is a biographical account of women of Fort Washakie, Wyoming.

Peterson, Susan. *Maria Martinez: Five Generations of Potters*. Washington, D.C.: Renwick Galleries, 1978.

Presents brief biographical information about Maria Martinez and specific information about the pottery. Illustrated.

Phillips, Leon. *First Lady of America: A Romanticized Biography of Pocahontas*. Richmond, VA: Westover Publishing, 1973.

Phillips attempts to tell, free from legend, the story of the historical Pocahontas.

Reichard, Gladys A. *Dezba, Woman of the Desert: Life among the Navajo Indians*. Glorieta, NM: Rio Grande Press, 1971.

First published in 1939 to tell the story of an Indian woman over 60 years old, the incidents and details are true, but the relationships and specific episodes are fictionalized.

Reid, Russell. "Sakakawea." *North Dakota History* 30 (January–October 1963): 101–10.

Reid discusses Sacajawea's identity based on the 1812 journal of John Luttig, a clerk for the Missouri Fur Company.

Richey, Elinor. "Sagebrush Princess with a Cause: Sarah Winnemucca." *American West* 12 (November 1975): 30–33, 57–63.

Discussion of the life of Paiute Sarah Winnemucca and her involvement with whites, her fondness for them, and her realization of the injustices her people had suffered since the white invasion. Her dream that the Indian hope of survival lay in emulating whites was shattered by indiscriminate killing of her people and the eventual relocation of her people in the Washington Territory.

Robertson, Wyndam. *Pocahontas, Alias Matoaka, and Her Descendants*. Baltimore: 1887; reprinted Genealogical Publishing, 1968.

Genealogy of Pocahontas.

Sargent, Daniel. *Catherine Tekakwitha*. New York: Longmans, Green, 1937.

Biography of Iroquois woman who lived the life of a nun. Her tomb was visited by Indians who followed her Christian example, and she was believed by some to have been a saint.

Schultz, James Willard. *Birdwoman (Sacajawea): The Guide of Lewis and Clark*. Boston: Houghton Mifflin, 1918.

Schultz tells the story of Sacajawea through the tales he received from older friends.

Seymour, Flora Warren. *Women of Trail and Wigwam*. New York: Woman's Press, 1930.

After a general introduction, Seymour provides chapters on Sacajawea (Shoshone), Wih-munke Wakan (Sioux), Madame Montour (Seneca captive), Seneca Sisters (captors of Mary Jemison), Molly Brant (Mohawk), Daughters of the Wind Clan (Creek), Milly (Seminole), Margaret McLaughlin (Indian wife of a fur trader), Nellie Connolly (Oregon), Julia (Flathead), Owl Woman and Yellow Woman (Cheyenne), wives of mountain men, Appearing Day (Brulé Sioux), Sarah Winnemucca (Paiute), Winema (Modoc), Cherry and Magpie Outside (Crow). The stories are interesting but are not documented.

*Speaking Together: Canada's Native Women*. Ottawa: Secretary of State, 1975.

Published in conjunction with the celebration of International Women's Year. Includes brief biographical sketches, personal statements, and photographs of twenty-nine Canadian Indian women.

Stewart, Patricia. "Sarah Winnemucca." *Nevada Historical Society Quarterly* 14 (Winter 1971): 23–38.

Stewart summarizes the information available about the life of Sarah Winnemucca.

Tucker, Norma. "Nancy Ward, Ghighau of the Cherokees." *Georgia Historical Quarterly* 53 (June 1969): 192–200.

This is a biography of Nancy Ward, "beloved woman" of the Cherokee.

Vanderburgh, Rosamund M. *I Am Nokomis Too: The Biography of Verna Patronella Johnston*. Don Mills, Ontario: General Publishing, 1977.

This is a popular account of the life of Verna Johnston (Ojibwa) based on her recollections and community memories of Cape Croker, Ontario. She is interested in Indian adaptation to urban life and had a boarding house in Toronto during part of her life. In 1976 she was named Indian Woman of the Year by the Native Women's Association of Canada. Includes taped interview with Johnston.

Waltrip, Lela, and Rufus Waltrip. *Indian Women*. New York: David McKay, 1964.

Biographical sketches of thirteen Indian women from 1535 to the present are included: Big Eyes, Pocahontas, Sacajawea, Winema, Cynthia Ann Parker, Sara Winnemucca, Indian Emily, Dot-so-la-lee, Tomasse, Neosho, Maria Martinez, Annie Dodge Wauneka, Pablita Velarde.

Wilson, Dorothy Clarke. *Bright Eyes: The Story of Suzette La Flesche, an Omaha Indian*. New York: McGraw-Hill, 1974.

This is a fictionalized biography of La Flesche, who in the 1870s was a spokeswoman for her tribe as well as for the Poncas.

Wood, Beth, and Tom Barry. "The Story of Three Navajo Women." *Integrateducation* 16, no. 2 (March–April 1978): 33–35.

Focuses on the lives of Emmie Yazzie, Claudeen Bates Arthur, and Elva Benson. These women are concerned with Indian rights, the environment, legal rights, and education.

Woodward, Grace Steele. *Pocahontas*. Norman: University of Oklahoma Press, 1969.

Presented by the author as a new evaluation of the role of Pocahontas in history.

## III. ETHNOGRAPHIC AND HISTORICAL STUDIES

Aberle, S. B. D. "Child Mortality among Pueblo Indians." *American Journal of Physical Anthropology* 16 (January–March 1932): 339–49.

Aberle describes childbirth among Pueblo women on the basis of his studies done at two Tanoan pueblos in New Mexico.

———. "Maternal Mortality among the Pueblos." *American Journal of Physical Anthropology* 18 (January–March, 1934): 431–35.

This study of five Pueblo villages tells of the events associated with childbirth. It provides statistic of child mortality and the death rate of Pueblo women from causes attributed to pregnancy.

Apes, William. *The Experiences of Five Christian Indians of the Pequod Tribe*. Boston: James B. Dow, 1933.

This religious tract by Apes includes personal religious testimonies of four Indian women who converted to Christianity and preached among their people.

Basso, Keith. *The Cibecue Apache*. New York: Holt, Rinehart and Winston, 1970.

Chapter Five is about the girl's puberty ceremony and includes personal accounts. It discusses the relationship of the ceremony to the figure of Changing Woman, who gives longevity and the physical capabilities of perpetual youth.

———. "The Gift of Changing Woman." *BAE Bulletin* 196. Washington, D.C.: Smithsonian Institution, 1966, pp. 119–73.

For this discussion of Apache girls' puberty rites, information was gathered at Cibecue (Arizona). The ceremony gives power to the community through the girl who participates.

Beauchamp, W. M. "Iroquois Women." *Journal of American Folklore* 13 (April–June 1900): 81–91.

Discusses the position of women among the Iroquois, their roles, responsibilities, and prestige.

Beck, Peggy V., and Anna Lee Walters (Pawnee-Oto). *The Sacred Ways of Knowledge: Sources of Life*. Tsaile, AZ: Navajo Community College, 1977.

Information about sacred ways gathered through interviews, speeches, prayers, songs, and conversations. Includes chapters on girls' puberty ceremonies, peyote, and studies of selected tribes.

Blanchard, Kendall. "Changing Sex Roles and Protestantism among the Navajo Women in Ramah." *Journal for the Scientific Study of Religion* 14 (March 1975): 43–50.

Author postulates that economic and social changes have had more negative impact on traditional life styles of Navajo females than males.

Women affiliating with the missions are less traditional than other Navajo women who have suffered a "loss of prestige and security within the family."

Bloom, Joseph D. "Migration and Psychopathology of Eskimo Women." *American Journal of Psychiatry* 130 (April 1973): 446–49.

Author theorizes that Eskimo women migrate to the cities because of dissatisfaction with their low standing in the native culture. The uprooting and often unsatisfactory integration into the city results in increased psychological problems for Eskimo women.

Briggs, Jean L. "Kapluna Daughter: Living with Eskimos." *Transaction* 7 (June 1970): 12–24.

Experiences of a white woman "adopted" by an Eskimo family and treated as their "daughter" are discussed as anthropological role playing.

Brown, Judith K. "A Cross-Cultural Study of Female Initiation Rites." *American Anthropologist* 65 (August 1963): 837–53.

In this study of fifty-five areas of the world, one hundred societies, thirteen in North American, are examined.

———. "Economic Organization and the Powers of Women among the Iroquois." *Ethnohistory* 17 (Summer–Fall, 1970): 151–67.

This is a study of the relationship between the position of Iroquois women and their economic status. Their high status reflects their control of the tribe's economic organization.

Carr, Lucien. "On the Social and Political Position of Women among the Huron Iroquois Tribes." *16th Annual Report of the Peabody Museum of American Archaeology and Ethnography*. Cambridge: Harvard University Press, 1884, pp. 207–32.

This is an interesting but dated view of Indian women. Many later sources rely on this interpretation of women's roles.

Christensen, Rosemary A. "Indian Women: An Historical and Personal Perspective." *Pupil Personnel Services* 4 (July 1975): 12–22.

Christensen begins by pointing out that the first Anishinabe created by Gitchee Manitou was a woman and discusses the roles of Indian women, the differences between Indian and white women in relation to the women's movement, and the literary views of Indian women. "Accounts of Indian women are based on the biased and one-sided views of . . . the trader, the missionary, and the anthropologist."

Cruikshank, Julie. "Becoming a Woman in Athapaskan Society: Changing Traditions on the Upper Yukon River." *Western Canadian Journal of Anthropology* 5, no. 2 (1975): 1–14.

Includes comments from Indian women of the Yukon familiar with the traditions of seclusion during menstruation. Cruikshank discussed how changes in tradition have affected women's roles in Athapaskan society.

———. "Native Women in the North: An Expanding Role." *North/Nord* 18 (November–December, 1971): 1–7.

This article discusses the role of Canadian Indian men and women, the laws which affect Indian women, and women's role in the family as well as at work and in politics.

Downs, James F. "The Cowboy and the Lady: Models as a Determinant of the Rate of Acculturation among the Piñon Navajo." In *Native Americans Today: Sociological Perspectives,* edited by Howard M. Bahr, Bruce A. Chadwick, and Robert C. Day. New York: Harper and Row, 1972.

Discusses traditional behavior of Navajo women.

Driver, Harold E. "Girls' Puberty Rites and Matrilocal Residence." *American Anthropologist* 71 (October 1969): 905–8.

Challenges the view that matrilocal residence causes girls' puberty rites to be part of the culture.

———. "Girls' Puberty Rites in Western North America." *Publications in Anthropological Records* 6 (1941–42): 21–90. Berkeley: University of California Press, 1942.

This is a comparative study of puberty rites.

———. "Reply to Opler on Apachean Subsistence, Residence, and Girls' Puberty Rites." *American Anthropologist* 74 (October 1972): 1147–51.

In this article Driver responds to Morris E. Opler's article in the same volume.

Ewers, John C. "Deadlier than the Male." *American Heritage* 16 (1965): 10–13.

Four Indian women's stories are given: Other Magpie, Woman Chief, Throwing Down, Running Eagle. The stories are about their exploits as warriors, not complete biographical accounts.

———. "Mothers of the Mixed-Bloods: The Marginal Woman in the History of the Upper Missouri." In *Probing the American West,* edited by Kenneth Ross Toole, pp. 62–70. Santa Fe: Museum of New Mexico, 1962.

Ewers here assumes the duties of women to be inferior; he ignores the division of labor as part of a culture.

Flannery, Regina. "The Position of Women among the Mescalero Apache." *Primitive Man* 5 (April–July, 1932): 26–32.

Discusses arranged marriages as well as economic, social, and religious lives of Mescalero Apache women.

Frisbie, Charlotte J. *Kinaalda: A Study of the Navajo Girl's Puberty Ceremony.* Middletown, CT: Wesleyan University Press, 1967.

Frisbie provides a record of four ceremonial days—what happens and why. The ceremony is part of the Blessing Way.

Garbarino, Merwyn S. *Big Cypress, A Changing Seminole Community.* New York: Holt, Rinehart and Winston, 1972.

This is a general study of the Seminoles; it includes a section on social organization that deals in part with women's roles.

———. "Life in the City: Chicago." In *The American Indian in Urban Society,* edited by Jack O. Wadell and O. Michael Watson, pp. 168–205. Boston: Little, Brown, and Co., 1971.

This study includes statements by both male and female American Indians living in Chicago. They talk of housing, education, children, family relationships, and Indian identity.

Gilmore, Melvin R. "Notes on Gynecology and Obstetrics of the Akrikara Tribe." *Michigan Academy of Science, Arts and Letters, Papers* 14 (1930): 71–81.

Information recorded in 1926 from Stesta-Kata, an eighty-six-year-old midwife of Arikara, tells of the life of an Arikara girl through childhood, puberty, pregnancy, and childbirth.

Goldenweiser, A. A. "Functions of Women in Iroquois Society." *American Anthropologist* 17 (1915): 376–77.

This account of the minutes of a 1914 meeting reviews the paper presented by Goldenweiser on Iroquois women and their power within the tribe. He believes that the status of women in "primitive societies" is higher than that in other cultures.

Griffin, Naomi Musmaker. *The Roles of Men and Women in Eskimo Culture.* Chicago: University of Chicago Press, 1930.

Discusses roles and division of labor. Includes chart of activities indicating whether men or women participate.

Grinnell, George Bird. "Cheyenne Woman Customs." *American Anthropologist,* n.s. 4 (January–March 1902): 13–16.

These customs associated with puberty and childbirth were communicated to Grinnell by older Cheyenne women.

Haas, Mary R. "Men's and Women's Speech in Koasati." In *Language in Culture and Society,* edited by Dell Hymes, pp. 228–33. New York: Harper and Row, 1964.

Discusses male and female differences in vocabulary and pronunciation.

Hallowell, A. Irving. "Shabwan: A Dissocial Indian Girl." *American Journal of Orthopsychiatry* 8 (April 1938): 329–40.

Interesting account of a young girl who was presumed "crazy" by the tribe and of her subsequent interaction with the author. The article includes comments about the attitudes toward women and girls in Ojibwa culture. Shabwan was a Saulteaux Indian living east of Lake Winnipeg.

Hammond, Dorothy, and Alta Jablow. *Women: Their Economic Role in Traditional Societies*. Reading, MA: Addison-Wesley Publishing, Module in Anthropology No. 35, 1973.

The authors discuss the assignment of women's work as a matter of tradition rather than biology or predisposition. They acknowledge that the work of women always gets attention but that it does not elicit the public esteem accorded the work of men.

Hanasy, Laila Shukry. "The Role of Women in a Changing Navajo Society." *American Anthropologist* 59 (February 1957): 101–11.

This study done in New Mexico during 1951–52 suggests that women's roles have been adversely affected by recent social and economic changes.

Hewitt, J. N. B. "Status of Women in Iroquois Polity before 1784." *Smithsonian Annual Reports for the Year Ending 30 June 1932*. Washington, D.C.: Smithsonian Institue, 1933, pp. 475–588.

Discusses matrilineal features of Iroquois internal organization and kinship relations. "The life of a woman was regarded as of double value of that of a man to the community." Points to the change in the power of women as a result of white contact.

Hilgar, M. Inez. "Chippewa Pre-natal Food and Conduct Taboos." *Primitive Man* 9 (July 1936): 46–48.

Reports information collected in Minnesota, Wisconsin, and Michigan during the 1930s.

Hill, Jane H., and Rosinda Nolasquez. *Mulu'wetum: The First People, Cupeno Oral History and Language*. Banning, CA: Malki Museum Press, 1973.

Recollections and stories of Cupeno people in both English and Cupeno.

Hippler, Arthur E. "Additional Perspectives on Eskimo Female Infanticide." *American Anthropologist* 74 (October 1972): 1318–19.

Further discussion of Milton Freeman's article on female infanticide among the Netsilik Eskimos.

Honigmann, John J. *Culture and Ethos of Kaska Society*. Yale University Publications in Anthropology, no. 40. New Haven: Yale University Press, 1949.

This study of Dease Lake in British Columbia includes autobiographical sketches with Rorschach analysis, dream interpretation, and discussion in depth of Dorothy Plover's personality and life.

"Hopi Womanpower." *Human Behavior* 3 (November 1974): 49–50.

In this brief discussion of the matrilineal, matrilocal society of Hopi, women's duties and the education of children are explained.

Howard, Oliver O. *My Life and Experiences among Our Hostile Indians.* Hartford, CT: A. T. Worthington, 1907; reprinted ed., New York: Da Capo Press, 1972.

In this autobiography of Oliver Howard, major general in the U.S. Army, he includes a chapter on "Squaw Men" and a chapter on Sarah Winnemucca. This book provides a military view of Indian women.

Hunter, Lois Marie. *The Shinnecock Indians.* Islip, NY: Buys Brothers, 1952.

One chapter, "Only a Squaw," tells of the role of women in Shinnecock culture.

Jacobs, Melville. *Clackamas Chinook Texts.* Bloomington: Indiana University Research Center in Anthropology, Folklore and Linguistics, 1958.

The informant is Mrs. Victoria Howard of West Linn, Oregon. Information was gathered during the period 1929–30.

Jacobs, Sue-Ellen. *Women in Perspective: A Guide for Cross-Cultural Studies.* Urbana: University of Illinois Press, 1974.

This general study includes material on American Indian women as well as a bibliography.

Jamieson, Kathleen. "Sisters under the Skin: An Exploration of the Implication of Feminist Materialist Perspective Research." *Canadian Ethnic Studies* 13, no. 1 (1981): 130–43.

Jamieson analyzes the position of Canadian Indian women from a feminist historical perspective. She argues that the social and economic positions of Indian women make them more like Indian men than like non-Indian women.

Kingston, C. S. "Sacajawea as Guide: The Evaluation of a Legend." *Pacific Northwest Quarterly* 35 (January 1944): 3–18.

Kingston examines the articles which led to the legend of Sacajawea's role as a guide on the Lewis and Clark Expedition. The article discusses Grace Raymond Hebard's book and Sacajawea's role in school texts. The place to arrive at the facts is in the Lewis and Clark journals. She is cited as acting as a guide in only one instance: her main contribution was as a link between the whites and her people.

Kluckhohn, Clyde. "Navajo Women's Knowledge of Their Song Ceremonials." In *Culture and Behavior,* edited by Richard Kluckhohn, pp. 92–96. New York: Free Press, 1962.

This study showed Navaho women had little knowledge of ceremonies; there were no women singers or curers in the group interviewed.

La Flesche, Francis. "Osage Marriage Customs." *American Anthropologist,* n.s. 14 (January–March 1912): 127–30.

Two customs are recorded: *Mizhi* (marriage between young people) and *Omiha* (marriage between previously married persons).

Leacock, Eleanor. "Matrilocality in a Simple Hunting Economy (Montagnais-Naskapi)." *Southwestern Journal of Anthropology 11 (Spring 1955): 31–47.*

This is a study of Algonkian matrilocality based on historical records and contemporary accounts.

Lewis, Ann. "Separate Yet Sharing." *Conservationist* 30 (January–February 1976): 17.

This brief summary of the historical and contemporary role of Iroquois women shows their power within the tribe.

Lewis, Claudia. *Indian Families of the Northwest Coast: The Impact of Change.* Chicago: University of Chicago Press, 1970.

This is a study of a northwest coast Indian community with information on the roles of women, marriage, and the future of the community.

Lowie, Robert H. "The Matrilineal Complex." *University of California Publications in American Archaeology and Ethnology* 16 (1919–20): 29–45.

Lowie provides a detailed account of terminology and practice in matrilineal societies.

McSwain, Romola Mae. *The Role of Wives in the Urban Adjustment of Navaho Migrant Families to Denver, Colorado,* Navaho Urban Relocation Research Report no. 10, April 1965.

This study includes nine case studies of Navaho migrant women in Denver. The author suggests that wives play a crucial role in the adjustment of Navaho families to urban life.

Mason, Otis. *Woman's Share in Primitive Culture.* New York: Appleton, 1894.

Deals with roles of women all over the world. Although dated by its time of writing, a good overview of the roles of food bringer, weaver, skin dresser, potter, artist, and linguist and the importance of women in society and religion.

Mathes, Valerie Sherer. "American Indian Women and the Catholic Church." *North Dakota History* 47 (Fall 1980): 20–25.

Mathes reviews the lives of Katharine Tekakwitha and Louise Sighouin and discusses Indian women who joined various sisterhoods of the Catholic church.

———. "A New Look at the Role of Women in Indian Society." *American Indian Quarterly* 2 (Summer 1975): 131–39.

Mathes shows that generalizations about the inferiority of Indian women that are based on Catlin, Morgan, Denig, and Hodge, all white males, do not take into account the ethnocentrism of the observers or the division of labor in tribes that has been documented in other sources.

Mathur, Mary E. Fleming. "Who Cares That A Woman's Work Is Never Done . . . ?" *Indian Historian* 4 (Summer 1971): 11–16.

This is a review of the literature on women's roles with emphasis on the Iroquois culture.

Mead, Margaret. *The Changing Culture of an Indian Tribe.* New York: Columbia University Press, 1932.

In this examination of tribal women during the period of white contact, Mead used the Omaha (called "Antlers" in the study) to show the negative impact of white contact on traditional life.

Metcalf, Ann. "From Schoolgirl to Mother: The Effects of Education on Navajo Women." *Social Problems* 23 (June 1976): 535–44.

This study found that boarding school experiences of Navajo girls had detrimental effects on their adult self-esteem and maternal attitudes.

Metoyer, Cheryl A. "The Native American Woman." In *The Study of Women: Enlarging Perspectives of Social Reality,* edited by Eloise C. Snyder. New York: Harper and Row, 1979.

The chapter on Indian women is part of a longer study on contemporary women.

Niethammer, Carolyn. *Daughters of the Earth: The Lives and Legends of American Indian Women.* New York: Collier Books, 1977.

This is a collection of ethnographic, historical, and literary accounts of Indian women.

O'Meara, Walter. *Daughters of the Country: The Women of the Fur Traders and Mountain Men.* New York: Harcourt, Brace and World, 1968.

Discusses in detail the relationships between Indian women and white men on the frontier. O'Meara studied journals, memoirs, chronicles, and letters to gather information.

Opler, Morris E. "Cause and Effect in Apachean Agriculture, Division of Labor, Residence Patterns, and Girls' Puberty Rites." *American Anthropologist* 74 (October 1972): 1133–46.

Explanation for Apachean matrilocal residence is linked to agriculture and labor.

Oswalt, Wendall H. "Traditional Story Knife Tales of the Yuk Girls." *Proceedings of the American Philosophical Society* 108 (1964): 310–36.

Oswalt analyzes forty-one stories most of which feature the grandmother or granddaughter as the central character.

Parsons, Elsie Clews. *American Indian Life.* New York: Viking Press, 1922.

Twenty-four anthropologists each composed a story, incident, or life history characteristic of a tribe known to them.

———. "Mothers and Children at Zuni, New Mexico." *Man* 19 (November 1919): 168–73.

Parsons records customs of childbirth and childrearing at Zuni.

———. "Tewa Mothers and Children." *Man* 24 (October 1924): 148–51.

Tewa birth and childrearing customs, taboos, and rituals are presented.

———. "Waiyautitsa of Zuni, New Mexico." *Scientific Monthly* 9 (November 1919): 443–57.

Focuses attention upon differentiation of the sexes at Zuni by tracing the "typical" experiences of a girl growing up on the Zuni pueblo.

Randle, Martha Champion. "Iroquois Women, Then and Now." In *Symposium on Local Diversity in Iroquois Culture,* edited by William N. Fenton, pp. 169–80. Bureau of American Ethnology Bulletin no. 149, 1951.

Concludes that culture shock was felt more by males. Iroquois women have retained ancient security and efficiency.

Reichard, Gladys A. *Spider Woman: A Story of Navajo Weavers and Chanters.* Santa Fe: Rio Grande Press, 1968.

This is a reprint of the 1934 edition about Navajo textiles and women's roles.

Richards, Cara E. "Matriarchy or Mistake: The Role of Iroquois Women through Time." In *Cultural Stability and Cultural Change,* edited by Verne R. Ray, pp. 36–45. Seattle: American Ethnological Society, 1957.

Analyzes power positions of the sexes in Iroquois society, showing the gradual increase in the power of women and loss by the men through social change and time.

Schlegel, Alice. "The Adolescent Socialization of the Hopi Girl." *Ethnology* 12 (October 1973): 449–62.

Sees Hopi female adolescence as a time of crisis, strained relations, moodiness, and unpredictability, complicated by fear of rejection by a lover. Study of the period of socialization into womanhood.

Scott, Leslee M. "Indian Women as Food Providers and Tribal Counselors." *Oregon Historical Quarterly* 42 (1941): 208–19.

Women as food providers and figures of authority are interrelated subjects: their usefulness as food providers led to the tribal influence. Women were responsible for the basic essentials of food and shelter.

Scully, Vincent. "In Praise of Women: The Mescalero Puberty." *Art in America* 60 (July–August 1972): 70–77.

Ceremony celebrating coming of age of girls has been combined with the mountain spirits dance and is described in detail.

Sirdofshy, Arthur. "An Apache Girl Comes of Age." *Travel* 138 (July 1972): 40–43.

In the Apache Sunrise Dance, Winona Crawford dances three days to celebrate her becoming a woman. Illustrated.

Smithson, Carma Lee. *The Havasupai Woman.* Salt Lake City: University of Utah Press, 1959.

Data were obtained from three men and six women; emphasis is on the life cycle of the Havasupai woman. Discusses the limitations of social and economic roles within the patrilineal culture.

Speck, Frank G. *Catawba Texts.* New York: AMS Press, 1969.

First published in 1934. Informants about Catawba culture include three women: Mrs. Samson Owl, Mrs. Margaret Wiley Brown, and Mrs. Sally Gordon.

Spindler, Louise S. "Menomini Women and Culture Change." *Memoirs of the American Anthropological Association* 91 (1962): 14–20.

This is a study of the position and roles of Menomini women.

———. "Women in Menomini Culture." In *The North American Indians: A Sourcebook,* by Roger C. Owen et al., pp. 598–605. London: Macmillan, 1967.

Comments on the role of women among the Menominis of the Upper Great Lakes area.

Terrell, John Upton, and Donna M. Terrell. *Indian Women of the Western Morning: Their Life in Early America.* New York: Dial Press, 1974.

This book provides a look at the various roles of American Indian women with examples from different cultural groups.

Thompson, Laura, and Alice Joseph. *The Hopi Way.* Lawrence, KS: Haskell Institute, 1944.

This book includes discussion on matrilineal organization and clans.

Trigger, Bruce G. "Iroquoian Matriliny." *Pennsylvania Archaeologist* 48 (1978): 55–65.

Trigger uses historical and archaeological evidence to determine that men's and women's roles among the Iroquois complemented one another and that matrilocal residence was a result of activity patterns following the adoption of horticulture.

Van Kirk, Sylvia. "Thanadelthur." *The Beaver* (Spring 1974): 40–45.

Tells of a Chippewa woman who was captured by the Crees in 1713 and worked for the Hudson's Bay Company as an interpreter.

———. "Women and the Fur Trade." *The Beaver* (Winter 1972): 4–21.

Role of the Indian women during the 1800s as liaison between Indian and white culture during the fur trading period. Van Kirk discusses the advantages (economics and familiarity with languages) and the disadvantages (mixed-blood children and abandoned Indian wives).

Voeglin, C. F. *The Shawnee Female Deity.* 1936; reprint ed., New Haven: Human Relations Area Files, 1970.

Discusses the female creator called Our Grandmother by the Shawnee.

Wallace, Anthony F. C. "Women, Land, and Society: Three Aspects of Aboriginal Delaware Life." *Pennsylvania Archaeologist* 17 (1947): 1–35.

A history of Delaware culture (1600–1763) reconstructed through primary texts. Discusses power of women and the application of the term "women" to the Delaware, arguing that it was complimentary, meaning "mother, grandmother, or mother of nations."

Weist, Katherine M. "Plains Indian Women: An Assessment." In *Anthropology on the Great Plains,* edited by W. Raymond Wood and Margot Liberty, pp. 255–71. Lincoln: University of Nebraska Press, 1980.

Weist cites examples of the views about Plains Indian women perpetuated by anthropologists, discusses some of the reasons for the paucity of material about Plains Indian women, and analyzes the materials that are available.

Weslager, C. A. "The Delaware Indians as Women." *Journal of the Washington Academy of Science* 37 (15 September 1947): 298–304.

Discusses the controversy over the subjugation of the Delaware Indians by the Five Nations in the 1700s and the subsequent "feminization" of the tribe.

———. "Further Light on the Delaware Indians as Women." *Journal of the Washington Academy of Science* 37 (15 September 1947): 298–304.

This is further discussion and clarification of the meaning of "feminization" of the Delaware by the Five Iroquois Nations.

Winnemucca, Sarah (Paiute). "The Pah-Utes." *Californian* 6 (1882): 252–56.

Winnemucca provides information on foods, the courage of the people, the oral language, traditions, ranking systems and customs affecting Indian girls, and the ceremony of courtship.

## IV. CONTEMPORARY LITERATURE AND CRITICISM

Ackerman, Maria (Tlingit). *Tlingit Stories.* Anchorage: Alaska Methodist University Press, 1977.

Collection of stories.

Allen, Minnerva (Assiniboine). *Like Spirits of the Past Trying to Break Out and Walk to the West.* Albuquerque: Wopai Books, 1974.

Poetry and a story on traditional Indian themes.

Allen, Paula Gunn (Laguna). *The Blind Lion.* Berkeley: Thorys Springs Press, 1975.

Poetry.

———. *A Cannon between My Knees.* New York: Strawberry Press, 1978.

Poetry.

———. "The Mythopoetic Vision in Native American Literature." *American Indian Culture and Research Journal* 1 (1974): 3–12.

According to Allen, the term *myth* has been misused and misunderstood. Used correctly, the term can be applied to mythic narratives and shown to be related to native American religions. Black Elk's vision is cited as an example.

———. "The Psychological Landscape of *Ceremony*." *American Indian Quarterly* 5 (1979): 7–12.

Allen discusses the male/female principles of Leslie Silko's book *Ceremony* in relation to the characters and the reverence for the land.

———. "The Sacred Hoop: A Contemporary Indian Perspective on American Indian Literature." In *Literature of the American Indians: Views and Interpretations,* edited by Abraham Chapman, pp. 111–35. New York: New American Library, 1975.

This examination of native American cultures helps explain the differences between Indian literature and western literature, particularly in the differing views of religion, nature, and language. Allen also discusses the importance of ceremony and its relationship to the literature.

———. *Star Child.* Marvin, SD: *Blue Cloud Quarterly* 27 (1981).

Poetry.

———. "A Stranger in My Own Life: Alienation in Native American Prose and Poetry." *ASAIL Newsletter* 3 (Spring 1979): 16–23; reprint, *MELUS* 7 (1980) 3–19.

In this discussion of the mixed-blood in life and literature, Allen makes brief references to comments made by N. Scott Momaday and James Welch and discusses at length the role of Tayo in Leslie Silko's *Ceremony.*

———. *The Woman Who Owned Shadows.* San Francisco: Spinster's Inc., 1983.

In this novel, which incorporates oral tradition, the female protagonist searches for personal stability and tribal identity in a contemporary context; narrative is interiorized.

Bannan, Helen M. "Spider Woman's Web: Mothers and Daughters in Southwestern Native American Literature." In *The Lost Tradition: Mothers and Daughters in Literature,* edited by Cathy Davidson and E. M. Broner, pp. 268–79. New York: Ungar, 1980.

Bannan cites several traditional tales that establish the mother-daughter relationship that is expected behavior. She links traditional roles to the expression of female images in contemporary poetry by Silko, Allen, and others.

Beavert, Virginia (Yakima). *The Way It Was (Anaku Iwacha): Yakima Legends.* Yakima, WA: Consortium of Johnson O'Malley Committees of Region IV, 1974.

A collection of Yakima legends translated into English.

Bennett, Kay (Navajo). "Letter to the Editor." In *The American Indian Speaks*, edited by John R. Milton, pp. 171–72. Vermillion: University of South Dakota Press, 1969.

Bennett discusses her reason for writing: "to preserve a part of our history and culture."

Blicksilver, Edith. *The Ethnic American Woman: Problems, Protests, Lifestyle*. Dubuque, IA: Kendall-Hunt Publishing, 1978.

This anthology contains works by several Native American women: Rose Mary (Shingobe) Barstow, Joy Harjo, Nila Northsun, Buffy Sainte-Marie, Leslie Silko, Virginia Driving Hawk Sneve, Liz Sohappy, and Anne Webster.

———. "Traditionalism vs. Modernity: Leslie Silko on American Indian Women." *Southwest Review* 64 (Spring 1979): 149–60.

Silko is seen as a link from the past to the present in the way she blends traditionalism with contemporary experiences in her fiction and poetry. Discusses "Lullaby," "Yellow Woman," "The Man to Send Rain Clouds," and poetry from *Laguna Woman*.

Brigham, Besmilr. *Heaved from the Earth*. New York: Alfred A. Knopf, 1971.

Poetry by a part-Choctaw woman from Mississippi.

Cameron, Anne. *Daughters of Copper Woman*. Vancouver: Press Gang Publishers, 1981.

A collection of stories told to the author by women of Vancouver Island. The women remain anonymous by choice. Includes creation tales, hero tales, and stories of the women's secret society. The book is influenced by a contemporary feminist perspective.

Cardiff, Gladys (Cherokee). *To Frighten a Storm*. Port Townsend, WA: Copper Canyon Press, 1976.

Poetry.

Chanin, Abe, with Mildred Chanin. *This Land, These Voices*, pp. 3–10, 17–34. Flagstaff: Northland Press, 1977.

In an interview Elizabeth White, an eighty-four-year-old Hopi woman, tells of her life in Old Oraibi and her early experiences as a teacher in Hotevilla ("The Stars That Guided Her Life"). Annie Dodge Wauneka was the first woman elected to the Navajo Tribal Council, and in this interview she talks of her father, Chee Dodge, and the Long Walk. She has worked with the Navajo to prevent tuberculosis and to provide for better health and sanitary conditions ("The Daughter of the Lost Navajo Chief").

Cook, Elizabeth (Crow Creek Sioux). "American Indian Literature in Servitude." *Indian Historian* 10 (1977): 3–6.

Sioux woman's analysis of American Indian literature.

———. "Propulsives in Native American Literature." *CCC* 24 (1973); 271–74.

Discusses the roots of contemporary literature in the traditional philosophies and literatures of American Indians.

Cook-Lynn, Elizabeth (Crow Creek Sioux). *Then Badger Said This*. New York: Vantage Press, 1977.

Cook-Lynn's prose and poetry focus on the traditions and experiences of this Sioux woman.

Defender, Adelina (Pueblo). "No Time for Tears." In *An American Indian Anthology*, edited by Benet Tvedten, pp. 23–31. Marvin, SD: Blue Cloud Abbey, 1971.

Nine-year-old Moon Rainbow is aware of the religious conflicts at the pueblo where Catholicism and Protestantism are in competition with traditional pueblo beliefs.

Deloria, Ella C. (Sioux). *Dakota Texts*. Edited by Agnes Picotte and Paul N. Pavich. Vermillion: Dakota Press, 1978.

This edition, a reprint of the 1932 publication, provides background on Ella Deloria, who was born in 1889 on the Yankton Sioux reservation. She had collected materials for Franz Boas between 1927 and 1942. Included in this book are Dakota narratives and translations of traditional stories of Iktomi, Double-Face, Iya, Stone-Boy, and Rolling Skull, in addition to more contemporary stories.

———. *Speaking of Indians*. Edited by Agnes Picotte and Paul Pavich. New York: Friendship Press, 1944; reprint, Vermillion: Dakota Press, 1979.

The introduction provides information about Deloria, a Sioux woman whose text is influenced by tradition, by ethnology training at Columbia University, and by Christianity.

Downing, Linda (Cherokee). "Day of Confusion." *Arrows Four: Prose and Poetry by Young American Indians*, edited by T. D. Allen, pp. 57–59. New York: Pocket Books, 1974.

This short story tells of two sisters sent to live in an orphanage because their father could no longer care for them.

Evers, Lawrence, and Dennis Carr. "A Conversation with Leslie Marmon Silko." *Sun Tracks* 3 (Fall 1976): 28–33.

Evers and Carr interview the author of *Ceremony* as well as of several short stories.

Fisher, Dexter, ed. *The Third Woman: Minority Women Writers of the United States*. Boston: Houghton Mifflin, 1980.

In this comprehensive collection Fisher includes nineteen native American women writers. Myth, poetry, fiction, autobiography, and nonfiction are included.

———. "Zitkala-Sa: The Evolution of a Writer." *American Indian Quarterly* 5, no. 3 (August 1979): 229–38.

Fisher provides biographical data on Zitkala-Sa (Gertrude Bonnin) and describes her as "a curious blend of civilized romanticism and aggressive individualism."

Gerard, Mary Ann (Blackfeet). "It's My Rock." In *Arrows Four: Prose and Poetry by Young American Indians*, edited by T. D. Allen, pp. 31–39. New York: Pocket Books, 1974.

In this short story of a teenage girl's experiences with love, homosexuality, and drugs, the protagonist tries to place her feelings and frustrations within a reality outside of the mental institution where she has been placed.

Goudy, Irene (Yakima). "Yakimas." In *An American Indian Anthology*, edited by Benet Tvedten, pp. 63–65. Marvin, SD: Blue Cloud Abbey, 1971.

An account of the Cherokee Green Corn Dance, which is no longer performed as it was a century ago, is discussed by a Cherokee woman.

Hale, Janet Campbell (Coeur d'Alene). *Custer Lives in Humboldt County and Other Poems*. Greenfield Center, NY: Greenfield Review Press, 1978.

Poetry.

———. *The Owl's Song*. New York: Doubleday, 1974.

Hale's novel is about fourteen-year-old Billy who struggles with the white world and finds sustenance in his home environment.

Hart, Hazel (Chippewa). "Ge Chi Maung Won: The Life Story of an Old Chippewa Woman." In *Arrows Four: Prose and Poetry by Young American Indians*, edited by T. D. Allen, pp. 165–71. New York: Pocket Books, 1974.

In this short story of life and death, the grandmother tells the story of her grandmother and her mother, Gesis. She tells of being raised by her grandparents. The importance of the oral tradition and of relatives is stressed.

Hogan, Linda (Chickasaw). *Calling Myself Home*. Greenfield Center, NY: Greenfield Review Press, 1978.

Poetry.

———. *Daughters, I Love You*. Denver: Research Center on Women, 1981.

Poetry inspired by the Black Hills survival gathering, 1980.

Harjo, Joy (Creek). *The Last Song*. Las Cruces, NM: Puerto Del Sol Press, 1975.

Poetry.

———. *What Moon Drove Me to This*. Berkeley: Reed and Cannon, 1979.

Poetry.

Jaskoski, Helen. " 'My Heart Will Go Out': Healing Songs of Native American Women." *International Journal of Women's Studies* 4, no. 2 (March–April 1981): 118–34.

Demonstrates the use of poetry and song as a healing agent as used by American Indian women in Papago, Crow, Tlingit, Comanche, Mandan, and Apache ceremonies and rites. Discusses the role of the woman healer in traditional societies.

Johnson, E. Pauline [Tekahionwake] (Mohawk). *Flint and Feather*. Toronto: Musson Book Co., 1912.

This is a collection of poetry by a Mohawk woman born in 1862. Her works are difficult to find, but include the following: *The White Wampum* (1895), *Canadian Born* (1903), *Legends of Vancouver* (1911), *The Shagganappi* (1913), and *The Moccasin Maker* (1913).

———. *The Moccasin Maker*. Toronto: William Briggs, 1913.

Johnson lived on the Canadian Iroquois Reserve for many years and was a poet and writer. She was part white but identified with her mother's life as she told it. Her mother, Lydia Bestman, had come from England and lived among the Indians in Canada, marrying the Mohawk George Mansion. The book also relates stories of Canadian Indian legends.

———. *The Shagganappi*. Toronto: William Briggs, 1913.

This is a collection of short stories by the woman who preferred to be called Tekahionwake.

Jones, Louis Thomas. "Eloquent Indian Women." In *Aboriginal American Oratory*, pp. 113–20. Los Angeles: Southwest Museum, 1965.

Jones gives examples from the writings of Celsa Apapas (Cupeno), Warcaziwin (Sioux), and Gertrude Bonnin (Zitkala-Sa, Sioux).

Kaczkurkin, Mini Walenquela (Yaqui). *Yoeme: Lore of the Arizona Yaqui People*. Tucson: Sun Tracks, 1977.

Stories heard from the author's grandmother, Mrs. Carmen Garcia, are printed to preserve the oral tradition for the children. They are in English because so many of the children have not learned the Yaqui language.

Katz, Jane B. *I Am the Fire of Time: The Voices of Native American Women*. New York: E. P. Dutton, 1977.

This anthology of literature by American Indian women from various tribes includes ninety examples of autobiography, poetry, oral history fiction, prayer, and essay. While there are no full-length personal narratives, the book generally provides a comprehensive picture of the roles of Indian women from traditional tribal times to contemporary. Variety of forms, experiences, and tribal and regional representation are good.

McDowell, Leonora Hayden (Cree). *Moccasin Meanderings*. New York: Gusto Press, 1979.

Poetry.

McLaughlin, Marie L. (Sioux). *Myths and Legends of the Sioux.* Bismarck: Bismarck Tribune Co., 1916.

The author is one-quarter Sioux. She was born in 1842 in Wabasha, Minnesota, married an Indian agent, and lived on reservations for forty years. In this collection she repeats stories told to her by older Indians.

Manychildren, Selena (Navajo). "My Mother." *In Arrows Four,* edited by T. D. Allen, pp. 50–54. New York: Washington Square Books, 1974.

This tribute to her mother was written by a Navajo high school senior at the Phoenix Indian School.

Marriott, Alice. *The Ten Grandmothers.* Norman: University of Oklahoma Press, 1945.

Legends of ten medicine bundles of the Kiowa are included. The bundles were called the Ten Grandmothers. Spear Woman and Eagle Plume are the two principle women informants for Marriott about Kiowa history and experience.

Milton, John R., ed. *Four Indian Poets.* Vermillion: Dakota Press, 1974.

Milton includes a biographical sketch of Paula Gunn Allen and ten of her poems; Allen is Laguna.

Mourning Dove [Hum-ishu-ma] (Okanogan). *Cogewea, the Half Blood.* Boston: Four Seas, 1927; reprint, Lincoln: University of Nebraska Press, 1981.

Mourning Dove was among the first of Indian women to write fiction. This novel is based on her life and the Indian experience on the cattle ranges. Cogewea, a mixed-blood girl, ultimately chooses her Indian identity over her white heritage.

———. *Tales of the Okanogans.* Edited by Donald M. Hines. Fairfield, WA: Ye Galleon Press, 1976.

Mourning Dove retells thirty-eight traditional tales of the Okanogan Indians who live on the border area of Washington state and Canada. Mourning Dove had collected the tales from her parents, friends, and relatives and translated them into English. The tales come from the Kettle Falls area near the confluence of the Colville, Columbia, and Kettle Rivers in Eastern Washington. The preface is personal narrative.

North Sun, Nila. *Diet Pepsi and Nacho Cheese.* Fallon, NE: Duck Down Press, 1977.

Poetry.

Platero, Juanita (Navajo), and Siyowin Miller. "Chee's Daughter." In *Literature of the American Indian,* edited by Thomas E. Sanders and Walter W. Peek, pp. 471–81. Beverly Hills: Glencoe Press, 1974.

This short story portrays the conflicts between traditional and progressive Navajos and the particular impact of tradition on one family when Chee must give up his daughter to his in-laws.

Popkes, Opal Lee (Choctaw). "Zuma Chow's Cave." In *The Man to Send Rain Clouds: Contemporary Stories by American Indians,* edited by Kenneth Rosen, pp. 109–27. New York: Viking, 1974.

In this short story, Chowt hides out in a canyon north of Santa Monica in 1903.

Rose, Wendy (Hopi). *Academic Squaw: Reports to the World from the Ivory Tower*. Marvin, SD: *Blue Cloud Quarterly,* 1977.

Poetry.

———. *Builder Kachina: A Home-Going Cycle*. Marvin, SD: Blue Cloud Press, 1979.

Poetry.

———. *Hopi Roadrunner Dancing*. Greenfield Center, NY: Greenfield Review Press, 1973.

Poetry.

———. *Long Division: A Tribal History*. New York: Strawberry Press, 1976.

Poetry.

———. *Lost Copper*. Morongo Indian Reservation, CA: Malki Museum Press, 1980.

Poetry.

———. *Poetry of the American Indian: Wendy Rose*. Sacramento: American Visual Communication Bank, 1978.

Poetry.

———. *What Happened When the Hopi Hit New York*. New York Contact II Publications, 1982.

Poetry.

Ruoff, A. Lavonne. "Ritual and Renewal: Keres Traditions in the Short Fiction of Leslie Silko." *MELUS* 5 (1978): 2–17.

Ruoff discusses the relationship between oral tradition and Silko's fiction.

Sanchez, Carol Lee (Laguna-Sioux). *Conversations from the Nightmare*. Berkeley: Casa Editorial Publications, 1975.

Poetry.

———. *Message Bringer Woman*. San Francisco: Taureen Horn, n.d.

Poetry.

Seyersted, Per. *Leslie Marmon Silko*. Boise: Boise State University Western Writers Series no. 45, 1980.

History of Laguna, biographical notes, description and evaluations of Silko's *Ceremony* and short stories.

Silko, Leslie (Laguna). *Ceremony*. New York: Viking Press, 1977.

In this novel, Tayo, a World War II veteran, returns to Laguna and must find the right "way" to live there again; he must find the right ceremony.

———. *Laguna Woman.* Greenfield Center, NY: Greenfield Review Press, 1974.

Poetry.

———. *The Man to Send Rain Clouds: Contemporary Stories by American Indians,* edited by Kenneth Rosen. New York: Viking, 1974.

"Bravura," pp. 149–54. Bravura, a poet, leaves the university and goes to the Southwest searching for inspiration. Once there, he settles into an appreciative state of the country, but he does not write.

"A Geronimo Story," pp. 128–44. A subtly humorous account of a group of Laguna scouts who reluctantly accompany the U.S. cavalry on an expedition to capture Geronimo. The story, told through the eyes of one of the scouts, reveals their relief when Geronimo is not to be found and relates their feelings toward the white men searching for him.

"Humaweepi, the Warrior Priest," pp. 161–68. At age nineteen, Humaweepi discovers that he is being prepared to be a priest and medicine man to take over after his grandfather dies.

"The Man to Send Rain Clouds," pp. 3–8. The death of old Teofilo and his burial illustrate the Indian blending of old tradition and new knowledge. Teofilo is sent on his way in accordance with tradition but with one added element—holy water from a Catholic priest—to doubly ensure his returning as a cloud to bring rain to his people.

"Tony's Story," pp. 69–78. Leon, just returned from the service, is harrassed by the local law enforcement officer, but, ironically, it is Leon's friend Tony who kills the officer as the "evil force."

"Uncle Tony's Goat," pp. 93–100. A young boy learns a valuable lesson about respect and freedom. He and his friends torment the goats, and later, when he is to put the goats in a pen, the billy attacks him and then runs away.

"Yellow Woman," pp. 33–45. An Indian woman tries to persuade herself that the cattle rustler with whom she is having an affair is one of the Ka'tsina spirits. Although she leaves her husband and children for him, later she is forced to leave him or be arrested herself.

———. *Storyteller.* New York: Richard Seaver, Random House and Grove Books, 1981.

Using a mixed format of family photographs, traditional stories, short fiction, and poetry, Silko structures this work and unifies it by autobiographical fragments that point to the interplay of remembrance and creative writing. The work includes all of the author's short stories and most of her poetry.

"Special Issue: Native Women of New Mexico." *A* 3 (Fall 1973).

This issue is devoted to poetry and prose by American Indian women.

Sullivan, Elizabeth (Creek). *Indian Legends of the Trail of Tears and Other Creek Stories*. Tulsa, OK: Giant Services, 1974.

Legends and stories told to the author by her great-grandmother and other elders are collected in this volume.

Tall Mountain, Mary (Koyukons). *There Is No Word for Goodbye*. Marvin, SD: *Blue Cloud Quarterly* 27 (1981).

Poetry.

Walters, Anna Lee (Pawnee-Oto). "Chapter 1." *The Man to Send Rain Clouds: Contemporary Stories by American Indians*, edited by Kenneth Rosen, pp. 82–92. New York: Viking, 1974.

This story is set in Canyon de Chelly in 1863; the threat of soldiers taking over the land is ever present.

Volborth, Judith Ivaloo (Apache-Comanche). *Thunder Root: Traditional and Contemporary Native American Verse*. Los Angeles: UCLA American Indian Culture and Research Center, 1978.

Poetry; introduction by Kenneth Lincoln.

Walsh, Marnie (Sioux). *A Taste of the Knife*. Boise, ID: Ahsahta Press, 1976.

Poetry.

Washburne, Heluiz, and Anauta (Eskimo). *Children of the Blizzard*. London: Dennis Dobson, 1960.

This collection of stories recorded by Washburne is based on the experiences of Anauta, an Eskimo woman from Baffin Island. The stories tell primarily of the life of Eskimo children.

Yazzie, Ethelou, ed. (Navajo). *Navajo History*. Mary Farms, AZ: Navajo Community College Press, 1971.

This collection includes previously unrecorded history of the Navajos with photographs and illustrations. It includes certain myths, tales of monsters, the story of Changing Woman, and stories of the twins and Spider Woman. The stories are recorded from those obtained from Navajo storytellers.

Zitkala-Sa [Gertrude Bonnin] (Dakota Sioux). *American Indian Stories*. 1921; reprint, Glorieta, NM: Rio Grande Press, 1976.

This collection includes reprints from the *Atlantic Monthly, Harper's Magazine,* and *Everybody's Magazine*. There are ten stories of Indian life that are laced with the resentment toward the Bureau of Indian Affairs that characterized Bonnin's lectures and writing.

———. "The Indian's Awakening." *American Indian Magazine* 4 (January–March 1916): 57–59.

Poem which tells of the cutting of her hair and loss of traditional clothing but reaffirms that her heart was left unchanged.

———. *Old Indian Legends*. Boston: Ginn, 1901.

Collection of Sioux legends.

———. "A Sioux Woman's Love for Her Grandchild." *American Indian Magazine* 4 (October–December 1917): 230.

Poem reflecting about Custer and the Battle of the Little Big Horn.

———. "The Soft-Hearted Sioux." *Harper's Magazine* 102 (March 1902): 505–8.

This story is told in the first person about a young boy who was sent to the mission school, learned to be a Christian, and returned home to find his father dying. His attempt to secure meat for his starving parents ended in the murder of a white man and his eventual imprisonment.

———. "The Trial Path." *Harper's Magazine* 103 (October 1901): 741–44.

In this story of two Dakota women, a grandmother is telling a story to a young woman about the tribal history and the death of the young woman's grandfather.

## V. ADDITIONAL ARTICLES AND BOOKS ABOUT AMERICAN INDIAN WOMEN

Alilkatuktuk, Jeela. "Canada: Stranger in My Own Land." *MS* 3 (February 1974): 8–10.

A native woman of Canada comments about the role of Indian women in her country.

Barrett, S. M. *Hoistah: An Indian Girl.* New York: Duffield, 1913.

This is a fictionalized story of a Cheyenne woman born in the early 1800s.

Bowman, John Clarke. *Powhatan's Daughter.* New York: Viking, 1973.

This historical novel is based on legendary accounts of Pocahontas and John Smith.

Braudy, Susan. "Buffy Sainte-Marie: 'Native North American Me.' " *MS* 4 (March 1975): 14–18.

Braudy writes about the Cree singer and entertainer who has also been an activist for Indian people.

———. " 'We Will Remember' Survival School: The Women and Children of the American Indian Movement." *MS* 5 (July 1976): 77–80, 94, 120.

Women involved in the American Indian Movement tell of their desires to educate their children in the traditions of their people.

Broussand, C. "Mohawk Beauty with a Mission." *Look* 28 (28 January 1964): 91–94.

This is a brief, illustrated account of Kahn Tineta Horn, a Canadian Mohawk woman who was active as a spokesperson for her people.

Brown, Dee. *Creek Mary's Blood.* New York: Holt, Rinehart, and Winston, 1980.

Brown's book is a novel of four generations of American Indian life told through the life of one family. Creek Mary is the daughter of a Muskogee chief who first married a white trader and later a Cherokee. The novel is the story of Creek Mary and her descendents.

Child Study Association of America. *The Indian Girl: Her Social Heritage, Her Needs and Her Opportunities*. Washington, D.C.: U.S. Government Printing Office, c. 1934.

A brief pamphlet which outlines the problems Indian girls may have at government schools and how teachers and administrators in those schools can help the girls adjust. The pamphlet assumes the girls will need to know how to adjust to white society.

Dunn, Dorothy. "Pablita Velarde, Painter of Pueblo Life." *El Palacio* 59 (1952): 335–41.

Pablita Verlarde continues in the traditional two-dimensional style of Pueblo painting.

Fleming, E. McClung. "Symbols of the U.S. from Indian Queen to Uncle Sam." In *Frontiers of American Culture,* edited by Ray B. Browne, pp. 1–24. Lafayette: Purdue University Press, 1968.

The first part of the chapter discusses the use of the Indian woman to represent America. The use of the Indian princess image began in the 1760s and lasted into the nineteenth century.

Fuller, Iola. *The Loon Feather*. New York: Harcourt, Brace, 1941.

In this fictionalized account of the life of Tecumseh's daughter, she is torn between her Indian heritage and the life of her French stepfather.

Goodwill, Jean. "A New Horizon for Native Women in Canada." In *Citizen Participation: Canada, a Book of Readings,* edited by James A. Draper, pp. 362–70. Toronto: New Press, 1971.

Goodwill discusses the increased involvement in politics and education by Canadian Indian women in order to retain their heritage and preserve their rights.

Green, Rayna. *Native American Women: A Bibliography*. Wichita Falls, TX: Ohoyo Resource Center, 1981.

A lengthy bibliography divided into several sections; includes books for children and films.

———. "Native American Woman: Review Essay." *Signs* 6 (Winter 1980): 248–67.

Green discusses the scholarship and popular literature written about American Indian women since the seventeenth century in the United States and Canada. She organizes the material chronologically, enabling readers to understand the various trends and cycles of interest in Indian women's lives.

———. "The Pocahontas Perplex: The Image of Indian Women in Popular Culture." *Massachusetts Review* 16 (Autumn 1975): 698–714.

Green discusses the princess and squaw images in literature and folklore.

Halsell, Grace. *Bessie Yellowhair*. New York: Warner Books, 1974.

This novel, with an Indian woman as the main character, tells of life both on and off the reservation.

Hilger, Sister Mary Ione. *The First Sioux Nun: Sister Marie-Josephine Nebraska, S.G.M., 1859–1884*. Milwaukee: Bruce Publishing Co., 1963.

In this partially fictionalized story, Anapo, Little Dawn, became a sister with the Grey Nuns in 1884. She had been brought up at the Catholic orphanage and joined the sisterhood at St. Boniface, Manitoba.

Irwin, Hadley. *We Are Mesquakie; We Are One*. Old Westbury, NY: Feminist Press, 1980.

This fictional account of a young Mesquakie woman tells of the return of the Mesquakie people from the reservation in Kansas to their home in Iowa. Although written for a high school audience, the book is a compelling and accurate record of Mesquakie history.

Kidwell, Clara Sue. Review of *Bright Eyes: The Story of Susette La Flesche, an Omaha Indian*, by Dorothy Clarke Wilson. *Journal of Ethnic Studies* 2 (Winter 1975): 118–22.

Although this is primarily a book review, Kidwell places emphasis on the roles of Indian women.

———. "The Power of Women in Three American Indian Societies." *Journal of Ethnic Studies* 6 (1979): 113–21.

In this study of Indian women's roles Kidwell discusses Ojibwa, Winnebago, and Menominee cultures.

LaDuke, Winona (Anishnabe). "In Honor of Women Warriors." *off our backs* 11 (February 1981): 3–4.

Anishnabe woman discusses problems facing contemporary Indian women and the historical antecedents of the problems.

LaRoque, Emma. *Defeathering the Indian*. Agincourt, Canada: Book Society of Canada, 1975.

LaRoque is a Cree-Métis woman born in 1950. She describes her book as "a commentary on education based on personal experience."

Lee, Pelican, and Jane Wing. "Rita Silk-Nauni vs. the State." *off our backs* 11 (February 1981): 2, 4.

Account of a Lakota woman and her experiences fleeing a husband who beat her and her encounter with police brutality in Oklahoma.

Lurie, Nancy Oestreich. "Indian Women: A Legacy of Freedom." In *Look to the Mountaintop*, edited by Robert Iacopi, pp. 29–36. San Jose: Gousha Publications, 1972.

Lurie discusses some of the myths and legends about Pocahontas, stereotypes of Indian women, women's roles in tribal organization, and contemporary Indian women.

McCarty, Darlene. "A Day with Yaha." In *The American Indian Speaks,* edited by John R. Milton, pp. 119–25. Vermillion: University of South Dakota Press, 1969.

Memories of her grandmother Yaha blend the traditional and contemporary experiences.

Medicine, Bea (Sioux). "The Anthropologist as the Indian's Image Maker." *Indian Historian* 4 (Fall 1971): 27–29.

Medicine discusses how the Indian image has been created by outsiders and that when the Indian presents his or her own history, there are accusations of subjectivity or ethnocentrism.

———. *The Native American Woman: A Perspective.* Austin, TX: National Educational Laboratory Publishers, March, 1978.

A contemporary perspective by a Lakota woman who has been a spokeswoman for Indian women's rights and who is also an anthropologist. The book includes comments on anthropologists and historians, changes Indian women have undergone, and expectations for the future. There are lengthy quotations and photographs to supplement the text.

———. "Role and Function of Indian Women." *Indian Education* 7 (January 1977: 4–5.

These are excerpts from Medicine's address to the Eighth National Indian Education Association Convention.

———. "The Role of Women in Native American Societies: A Bibliography." *Indian Historian* 8 (Summer 1975): 50–53.

Medicine includes 100 citations of books and articles on American Indian women.

Miller, Dorothy I. "Native American Women: Leadership Images." *Integrateducation* 16 (January–February 1978): 37–39.

This is a discussion of the bicultural role of Indian women who are in leadership roles in the majority society.

Nahanee, Theresa. "Canadian Women Demand Equal Rights." *Indian News* 15 (January 1973): 1, 6–7.

Reports on a meeting of Canadian Indian women concerned with their status accorded by the Canadian government.

North American Indian Women's Association. *Special Needs of Handicapped Indian Children and Indian Women's Problems.* Washington, D.C.: Social Services, Bureau of Indian Affairs, May 1978.

This is a project report on data gathering, interviews, and recommendations. The report deals with physical and mental handicaps, child abuse, abuse of Indian women, school-age parenthood, solo parenthood, unwanted pregnancies, malnutrition, and alcoholism. Indian women were trained to gather the information for the report. Although it is a collection of statistics and often unanalyzed information, the report is interesting for its comments on contemporary Indian women's experiences.

Ohoyo Resource Center Staff. *Resource Guide of American Indian—Alaskan Native Women*. Newton, MA: WEEA Publishing Center, 1980.

A listing of contemporary American Indian and Alaskan women who have served in a variety of occupations and services and who have improved the lives of Indian people.

———. *Words of Today's American Indian Women: Ohoyo Makachi*. Wichita Falls, TX: Ohoyo Resource Center, 1981.

Presentations by American Indian and Alaskan Indian women from the April 1981 Ohoyo Resource Center Conference on Educational Equity Awareness, as well as other selected conference speeches. *Ohoyo* is the Choctaw word for *woman; Ohoyo Makachi* is translated as "women speak."

Sainte-Marie, Buffy. *The Buffy Sainte-Marie Songbook*. New York: Grosset and Dunlap, 1971.

This collection includes a brief account by Sainte-Marie on song writing in addition to the words and music to her songs. Illustrated. Specific introductions to some songs explain the background.

Smith, Dana Margaret [Mrs. White Mountain Smith] (Hopi). *Hopi Girl*. Palo Alto: Stanford University Press, 1931.

This fictional account tells of Po-la-ma-na, Butterfly Girl of Hopi Land, who was sent away to government schools and came back to live with her people.

Steiner, Stan. *The New Indians*. New York: Harper and Row, 1968.

Steiner includes one chapter specifically on Indian women.

U.S. Department of Labor. *Native American Women and Equal Opportunity: How to Get Ahead in the Federal Government*. Washington, D.C.: U.S. Government Printing Office, 1979.

This is a publication of the Women's Bureau that resulted from federal training seminar for American Indian women. Includes an essay, "Native Women in the World of Work," by Shirley Hill Witt.

Watson, Virginia. *The Princess Pocahontas*. Philadelphia: Penn Publishing, 1916.

This is a fictional account of the life of Pocahontas from the forests of Virginia to the courts of England.

Wauneka, Annie D. "The Dilemma for Indian Women." *Wassaja 4 (September 1976): 8.*

Wauneka asserts that Indian women's first priorities are "equal treatment, opportunity and recognition of the Indians and Tribal Government." She believes that women's roles cannot be assessed until the legal status of all Indians is reaffirmed and strengthened.

Welter, Barbara, ed. *The Woman Question in American History*. Hinsdale, IL: Dryden Press, 1973.

Welter includes one chapter on American Indian women, excerpts from *Daughters of the Country*, by Walter O'Meara. It is unfortunate that only O'Meara's narrow view is presented.

Witt, Shirley Hill. "The Brave-Hearted Women." *Akwesasne Notes* 8 (Early Summer 1976): 16–17.

Witt relates the strength of Indian women to traditional positions within tribes.

———. "Native Women Today: Sexism and the Indian Woman." *Civil Rights Digest* 6 (Spring 1974): 29–35.

Discusses the origins of "squaw" and other stereotypes. Facts and statistics on roles of traditional and contemporary Indian women in education, employment, and health are presented.

*Women of All Red Nations*. Porcupine, SD: We Will Remember Group, 1978.

Reports on the conference of Women of All Red Nations (W.A.R.N.) and includes articles on personal experiences of American Indian women concerning contemporary issues.

Young, Philip. "The Mother of Us All: Pocahontas Reconsidered." *The Kenyon Review* 24 (Summer 1962): 391–415.

In this discussion of what "facts" are known about Pocahontas, Young points out how she has become a "goddess" and "myth" of literature.

Zastro, Leona M. "American Indian Women as Art Educators." *Journal of American Indian Education* 18 (October 1978): 6–10.

Zastro discusses Pima, Papago, and Pueblo women as art educators teaching their children traditional arts.

# Index


Adams, Hank, 133
Adams, Henry, 4
*Agriculture of the Hidatsa Indians: An Indian Interpretation,* 43
Alberta Métis League, 122
Alcatraz, 135
Allen, Paula Gunn, 140
American Indian Institute, 135
*American Indian Life,* 34
Antone, Ella Lopez, 52, 56–57, 62–63
Arizona Hall of Fame, 99
As-told-to autobiography, 10–12, 14, 21, 24, 49–68, 140
"Autobiography of a Fox Woman, The," 31–39
"Autobiography of a Winnebago Family," 135
*Autobiography of a Winnebago Indian, The,* 82
*Autobiography of Delfina Cuero, The,* 12

Bad Soldier, 76
Beckwourth, James, 6
*Belle Highwalking: The Narrative of a Northern Cheyenne,* 132
*Big Falling Snow,* 9
Bizzett, Irma, 77, 79
Black Hawk War, 75
Black Vomit, 91
Boas, Franz, 30
*Bobbi Lee: Indian Rebel,* 24, 116, 132, 136
Bonnin, Gertrude (Zitkala Sa), 12, 116
Boone, Daniel, 6
Buffalo Bird Woman (Waheenee; Maxi'diwiac; Mahidiwia, 43–45
Bunzel, Ruth, 42–43, 45
Bureau of Indian Affairs, 93

Campbell, Maria, 23, 116–26
Canada, 116–26, 132–33
Captivity narrative, 4–6
Cheechum, 118–26
Chehia (Anna Moore Shaw), 85–112
*Cheyenne Memories,* 132
Chona, Maria, 12, 49–68, 86
Cloud North, Woesha, 76–77, 79, 135
Cody, William F., 6
Colson, Elizabeth, 20
Con Quien, The Gambler, 52
Courlander, Harold, 9
Crashing Thunder, 73, 131
Crockett, Davey, 6
*Crying Wind,* 5
Cuero, Delfina, 22–23

Dalottiwa, 35
Daniels, Stan, 122
Deer, Ada, 129
Deloria, Vine, Sr., 18–19
*Diary* (Samuel Sewell), 5
Dowawisnima. *See* Sekaquaptewa, Helen
Dyk, Walter, 9

*Earthdivers: Tribal Narratives on Mixed Descent,* 117
Edwards, Jonathan, 5
Ethnographic autobiography, 10–11, 15, 29–46, 71–82

Fish Back (Mitchell Redcloud, Sr.), 82
*Folklore of the Musquakie Indians of North America,* 34

Frank, Gelya, 29
Franklin, Benjamin, 4, 6

Gadsden Purchase, 86
Gila Crossing Day School, 92
Gila River Reservation, 86, 98
Goodbird, Edward (Tsaka'Kasakic), 43–44
Great Pueblo Revolt, 87
Grinnell, George Bird, 40–41

Haag, Mack, 39
"Half-breed," 117
*Halfbreed,* 23, 116–26
Hardin, Helen, 129
Harris, LaDonna, 129
Hartland, E. Sidney, 34
*Hawk over Whirlpools,* 54, 65
Herold, Joyce, 64
Hidatsa, 43
Highwalking, Belle, 132
Hopi, 85–112
Hopkins, Sarah Winnemucca, 10, 12, 21
"How Meskwaki Children Should Be Brought Up," 33
Hungry Wolf, Beverly, 136

Indian Act of 1951, 119
Indian Reorganization Act, 36

Jones, David, 71–72, 131
Jones, William, 35

*Karnee, a Paiute Narrative,* 12
Keams Canyon, 88
Keams Canyon Agency, 104
Kidwell, Clara Sue, viii
Kluckhohn, Clyde, 9, 61
Kroeber, A. L., 30, 39, 42
Krupat, Arnold, 10

Landes, Ruth, 21
Langness, L. L., 9, 29
LaRoque, Emma, 133
*Life among the Paiutes,* 21
Life-history studies, 115
Life-passage studies, 115
Lincoln, Harry, 33, 35–36
Linderman, Frank, 42, 45
Littlebear, Minnie, 79
*Lives: An Anthropological Approach to Biography,* 29
Longest Walk, 132
Lowry, Annie, 12
Lucas, Governor Robert, 34
Lurie, Nancy O., 11, 66–67, 71–82, 131

Male autobiography, 6
Mandelbaum, David G., 115
Maricopa Indian Reservation, 99
*Me and Mine,* 10, 12, 22, 54, 85–112
Medicine, Bea, viii, 129
Medicine Dance, 79
Medicine Lodge, 80
Menstruation, 36–37
Mesquakie (Fox), 31–39
Métis, 116–26
Michelson, Truman, 21, 31–42, 115
Mixed-blood, 117
Montana Council for Indian Education, 132
Montezuma, Carlos, 97
Moore, Joshiah (Red Arrow), 90
Mormonism, 107–9
Mountain Wolf Woman, 54, 72–82, 131
*Mountain Wolf Woman,* 12, 72–82, 115

Naming Ceremony, 79
"Narrative of an Arapaho Woman," 31, 39–42
"Narrative of a Southern Cheyenne Woman, The," 31–32, 39–42
Native American Church, 79–80
*No Turning Back,* 12, 21

*Ojibwa Women,* 21
Oraibi, 86
Oral tradition, 3–4, 81
"Out of the Past," 21
Owen, Mary Alicia, 34–35

Papago, 49–68
*Papago Woman,* 12, 49–68
Parsons, Elsie Clews, 34
*Personal Narrative* (Jonathan Edwards), 5
"Personal Narrative of Anna Price," 21
Peyote, 79–80, 131
Phoenix High School, 88, 95
Phoenix Indian School, 88, 93, 105
Pima, 85–112

*Pima Legends,* 89, 98
*Pima Past, A,* 22–23, 54, 85–112
Poweshiek, Horace, 35–36
Pretty-shield, 8, 45, 54
*Pretty-shield: Medicine Woman of the Crows,* 45
Puberty rite, 62

Qoyawayma, Polingaysi, 12, 21

Radin, Paul, 30, 73, 79, 82
Red Arrow (Joshiah Moore), 90
*Red Mother,* 45
Red Power, 136
Rice, Fred, 81
Riel Rebellion, 126
Rowlandson, Mary, 5
Rowlodge, Jesse, 40
Russell, Adeline Shaw, 89

Sacrifice Offering Ceremony, 39
Sah-Gan-De-Oh, 23
*Sah-Gan-De-Oh: The Chief's Daughter,* 24
Sainte-Marie, Buffy, 129
Salt River Pima Reservation, 98
Sanapia, 71–72, 131
Scheick, William J., 117
Sekaquaptewa, Emory, 100, 105
Sekaquaptewa, Helen, 10, 22, 78, 85–112
Sewell, Samuel, 5
Shaw, Anna, 22–23, 78, 85–112
Shaw, Ross, 89
Shipek, Florence, 22
Silko, Leslie Marmon, 129, 139–40
Slave narrative, 6–7
Snake Dance, 86
*Son of Old Man Hat,* 9
*Sovereignty and Goodness of God, The,* 5
Spicer, Edward, 22
Stands in Timber, John, 132
*Storyteller,* 139–40

Thoreau, Henry David, 4, 6
*Three Pomo Women,* 20
Thure, Karen, 89, 97
Tipi Decorators, 40
Trail of Broken Treaties, 132

Udall, Louise, 12, 99–112
Underhill, Ruth, ix, 11, 49–68, 73
University of Arizona Press, 100, 111

Vizenor, Gerald, 117

Waheenee, 19–21
*Waheenee: An Indian Girl's Story,* 21, 44
Walters, Anna Lee, 137–39
Wanatee, Adeline, 36–37
Wauneka, Annie, 129
*Ways of My Grandmothers, The,* 136
Weist, Katherine M., viii
Wentz, Frances, 74
Wilson, Frederick, 43
Wilson, Gilbert, 19–20, 42–46
Winnebago, 71–82
Winnie, Lucille, 24
*Woman Who Owned the Shadows, The,* 140
Wounded Knee, 132
Written autobiography, 13

Yava, Albert, 9
Yoimut, 21
"Yoimut's Story, the Last Chunut," 21
Young, Lucy, 21

Zitkala Sa. *See* Bonnin, Gertrude
Zuni, 45
Zuni, Flora, 45
Zuni, Lina, 45–46